/991

SPECIAL NEEDS IN ORDINARY SCI
General Editor: Peter Mittler

The Visually Handicapped Child in Your Classroom

Special Needs in Ordinary Schools

General editor: Peter Mittler
Associate editors: James Hogg, Peter Pumfrey, Tessa Roberts, Colin Robson
Honorary advisory board: Neville Bennett, Marion Blythman, George Cooke, John Fish, Ken Jones, Sylvia Phillips, Klaus Wedell, Phillip Williams

Titles in this series

The Visually Handicapped Child in your Classroom

Elizabeth K. Chapman
Juliet M. Stone

CASSELL

Cassell Educational Limited
Artillery House
Artillery Row
London SW1P 1RT

British Library Cataloguing in Publication Data

Chapman, Elizabeth K.
The visually handicapped child in your
classroom.—(Special needs in ordinary
schools).
1. Visually handicapped children—
Education
I. Title   II. Stone, Juliet M.   III. Series
371'.91'1   HV1626

ISBN 0–304–31400–5

Phototypesetting by Activity Ltd, Salisbury, Wilts
Printed and bound in Great Britain by
Biddles Ltd, Guildford and King's Lynn

First published 1988
Reprinted 1989

Copyright © 1988 by Elizabeth Chapman and Juliet M. Stone

Last digit is print no: 9 8 7 6 5 4 3 2

Contents

Foreword: Towards education for all

AIMS

This series aims to support teachers as they respond to the challenge they face in meeting the needs of all children in their school, particularly those identified as having special educational needs.

Although there have been many useful publications in the field of special educational needs during the last decade, the distinguishing feature of the present series of volumes lies in their concern with specific areas of the curriculum in primary and secondary schools. We have tried to produce a series of conceptually coherent and professionally relevant books, each of which is concerned with ways in which children with varying levels of ability and motivation can be taught together. The books draw on the experience of practising teachers, teacher trainers and researchers and seek to provide practical guidelines on ways in which specific areas of the curriculum can be made more accessible to all children. The volumes provide many examples of curriculum adaptation, classroom activities, teacher–child interactions, as well as the mobilisation of resources inside and outside the school.

The series is organised largely in terms of age and subject groupings, but three 'overview' volumes have been prepared in order to provide an account of some major current issues and developments. Seamus Hegarty's *Meeting Special Needs in Ordinary Schools* gives an introduction to the field of special needs as a whole, whilst Sheila Wolfendale's *Primary Schools and Special Needs* and John Sayer's *Secondary Schools for All?* address issues more specifically concerned with primary and secondary schools respectively. We hope that curriculum specialists will find essential background and contextual material in these overview volumes.

In addition, a section of this series will be concerned with examples of obstacles to learning. All of these specific special needs can be seen on a continuum ranging from mild to severe, or from temporary and transient to long-standing or permanent. These include difficulties in learning or in adjustment and behaviour, as well as problems resulting largely from sensory or physical impairments or from difficulties of communication from whatever cause. We hope that teachers will consult the volumes in this section for guidance on working with children with specific difficulties.

The series aims to make a modest 'distance learning' contribution to meeting the needs of teachers working with the whole range of pupils with special educational needs by offering a set of resource materials relating to specific areas of the primary and secondary curriculum and by suggesting ways in which learning obstacles, whatever their origin, can be identified and addressed.

We hope that these materials will not only be used for private study but be subjected to critical scrutiny by school-based inservice groups sharing common curricular interests and by staff of institutions of higher education concerned with both special needs teaching and specific curriculum areas. The series has been planned to provide a resource for Local Education Authority (LEA) advisers, specialist teachers from all sectors of the education service, educational psychologists, and teacher working parties. We hope that the books will provide a stimulus for dialogue and serve as catalysts for improved practice.

It is our hope that parents will also be encouraged to read about new ideas in teaching children with special needs so that they can be in a better position to work in partnership with teachers on the basis of an informed and critical understanding of current difficulties and developments. The goal of 'Education for All' can only be reached if we succeed in developing a working partnership between teachers, pupils, parents, and the community at large.

ELEMENTS OF A WHOLE-SCHOOL APPROACH

Meeting special educational needs in ordinary schools is much more than a process of opening school doors to admit children previously placed in special schools. It involves a radical re-examination of what all schools have to offer all children. Our efforts will be judged in the long term by our success with children who are already in ordinary schools but whose needs are not being met, for whatever reason.

The additional challenge of achieving full educational as well as social integration for children now in special schools needs to be seen in the wider context of a major reappraisal of what ordinary schools have to offer the pupils already in them. The debate about integration of handicapped and disabled children in ordinary schools should not be allowed to overshadow the movement for curriculum reform in the schools themselves. If successful, this could promote the fuller integration of the children already in the schools.

If this is the aim of current policy, as it is of this series of unit texts, we have to begin by examining ways in which schools and school policies can themselves be a major element in children's difficulties.

Can schools cause special needs?

Traditionally, we have looked for causes of learning difficulty in the child. Children have been subjected to tests and investigations by doctors, psychologists and teachers with the aim of pinpointing the nature of the problem and in the hope that this might lead to specific programmes of teaching and intervention. We less frequently ask ourselves whether what and how we teach and the way in which we organise and manage our schools could themselves be a major cause of children's difficulties.

The shift of emphasis towards a whole-school policy is sometimes described in terms of a move away from the deficit or medical model of special education towards a more environmental or ecological model. Clearly, we are concerned here with an interaction between the two. No one would deny that the origins of some learning difficulties do lie in the child. But even where a clear cause can be established – for example, a child with severe brain damage, or one with a serious sensory or motor disorder – it would be simplistic to attribute all the child's learning difficulties to the basic impairment alone.

The ecological model starts from the position that the growth and development of children can be understood only in relation to the nature of their interactions with the various environments which impinge on them and with which they are constantly interacting. These environments include the home and each individual member of the immediate and extended family. Equally important are other children in the neighbour-hood and at school, as well as people with whom the child comes into casual or closer contact. We also need to consider the local and wider community and its various institutions – not least, the powerful influence of television, which for some children represents more hours of informa-tion intake than is provided by teachers during eleven years of compul-sory education. The ecological model thus describes a gradually widening series of concentric circles, each of which provides a powerful series of influences and possibilities for interaction – and therefore learning.

Schools and schooling are only one of many environmental influences affecting the development and learning of children. A great deal has been learned from other environments before the child enters school and much more will be learned after the child leaves full-time education. Schools represent a relatively powerful series of environments, not all concerned with formal learning. During the hours spent in school, it is hard to estimate the extent to which the number and nature of the interactions experienced by any one child are directly concerned with formal teaching and learning. Social interactions with other children also need to be considered.

Questions concerned with access to the curriculum lie at the heart of any whole-school policy. What factors limit the access of certain children to the curriculum? What modifications are necessary to ensure fuller curriculum access? Are there areas of the curriculum from which some children are excluded? Is this because they are thought 'unlikely to be able to benefit'? And even if they are physically present, are there particular lessons or activities which are inaccessible because textbooks or work-sheets demand a level of literacy and comprehension which effectively prevent access? Are there tasks in which children partly or wholly fail to understand the language which the teacher is using? Are some teaching styles inappropriate for individual children?

Is it possible that some learning difficulties arise from the ways in which schools are organised and managed? For example, what messages are we conveying when we separate some children from others? How does the language we use to describe certain children reflect our own values and assumptions? How do schools transmit value judgements about children who succeed and those who do not? In the days when there was talk of comprehensive schools being 'grammar schools for all', what hope was there for children who were experiencing significant learning difficulties? And even today, what messages are we transmitting to children and their peers when we exclude them from participation in some school activities? How many children with special needs will be entered for the new General Certificate of Secondary Education (GCSE) examinations? How many have taken or will take part in Technical and Vocational Education Initiative (TVEI) schemes? The argument here is not that all children should have access to all aspects of the curriculum. Rather it is a plea for the individualisation of learning opportunities for all children. This requires a broad curriculum with a rich choice of learning opportunities designed to suit the very wide range of individual needs.

Curriculum reform

The last decade has seen an increasingly interventionist approach by Her Majesty's Inspectors of Education (HMI), by officials of the Department of Education and Science (DES) and by individual Secretaries of State. The 'Great Debate', allegedly beginning in 1976, led to a flood of curriculum guidelines from the centre. The garden is secret no longer. Whilst Britain is far from the centrally imposed curriculum found in some other countries, government is increasingly insisting that schools must reflect certain key areas of experience for all pupils, and in particular those concerned with the world of work (*sic*), with science and technology, and with economic awareness. These priorities are also reflected in the prescriptions for teacher education laid down with an increasing degree of firmness from the centre.

There are indications that a major reappraisal of curriculum content and access is already under way and seems to be well supported by teachers. Perhaps the best known and most recent examples can be found in the series of Inner London Education Authority (ILEA) reports concerned with secondary, primary and special education, known as the Hargreaves, Thomas and Fish Reports (ILEA, 1984, 1985a, 1985b). In particular, the Hargreaves Report envisaged a radical reform of the secondary curriculum, based to some extent on his book *Challenge for the Comprehensive School* (Hargreaves, 1982). This envisages a major shift of emphasis from the 'cognitive–academic' curriculum of many secondary schools towards one emphasising more personal involvement by pupils in selecting their own patterns of study from a wider range of choice. If the proposals in these reports were to be even partially implemented, pupils with special needs would stand to benefit from such a wholesale review of the curriculum of the school as a whole.

Pupils with special needs also stand to benefit from other developments in mainstream education. These include new approaches to records of achievement, particularly 'profiling' and a greater emphasis on criterion-referenced assessment. Some caution has already been expressed about the extent to which the new GCSE examinations will reach less able children previously excluded from the Certificate of Secondary Education. Similar caution is justified in relation to the TVEI and the Certificate of Pre-Vocational Education (CPVE). And what about the new training initiatives for school leavers and the 14–19 age group in general? Certainly, the pronouncements of the Manpower Services Commission (MSC) emphasise a policy of provision for all, and have made specific arrangements for young people with special needs, including those with disabilities. In the last analysis, society and its institutions will be judged by their success in preparing the majority of young people to make an effective and valued contribution to the community as a whole.

A CLIMATE OF CHANGE

Despite the very real and sometimes overwhelming difficulties faced by schools and teachers as a result of underfunding and professional unrest, there are encouraging signs of change and reform which, if successful, could have a significant impact not only on children with special needs but on all children. Some of these are briefly mentioned below.

The campaign for equal opportunities

First, we are more aware of the need to confront issues concerned with civil rights and equal opportunities. All professionals concerned with human services are being asked to examine their own attitudes and practices and to question the extent to which these might unwittingly or even deliberately discriminate unfairly against some sections of the population.

We are more conscious than ever of the need to take positive steps to promote the full access of girls and women not only to full educational opportunities but also to the whole range of community resources and services, including employment, leisure, housing, social security and the right to property. We have a similar concern for members of ethnic and religious groups who have been and still are victims of discrimination and restricted opportunities for participation in society and its institutions. It is no accident that the title of the Swann Report on children from ethnic minorities was *Education for All* (Committee of Inquiry, 1985). This too is the theme of the present series and the underlying aim of the movement to meet the whole range of special needs in ordinary schools.

The equal opportunities movement has not itself always fully accepted people with disabilities and special needs. At national level, there is no legislation specifically concerned with discrimination against people with disabilities, though this does exist in some other countries. The Equal Opportunities Commission does not concern itself with disability issues. On the other hand, an increasing number of local authorities and large corporations claim to be 'Equal Opportunities Employers', specifically mentioning disability alongside gender, ethnicity and sexual orientation. Furthermore, the 1986 Disabled Persons Act, arising from a private member's Bill and now on the statute book, seeks to carry forward for adults some of the more positive features of the 1981 Education Act – for example, it provides for the rights of all people with disabilities to take part or be represented in discussion and decision-making concerning services provided for them.

These developments, however, have been largely concerned with children or adults with disabilities, rather than with children already in ordinary schools. Powerful voluntary organisations such as MENCAP (the Royal Society for Mentally Handicapped Children and Adults) and the Spastics Society have helped to raise political and public awareness of the needs of children with disabilities and have fought hard and on the whole successfully to secure better services for them and for their families. Similarly, organisations of adults with disabilities, such as the British Council of Organisations for Disabled People, are pressing hard for better quality, integrated education, given their own personal experiences of segregated provision.

Special needs and social disadvantage

Even these developments have largely bypassed two of the largest groups now in special schools: those with moderate learning difficulties and those with emotional and behavioural difficulties. There are no powerful pressure groups to speak for them, for the same reason that no pressure groups speak for the needs of children with special needs already in ordinary schools. Many of these children come from families which do not readily form themselves into associations and pressure groups. Many of their parents are unemployed, on low incomes or dependent on social security; many live in overcrowded conditions in poor quality housing or have long-standing health problems. Some members of these families have themselves experienced school failure and rejection as children.

Problems of poverty and disadvantage are common in families of children with special needs already in ordinary schools. Low achievement and social disadvantage are clearly associated, though it is important not to assume that there is a simple relation between them. Although most children from socially disadvantaged backgrounds have not been identified as low achieving, there is still a high correlation between social-class membership and educational achievement, with middle-class children distancing themselves increasingly in educational achievements and perhaps also socially from children from working-class backgrounds – another form of segregation within what purports to be the mainstream.

The probability of socially disadvantaged children being identified as having special needs is very much greater than in other children. An early estimate suggested that it was more than seven times as high, when social disadvantage was defined by the presence of all three of the following indices: overcrowding (more than 1.5 persons per room), low income (supplementary benefit or free school meals) and adverse family circumstances (coming from a single-parent home or a home with more than five children) (Wedge and Prosser, 1973). Since this study was published, the number of families coming into these categories has greatly increased as a result of deteriorating economic conditions and changing social circumstances.

In this wider sense, the problem of special needs is largely a problem of social disadvantage and poverty. Children with special needs are therefore doubly vulnerable to underestimation of their abilities: first, because of their family and social backgrounds, and second, because of their low achievements. A recent large-scale study of special needs provision in junior schools suggests that while teachers' attitudes to low-achieving children are broadly positive, they are pessimistic about the ability of such children to derive much benefit from increased special needs provision (Croll and Moses, 1985).

Partnership with parents

The Croll and Moses survey of junior school practice confirms that teachers still tend to attribute many children's difficulties to adverse home circumstances. How many times have we heard comments along the lines of 'What can you expect from a child from that kind of family?' Is this not a form of stereotyping at least as damaging as racist and sexist attitudes?

Partnership with parents of socially disadvantaged children thus presents a very different challenge from that portrayed in the many reports of successful practice in some special schools. Nevertheless, the challenge can be and is being met. Paul Widlake's recent books (1984, 1985) give the lie to the oft-expressed view that some parents are 'not interested in their child's education'. Widlake documents project after project in which teachers and parents have worked well together. Many of these projects have involved teachers visiting homes rather than parents attending school meetings. There is also now ample research to show that children whose parents listen to them reading at home tend to read better and to enjoy reading more than other children (Topping and Wolfendale, 1985; see also Sheila Wolfendale's *Primary Schools and Special Needs*, in the present series).

Support in the classroom

If teachers in ordinary schools are to identify and meet the whole range of special needs, including those of children currently in special schools, they are entitled to support. Above all, this must come from the head teacher and from the senior staff of the school; from any special needs specialists or teams already in the school; from members of the new advisory and support services, as well as from educational psychologists, social workers and any health professionals who may be involved.

This support can take many forms. In the past, support meant removing the child for considerable periods of time into the care of remedial teachers either within the school or coming from outside. Withdrawal now tends to be discouraged, partly because it is thought to be another form of segregation within the ordinary school, and therefore in danger of isolating and stigmatising children, and partly because it deprives children of access to lessons and activities available to other children. In a major survey of special needs provision in middle and secondary schools, Clunies-Ross and Wimhurst (1983) showed that children with special needs were most often withdrawn from science and modern languages in order to find the time to give them extra help with literacy.

Many schools and LEAs are exploring ways in which both teachers and children can be supported without withdrawing children from ordinary classes. For example, special needs teachers increasingly are working alongside their colleagues in ordinary classrooms, not just with a small group of children with special needs but also with all children. Others are working as consultants to their colleagues in discussing the level of difficulty demanded of children following a particular course or specific lesson. An account of recent developments in consultancy is given in Hanko (1985), with particular reference to children with difficulties of behaviour or adjustment.

Although traditional remedial education is undergoing radical reform, major problems remain. Implementation of new approaches is uneven both between and within LEAs. Many schools still have a remedial department or are visited by peripatetic remedial teachers who withdraw children for extra tuition in reading with little time for consultation with school staff. Withdrawal is still the preferred mode of providing extra help in primary schools, as suggested in surveys of current practice (Clunies-Ross and Wimhurst, 1983; Hodgson, Clunies-Ross and Hegarty, 1984; Croll and Moses, 1985).

Nevertheless, an increasing number of schools now see withdrawal as only one of a widening range of options, only to be used where the child's individually assessed needs suggest that this is indeed the most appropriate form of provision. Other alternatives are now being considered. The overall aim of most of these involves the development of a working partnership between the ordinary class teacher and members of teams with particular responsibility for meeting special needs. This partnership can take a variety of forms, depending on particular circumstances and individual preferences. Much depends on the sheer credibility of special needs teachers, their perceived capacity to offer support and advice and, where necessary, direct, practical help.

We can think of the presence of the specialist teacher as being on a continuum of visibility. A 'high-profile' specialist may sit alongside a pupil with special needs, providing direct assistance and support in participating in activities being followed by the rest of the class. A 'low-profile' specialist may join with a colleague in what is in effect a team-teaching situation, perhaps spending a little more time with individuals or groups with special needs. An even lower profile is provided by teachers who may not set foot in the classroom at all but who may spend considerable periods of time in discussion with colleagues on ways in which the curriculum can be made more accessible to all children in the class, including the least able. Such discussions may involve an examination of textbooks and other reading assignments for readability, conceptual difficulty and relevance of content, as well as issues concerned with the presentation of the material, language modes and complexity used to explain what is required, and the use of different approaches to teacher-pupil dialogue.

IMPLICATIONS FOR TEACHER TRAINING

Issues of training are raised by the authors of the three overview works in this series but permeate all the volumes concerned with specific areas of the curriculum or specific areas of special needs.

The scale and complexity of changes taking place in the field of special needs and the necessary transformation of the teacher-training curriculum imply an agenda for teacher training that is nothing less than retraining and supporting every teacher in the country in working with pupils with special needs.

Although teacher training represented one of the three major priorities identified by the Warnock Committee, the resources devoted to this priority have been meagre, despite a strong commitment to training from teachers,

LEAs, staff of higher education, HMI and the DES itself. Nevertheless, some positive developments can be noted (for more detailed accounts of developments in teacher education see Sayer and Jones, 1985 and Robson, Sebba, Mittler and Davies, 1988).

Initial training

At the initial training level, we now find an insistence that all teachers in training must be exposed to a compulsory component concerned with meeting special needs in the ordinary school. The Council for the Accreditation of Teacher Education (CATE) and HMI seem set to enforce these criteria; institutions that do not meet them will not be accredited for teacher training.

Although this policy is welcome from a special needs perspective, many questions remain. Where will the staff to teach these courses come from? What happened to the Warnock recommendations for each teacher-training institution to have a small team of staff specifically concerned with this area? Even when a team exists, they can succeed in 'permeating' a special needs element into initial teacher training only to the extent that they influence all their fellow specialist tutors to widen their teaching perspectives to include children with special needs.

Special needs departments in higher education face similar problems to those confronting special needs teams in secondary schools. They need to gain access to and influence the work of the whole institution. They also need to avoid the situation where the very existence of an active special needs department results in colleagues regarding special needs as someone else's responsibility, not theirs.

Despite these problems, the outlook in the long term is favourable. More and more teachers in training are at least receiving an introduction to special needs; are being encouraged to seek out information on special needs policy and practice in the schools in which they are doing their teaching practice, and are being introduced to a variety of approaches to meeting their needs. Teaching materials are being prepared specifically for initial teacher-training students. Teacher trainers have also been greatly encouraged by the obvious interest and commitment of students to children with special needs; optional and elective courses on this subject have always been over-subscribed.

Inservice courses for designated teachers

Since 1983, the government has funded a series of one-term full-time courses in polytechnics and universities to provide intensive training for designated teachers with specific responsibility for pupils with special needs in ordinary schools (see *Meeting Special Needs in Ordinary Schools* by Seamus Hegarty in this series for information on research on evaluation of their effectiveness). These courses are innovative in a number of respects. They bring LEA and higher-education staff together in a productive working partnership. The seconded teacher, headteacher, LEA adviser and higher-education tutor enter into a commitment to train and support the teachers in becoming change agents in their own schools. Students spend two days a week in their own schools initiating and implementing change. All teachers with designated responsibilities for pupils with special needs have the right to be considered for these one-term courses, which are now a national priority area for which central funding is available. However, not all teachers can gain access to these courses as the institutions are geographically very unevenly distributed.

Other inservice courses

The future of inservice education for teachers (INSET) in education in general and special needs in particular is in a state of transition. Since April 1987, the government has abolished the central pooling arrangements which previously funded courses and has replaced these by a system in which LEAs are required to identify their training requirements and to submit these to the DES for funding. LEAs are being asked to negotiate training needs with each school as part of a policy of staff development and appraisal. Special needs is one of nineteen national priority areas that will receive 70 per cent funding from the DES, as is training for further education (FE) staff with special needs responsibilities.

These new arrangements, known as Grant Related Inservice Training (GRIST), will change the face of inservice training for all teachers but time is needed to assess their impact on training opportunities and teacher effectiveness (see Mittler, 1986, for an interim account of the implications of the proposed changes). In the meantime, there is serious concern about the future of secondments for courses longer than one term. Additional staffing will also be needed in higher education to respond to the wider range of demand.

An increasing number of 'teaching packages' have become available for teachers working with pupils with special needs. Some (though not all) of these are well designed and evaluated. Most of them are school-based and can be used by small groups of teachers working under the supervision of a trained tutor.

The best known of these is the Special Needs Action Programme (SNAP) originally developed for Coventry primary schools (Muncey and Ainscow, 1982) but now being adapted for secondary schools. This is based on a form of pyramid training in which co-ordinators from each school are trained to train colleagues in their own school or sometimes in a consortium of local schools. Evaluation by a National Foundation for Educational Research (NFER) research team suggests that SNAP is potentially an effective approach to school-based inservice training, providing that strong management support is guaranteed by the headteacher and by senior LEA staff (see Hegarty, *Meeting Special Needs in Ordinary Schools*, this series, for a brief summary).

Does training work?

Many readers of this series of books are likely to have recent experience of training courses. How many of them led to changes in classroom practice? How often have teachers been frustrated by their inability to introduce and implement change in their schools on returning from a course? How many heads actively support their staff in becoming change agents? How many teachers returning from advanced one-year courses have experienced 'the re-entry phenomenon'? At worst, this is quite simply being ignored: neither the LEA adviser, nor the head nor any one else asks about special interests and skills developed on the course and how these could be most effectively put to good use in the school. Instead, the returning member of staff is put through various re-initiation rituals ('Enjoyed your holiday?'), or is given responsibilities bearing no relation to interests developed on the course. Not infrequently, colleagues with less experience and fewer qualifications are promoted over their heads during their absence.

At a time of major initiatives in training, it may seem churlish to raise questions about the effectiveness of staff training. It is necessary to do so because training resources are limited and because the morale and motivation of the teaching force depend on satisfaction with what is offered – indeed, on opportunities to negotiate what is available with course providers. Blind faith in training for training's sake soon leads to disillusionment and frustration.

For the last three years, a team of researchers at Manchester University and Huddersfield Polytechnic have been involved in a DES funded project which aimed to assess the impact of a range of inservice courses on teachers working with pupils with special educational needs (see Robson, Sebba, Mittler and Davies, 1988, for a full account and Sebba, 1987, for a briefer interim report). A variety of courses was evaluated; some were held for one evening a week for a term; others were one-week full time; some were award-bearing, others were not. The former included the North-West regional diploma in special needs, the first example of a course developed in total partnership between a university and a polytechnic which allowed students to take modules from either institution and also gave credit recognition to specific Open University and LEA courses. The research also evaluated the effectiveness of an already published and disseminated course on behavioural methods of teaching – the EDY course (Farrell, 1985).

Whether or not the readers of these books are or will be experiencing a training course, or whether their training consists only of the reading of one or more of the books in this series, it may be useful to conclude by highlighting a number of challenges facing teachers and teacher trainers in the coming decades.

1. We are all out of date in relation to the challenges that we face in our work.
2. Training in isolation achieves very little. Training must be seen as part of a wider programme of change and development of the institution as a whole.
3. Each LEA, each school and each agency needs to develop a strategic approach to staff development, involving detailed identification of training and development needs with the staff as a whole and with each individual member of staff.
4. There must be a commitment by management to enable the staff member to try to implement ideas and methods learned on the course.
5. This implies a corresponding commitment by the training institutions to prepare the student to become an agent of change.

6. There is more to training than attending courses. Much can be learned simply by visiting other schools, seeing teachers and other professionals at work in different settings and exchanging ideas and experiences. Many valuable training experiences can be arranged within a single school or agency, or by a group of teachers from different schools meeting regularly to carry out an agreed task.
7. There is now no shortage of books, periodicals, videos and audio-visual aids concerned with the field of special needs. Every school should therefore have a small staff library which can be used as a resource by staff and parents. We hope that the present series of unit texts will make a useful contribution to such a library.

The publishers and I would like to thank the many people – too numerous to mention – who have helped to create this series. In particular we would like to thank the Associate Editors, James Hogg, Peter Pumfrey, Tessa Roberts and Colin Robson, for their active advice and guidance; the Honorary Advisory Board, Neville Bennett, Marion Blythman, George Cooke, John Fish, Ken Jones, Sylvia Phillips, Klaus Wedell and Phillip Williams, for their comments and suggestions; and the teachers, teacher trainers and special needs advisers who took part in our information surveys.

Professor Peter Mittler   University of Manchester
                                                      January 1987

REFERENCES

Clunies-Ross, L. and Wimhurst, S. (1983) *The Right Balance: Provision for Slow Learners in Secondary Schools*. Windsor: NFER/Nelson.
Committee of Inquiry (1985) *Education for All*. London: HMSO (The Swann Report).
Croll, P. and Moses, D. (1985) *One in Five: The Assessment and Incidence of Special Educational Needs*. London: Routledge & Kegan Paul.
Farrell, P. (ed.) (1985) *EDY: Its Impact on Staff Training in Mental Handicap*. Manchester: Manchester University Press.
Hanko, G. (1985) *Special Needs in Ordinary Classrooms: An Approach to Teacher Support and Pupil Care in Primary and Secondary Schools*. Oxford: Blackwell.
Hargreaves, D. (1982) *Challenge for the Comprehensive School*. London: Routledge & Kegan Paul.
Hodgson, A., Clunies-Ross, L. and Hegarty, S. (1984) *Learning Together*. Windsor: NFER/Nelson.
Inner London Education Authority (1984) *Improving Secondary Education*. London: ILEA (The Hargreaves Report).
Inner London Education Authority (1985a) *Improving Primary Schools*. London: ILEA (The Thomas Report).
Inner London Education Authority (1985b) *Equal Opportunities for All?* London: ILEA (The Fish Report).
Mittler, P. (1986) The new look in inservice training. *British Journal of Special Education*, **13**, pp. 50–51.
Muncey, J. and Ainscow, M. (1982) Launching SNAP in Coventry. *Special Education: Forward Trends*, **10**, pp. 3–5.
Robson, C., Sebba, J., Mittler, P. and Davies, G. (1988) *Inservice Training and Special*

Needs: Running Short School-Focused Courses. Manchester: Manchester University Press.

Sayer, J. and Jones, N. (eds) (1985) *Teacher Training and Special Educational Needs.* Beckenham: Croom Helm.

Sebba, J. (1987) The development of short, school-focused INSET courses in special educational needs. *Research Papers in Education* (in press).

Topping, K. and Wolfendale, S. (eds) (1985) *Parental Involvement in Children's Reading.* Beckenham: Croom Helm.

Wedge, P. and Prosser, H. (1973) *Born to Fail?* London: National Children's Bureau.

Widlake, P. (1984) *How to Reach the Hard to Teach.* Milton Keynes: Open University Press.

Widlake, P. (1985) *Reducing Educational Disadvantage.* London: Routledge & Kegan Paul.

—1—
Educational issues relating to pupils with visual disabilities

Teachers will find that the educational goals which they set for their visually handicapped pupils are essentially the same as for the fully sighted children in their classes and that these goals are attainable. The expertise, professionalism and caring interest that are needed by all pupils from those who teach them give the best basis for the education and support of pupils with special needs, including those who have visual disabilities. It will be appreciated that a single developmental problem, such as defective vision, need not dominate the pupils' classroom activities, nor differentiate them unduly from the classmates with whom they work and play. It is the combination of different characteristics, strengths and weaknesses that leads to the development of the pupil's unique personality, and in common with other children, those with visual handicaps will show a range of character, ability and adjustment. Nor can potential school achievement or social competence be directly linked to levels of sight: pupils with little or no sight have shown that they can achieve well in school, be independent and happy, since the interaction of the child and the learning environment is as significant for them in helping to achieve these goals as it is for any pupil in school. Sometimes, learning materials will need to be presented in a different way, and emphasis given to particular aspects of learning, but an understanding of the pupil's needs can clarify issues of curriculum access and special adaptations can be made for those pupils who have sight problems.

THE SIGNIFICANCE OF THE WARNOCK REPORT AND THE 1981 EDUCATION ACT

Such specific measures need to be considered in the context of present educational philosophy and provision. The approaches to the education of children with special needs, culminating in the 1981 Education Act, are equally applicable to pupils with defective vision, some of whom will be included among those pupils who are defined as having learning disabilities significantly greater than the majority of their peers, or as having some disability which would prevent them from having their needs fully met without special educational adaptations or modification to their curriculum. In the procedures required to fulfil the special educational needs of visually handicapped pupils, as with any pupils with special needs, the local education authority must make a formal assessment culminating in a statement of the child's individual special needs. The previous categorising of pupils in terms of the medical aspects of their handicap is no longer the ruling factor in deciding educational placement, although a thorough understanding of the implications of visual loss or reduced vision is necessary in order to meet the pupils' needs effectively. The philosophy of the Warnock Report (Department of Education and Science, 1978) greatly influenced the content of the 1981 Education Act, particularly with its recommendation that varying and individual educational needs should be acknowledged, rather than prejudged on the basis of categories. It was recognised by the Warnock Committee that children with sensory impairments could indeed have special educational needs, but that these might be met within a range of different kinds of educational placements, for instance, in individual integration, in special units, or in special schools. In addition, this committee reflected the view of many educators of visually handicapped pupils that there is no distinct cut-off point between the fully and the partially sighted, nor between the partially sighted and the blind in terms of functioning. Aspects of personality and motivation, social and cognitive development could be as significant as sensory impairment in affecting the pupil's educational needs and influencing his progress.

The recommendations of the Warnock Report and the legislation of the 1981 Education Act are significant in the educational placement of visually handicapped pupils, especially since the presence of visual impairments is no longer considered to be sufficient reason for special school placement nor is special school placement an inevitable consequence of the ascertainment of visual impairment. The total and individual needs of each child are considered more fully, and the assessment procedure which precedes recommendations for educational placement calls for information from medical, psychological and educational sources as well as involving parents actively in the final decision about where and how the pupil is to be educated.

PROCEDURES LEADING TO EDUCATIONAL PLACEMENT

As part of the assessment, factors relating to the child's previous history, the medical diagnosis and prognosis and the home and school environment are considered. Any indications of present or potential learning difficulties are analysed. Recommendations in the light of this information will be proffered in terms of the resources, environmental adaptations, curriculum modifications and special teaching methods needed to meet the pupil's individual needs. A recommendation for appropriate school placement is subsequently given, and a draft statement of the child's individual educational needs and the suggested educational placement, together with the reports of the professionals involved in the assessment, are shown to the parents. If there is agreement on these recommendations, the final statement is authorised. The positive aspects of this procedure include the full and detailed consideration of the individual needs of each child. The drawback is that the procedure is time consuming and can result in a backlog of incomplete or unimplemented statements, with the possible consequence that there is undue delay before the pupil is appropriately placed or supported.

The particular needs of children with defective sight call for a report on the child's eye condition or cause of defective vision from an ophthalmologist, and a report is also requested from the educational advisory service for the visually handicapped. This should be constructive and include an assessment of the child's functional levels of vision, details of preferred lighting, and recommendations regarding the presentation of materials for learning. Details of any special equipment, such as tape recorders, typewriters and closed circuit television will need to be provided. The advisory service should also consider the curricular needs of the pupil, and the inclusion of special or additional areas such as keyboard skills or mobility and orientation that will enable the pupil to have full access to the curriculum and to take part in all aspects of school life. Recommendations may include safety factors in practical areas, for instance, home economics or chemistry, and suggested alternative activities in cases where sight loss is so severe that the general activity is inappropriate, for example, judo or weight lifting instead of football. The report should also include proposals for extra support teaching and welfare provision if necessary and a recognition that extra preparation time may be required by the pupil. A full report from a qualified teacher of the visually handicapped is required in order to ensure that the pupil's real needs are identified and provided for.

Parental choice in educational placement

The location of schools and services in relation to the child's home can still influence decisions about the pupil's educational placement despite the ideal of open choice on the part of parents. Since the 1981 Education Act requires that the wishes of the parents are fully taken into account when school placement is determined, it will be important for them to have access to consultation and discussion with a professional who is well informed about both the educational needs of visually handicapped children and the schools and support services available. Parents may be faced with the question of whether their child will be considered to be 'special' in an ordinary school, or 'ordinary' in a special school. Consideration will have to be given to the child's potential and limitations, but it must be remembered that the pupil is part of a family with wishes and ambitions for the child. Parents can be greatly helped if they have received early information and guidance on the needs of children with no sight or defective vision, and in addition the chance to see for themselves educational provision as well as receiving information about potential placements. A late identification of visual handicap calls for information and advice to be readily available and sympathetically discussed with parents who are often expected to come to a decision about their child's educational placement while they are still trying to come to terms with the implications of a medical prognosis for their child that may be depressing.

There may well be problems ahead both for the pupil and for the school if the child's family are not in agreement with the professionals' decisions about the educational placement proposed. The prolonged procedure of appeal which the parents are entitled to embark upon in such circumstances can consume time and energy that would be better used in effecting a workable solution to placement problems. Time given to listening to the parents' point of view at an early stage and to reducing their anxieties by giving well-founded information can be helpful in arranging a placement which satisfies them.

Educational provision for visually handicapped pupils

Once all the relevant information needed to make a placement decision has been obtained, it is necessary to consider what educational opportunities are at present available for the visually handicapped pupil and sometimes what new opportunities, especially in integrated provision, can be developed.

Since severe visual handicap, especially total blindness, has a low incidence among school-aged children in the United Kingdom, it is likely that there will be very few children in each local education authority whose education requires significant adaptation as a result of lack of sight or substantially defective vision. This fact has a profound effect on service provision.

Colbourne-Browne and Tobin (1982) surveyed the educational placement of educationally blind pupils in England and Wales. By 'educationally blind' pupils, these authors mean those children who use tactile methods for their learning. They discovered that the numbers of such children attending special schools for the visually handicapped and those attending other kinds of schools, including integration into mainstream provision, were not grossly divergent. There were approximately a thousand in each type of provision. Those pupils not in special schools for the visually handicapped included pupils with other sensory, learning or physical handicaps who were in some cases attending special schools for children who were deaf, physically handicapped or mentally handicapped. But an interesting fact revealed by this study is that each of these groups would form a body of pupils scarcely greater than that of a large comprehensive school in mainstream education.

This low incidence of visual handicap means, in effect, that not every local education authority in England and Wales will have a range of appropriate educational placements for the severely visually impaired pupil, and it may be necessary to look for a solution in regional terms, or perhaps attendance at a residential special school may be considered.

Special schools for visually handicapped pupils

There are special schools for visually handicapped pupils in different regions of the country and the majority of these cater for pupils within the full range of visual impairment from total blindness to useful but impaired vision, although in a minority of cases there still remains an emphasis on meeting the needs of pupils who require either tactile or visual methods of working. A detailed account of the development of special school provision for visually handicapped pupils in the United Kingdom is given in Chapman (1978) and the address and details of all special schools for visually handicapped pupils are listed in the *Directory of Resources for those working with visually handicapped children* (Travis, 1987), published by Birmingham University.

In most instances these special schools for visually handicapped pupils are for children of primary school age or for the full school age-range and they have in general terms a regional catchment. There is one selective co-educational secondary school at Worcester College and a large all-age school at Exhall Grange, Warwickshire, both of which draw from a national catchment. Two special schools sponsored by the RNIB cater for pupils who have significant handicaps in addition to blindness. Schools offering special education for visually handicapped pupils have in many cases a residential base but still accept pupils on a daily basis when this is practicable. In the major conurbations day special schools may be available (for example, London, Birmingham), but for pupils in rural or inaccessible areas weekly or half-termly residence at a special school may still be the only viable option. Parents should be given full information about special school and integrated provision when placement is being considered. Some will wish to press for more neighbourhood educational provision for visually handicapped pupils and will hope that their child can go to school on a daily basis from home like his fully sighted peers. Both the recommendations of the Warnock Report and the legislation of the 1981 Education Act give impetus to this demand. Other parents, however, may want their child to attend a special school and may have had positive information about children with visual handicap who have been happy and successful in these schools. The placement best suited to the individual family should be sought.

UNIT PROVISION

The integration of visually handicapped pupils into neighbourhood schools can be effected in different ways. Unit provision usually takes the form of providing a home base in a separate room for visually handicapped pupils with the mainstream school. These pupils divide their time between the special unit and the ordinary classroom. The relative amount of time spent in either by an individual pupil will depend on the need for specialised teaching; teaching in the special unit will often be concerned with basic subjects. The balance of the work and activities may vary from child to child. For example, a pupil who is mastering literacy and numeracy with few difficulties will spend a considerable amount of time in the ordinary classroom, but another may need a good deal of specialised help and be at a stage of going to only one or two lessons daily in the fully integrated situation. If the pupil needs to be withdrawn for specialist teaching for a substantial amount of schoolwork, unit provision has a lot to offer. It may be considered as a transitional stage between attendance at a special school and full integration into mainstream education, or as a stage leading towards more intensive specialised provision. Unit provision should enable pupils to have their special needs met in an individual way whilst they are benefiting from the environment of an ordinary school.

RESOURCE CENTRES

Pupils in resource centre provision usually have the ordinary classroom as their home base, with the responsibility for what they are taught resting with their classroom teacher. Curriculum adaptations and support teaching sessions are provided by the resource teacher, and these sessions may be given either on a withdrawal basis or within the classroom.

In both these settings the specialist teacher can organise, often at short notice, the preparation of appropriate materials or give teaching support in a particular lesson. Sometimes it is necessary for the specialist teacher to be available to help in providing solutions for specific problems that arise in the classroom or more generally in the school because of specific difficulties that the visually handicapped child encounters, for instance, in dealing with visual materials or in taking part in group activities. The special teacher will need appropriate training and experience in order to solve many of these problems, and co-operation between specialist and regular teachers is essential in effecting this. Staff relationships often seem to be most successful when the unit or resource teacher takes a full part as a member of the school staff and is involved in general activities in the school.

There are some practical considerations that must be faced in terms of support for visually handicapped pupils who are being educated in resource situations. These include consultations over timetables, planning the inclusion of additional areas of the curriculum (braille, typewriting) and working out accessible storage for specialised equipment and materials. Pupils may still have to travel appreciable distances in order to attend unit or resource provision. This is not only tiring but may also preclude the child from participating in sports clubs, choir, drama groups or other out-of-school activities. These considerations can be a factor in deciding whether to provide an individually based integrated situation which gives the visually handicapped pupil the chance to go to school with neighbourhood children. Problems in this case which require resolution can lie in the need to provide sufficient specialised teaching support together with enough resources and equipment for the individual pupil at the time when they are needed (Chapman, 1978). The ethos of the receiving school in terms of accepting pupils with special needs and the physical environment in terms of the school campus and classrooms should be realistically appraised prior to recommendations for individual placements.

It is not in the interest of visually handicapped pupils or their parents for special schools and integrated provision to be considered either as competitors or as exclusive alternatives. Transfer from special school to integrated provision as a pupil gains mastery of specialised skills or transfer from integrated provision to special provision for specific reasons should be neither surprising nor impossible. It is the quality and appropriateness of the educational placement that is truly significant for the pupil rather than the theoretical views of those who decide upon it.

Advisory and peripatetic services

The support of an advisory service should be available to teachers who have visually handicapped pupils in their classes in mainstream schools, but there is a particular need for this when implementing the recommendations for a pupil who has been the subject of a statement. It is likely that the specialised services for visually handicapped children will be part of the local education authority's educational services, although some advisers are based on a special school for visually handicapped children. The main criterion for an effective service must be that it is staffed by experienced professionals who are appropriately qualified. The Warnock Report (op. cit.) recognises that pupils with sensory handicaps need advisory services providing support at this level.

The way in which the advisory role is carried out can vary in different locations. The spread of population, the numbers of visually handicapped pupils in a particular area and the range of educational provision available to them will influence the way in which the advisory service is organised and implemented. The nature of the work undertaken will also be substantially determined by the size of the advisory team. For example, some newly established services consist of only one peripatetic teacher responsible for the support of the entire age and ability range of visually handicapped pupils throughout the authority. Large authorities, or ones with a well-established service, may have several qualified teachers for visually handicapped pupils who are able to specialise in specific areas of support. These range through the needs of visually handicapped children in the pre-school, primary or secondary stages of education to those of adolescents attending further education courses and the special needs of multi-handicapped children with defective vision.

Benton (1984) lists the specific areas which should be provided by advisory services for visually handicapped pupils; these include the assessment of the pupils and the evaluation of their needs, direct support for the pupils, consultancy support for their teachers, and advice and counselling for their parents.

The procedures for assessment and the evaluation of educational needs have become more formalised since the 1981 Education Act so that now a report from a qualified teacher of visually handicapped children is a requirement of the assessment procedure for a child whose learning or development is affected by defective sight. The implications of the medical diagnosis in so far as it is likely to affect the child's education will need to be considered and attention given to the prognosis, especially if it involves the possibility of progressive deterioration of sight. The child's functional vision, that is the way in which sight is used in day-to-day school activities, must be assessed in addition to clinical information. Assessing functional vision will involve careful observation of the child's visual behaviour and ability to cope with blackboard and demonstration work, close desk or table tasks, physical and practical activities and recreation and playtime activities. The optimum conditions for effective functioning in terms of the physical environment, the suitability of learning materials and the need for adaptations to the curriculum will need to be planned.

Recommendations for training visually handicapped pupils to use any sight that they have as effectively as possible should be given, as should training in the use of low vision aids (magnifiers, etc.) and special equipment (closed circuit television) and in techniques for personal independence and mobility if these are necessary. These aspects of the pupil's education will need to be included in the report by the special teacher and should be taken into consideration when placement decisions are made.

Another function of the advisory service for visually handicapped children involves working with parents and families, and this is of particular importance in the case of the pre-school child with defective vision. Fortunately, pre-school visually handicapped children are frequently referred to the advisory services by the relevant medical services and this is helpful, since early intervention programmes can then be formulated involving parents and teachers and the possibility of nursery or playgroup provision explored. It is in these pre-school years that language development, concept formation and early independent mobility should be growing, and advisory services can help parents to encourage these.

A further task for the special advisory team will be to act as consultant to teachers who have visually handicapped pupils in their classes. The adviser can help to promote confidence in meeting the needs of these pupils by emphasising the aspects of learning which they share with their fully sighted classmates and suggesting practical measures that can help to minimise difficulties and increase curriculum access. Teachers can be made aware of the real challenges that visually handicapped pupils have to face. Sometimes they will complete tasks more slowly, owing to a slower rate of informational input (Mason and Tobin, 1986), but this need not necessarily reflect a reduced level of comprehension, although it may be mistaken for this. In the ordinary classroom, class and subject teachers should maintain responsibility for the content of lessons. To put the matter simply, they have the role of deciding what should be taught and when, with the specialist teacher as adviser giving guidance in the case of the visually handicapped pupils as to 'how'. The way in which learning materials are presented to visually handicapped pupils will be the major concern of the specialist teacher or adviser. Making or adapting these materials can be a time-consuming business and the help of ancillary assistance can be welcome. Professional advice on the transcription of reading schemes and work schemes is essential. The problems that may arise from an individual pupil's needs must also be addressed, and possible solutions proffered.

Direct and regular contact between the class teacher and the specialist teacher/adviser is vital in order to anticipate problems before they arise. An unduly large caseload of pupils can make this difficult, with the possibility of resentment building up if requests for help are not promptly met. Forward planning can be helpful in minimising difficulties, especially if any problems that pupils have are briefly recorded in writing rather than simply passed on verbally.

The specialist teacher may find that some visually handicapped pupils require direct support teaching sessions. These take place in the classroom where the specialist teacher assists or, in the case of practical subjects, in the laboratory, craft or home economics room where the specialist support teacher works with a group of children including those who are visually handicapped.

Teaching sessions on a withdrawal basis may be frequently timetabled and, although these are usually helpful to the pupil mastering basic skills or concepts, they should be monitored carefully in order to maintain the balance of the curriculum. Physical education, aesthetic and practical areas of learning and expression should be enjoyed by visually handicapped pupils as much as any others and give valuable opportunities for self-expression and the mastery of practical skills. The curriculum areas in which direct support teaching is most likely to be needed are those of literacy and numeracy, usually throughout the primary stage and often at the secondary stage. If these basic skills have been mastered, additional explanatory services and individual demonstration of processes may be needed to clarify work in mathematics and the sciences. For those pupils who possess some vision, there will need to be an emphasis on helping them to use this effectively for learning, with special training as well as some adapted materials. Independence in terms of mobility and self-help will need to be encouraged and in some cases specifically taught. It may also be necessary to begin keyboard skills in the last year of primary school and to continue this as required at the secondary level.

There may be social aspects of the visually handicapped pupil's life at school that can be helped by a perceptive specialist teacher who is able to facilitate communication over matters that a sensitive child or adolescent may be embarrassed to disclose. Pupils can sometimes be diffident in expressing their anxieties about their visual condition and may be greatly helped if they can talk to someone knowledgeable and experienced in such matters who is unlikely to be surprised by incidents which can be a worry to some youngsters, such as, for instance, a glass eye lost in the swimming pool or the effect of strong light on a photophobic (averse to glare) pupil which makes him sit with closed eyes. The specialist teacher can help to explain and deal with such problems and increase the confidence of the pupil and the understanding of the regular teacher in unusual cases of anxiety that might otherwise be deemed trivial.

Sometimes the advisory services for visually handicapped pupils are involved in the work of special schools for pupils with learning or physical disabilities as well as defective vision. In these situations they are able to contribute information and guidance regarding the problems that pupils have with visual activities and to consider on an individual basis the compounding effect that these may have in terms of the other disabilities from which the child may suffer. Co-operation between the teachers and therapists involved with the child aims at ensuring the formulation of a programme which takes account of all the physical, sensory and cognitive aspects of the child's development. (The general guidance on environment and the implications of visual handicap described in this book are relevant to the needs of pupils with multiple handicap that includes defective vision. Such background information is to be used in conjunction with individually formulated programmes, since it is unlikely that severely multi-handicapped pupils will be able to follow the programme of an ordinary class.)

The advisory services may also be responsible for pupils from their authority who attend special schools for the visually handi-capped, especially in the case of residential placements. Links can be established between home, school and the relevant authority which can help to monitor the child's progress, review placement and promote a well co-ordinated plan for the pupil's education.

These varied functions of the educational advisory services for visually handicapped pupils can be summed up as 'enabling'. The advisory team should enable the flow of relevant information on the pupils' needs to reach the schools where they are placed and enable teachers and visually handicapped pupils to work in an effective way because they are well informed and well supported.

THE INTERACTION BETWEEN MEDICAL AND EDUCATIONAL FACTORS

Pupils who are blind or who have significant and serious problems of sight have special educational needs whilst at the same time sharing major areas of learning and development with their fully sighted classmates. These facts are by no means irreconcilable, but it requires skill and knowledge on the part of the teacher to fulfil the special needs within the framework of teaching in the ordinary classroom.

Current educational philosophy has moved away from focusing on the physical or sensory basis of disability and so it may initially appear that an understanding of the cause of a child's disability is primarily a medical matter and not one of concern to the educator. Certainly the pupil should not be considered primarily as a medical case, nor should preconceived conclusions drawn from information on medical records be used to channel activities or limit opportunities. It must be emphasised that many factors in the child's motivation and experience affect both development and learning. Moreover, in the interests of the pupil a balance needs to be struck between the extremes of over-preoccupation with the medical aspects of the pupil's visual condition and ignorance of facts that could help the teacher to understand the child's special needs and find ways to fulfil them.

Although levels of sight do not relate directly to levels of performance in many school activities, there are some direct links between some of the specific forms of visual handicap and the way in which educational materials can most usefully be presented to individual children. The responsible educator will want to consider this, and use the information to give as much practical help as possible to the pupil who is visually impaired. There is, in fact, no reason why attention to a particular cause of defective vision should reduce the teacher's appreciation of the child's total needs and, moreover, relevant information can be helpful in offering precise and effective solutions to some of the problems of using materials and developing learning strategies that are likely to give difficulty to visually handicapped pupils.

For this reason, some basic ophthalmic information is given that will, it is hoped, clarify the cause of some of the problems that visually handicapped pupils can face. Teachers may want to use this information for reference in the case of individual pupils with visual defects or to study it in order to increase their general understanding of the implications of visual handicaps in learning. It is also relevant to the teacher to have some information about the way in which visually handicapped pupils are identified since they will have passed through these procedures before being in their present school.

IDENTIFICATION AND SCREENING

Teachers with pupils with defective vision in their classes have an interest in knowing how such children are identified and what services and professionals are involved in this procedure.

Most children with severe visual handicaps will have been discovered within a few days of their birth or in their early infancy in hospital. At home it may in some cases be the parents who notice something 'odd' about their baby's eyes or feel an unease about the baby's visual behaviour. If they voice this concern to the general practitioner or health visitor this may result in the first step being taken in the identification of a visual problem, but unfortunately there can be instances in which the defective vision is not detected until the child has a pre-school medical. In the early stages of a child's development the visual problem can be masked. In the confined environment of pre-school life the infant may have appeared to be progressing normally, and it may not be until an objective screening test is given that the sight problem is recognised.

Screening tests for vision are given on average three times during a child's life. As it is estimated that 25 per cent of school-children will have a sight problem that needs attention (Optical Information Council) it is essential that vision screening procedures should be effective. To be so, the screening procedures are dependent on the co-operation of school heads and staff in order to ensure that proper facilities are available for the testing to be undertaken properly. A quiet, empty room is needed so that the testing can be undisturbed, a check must be made for absent children, and the eye charts to be used must be left in a place where pupils will not be able to see them beforehand.

Every pupil should have a basic screening test for vision, and if problems are detected, further and more specific testing will need to be undertaken. Basic testing will include an assessment of distance vision.

DISTANCE VISION

This may be simply defined as the ability to discriminate highly contrasted figures from a distance. It involves both sharpness and clarity of vision and this can be measured. The usual test that is given for this is the Snellen chart for visual acuity , which is well known to anyone who has had a routine medical examination. The chart itself should be hung on a well-lit, shadow-free wall at a distance of six metres from where the subject stands. It is placed at eve level with one eye occluded. The child is asked to name the letters on the chart beginning with the top line. (Symbols of equivalent size are used for children who cannot name letters.) The letters or symbols are exactly measured, of decreasing size and arranged in rows. Each represents a calculated angle which can be discriminated by a subject with normal vision at a specific distance (60, 36, 24, 12, 9, or 6 metres from the chart). When the subject standing at 6 metres from the chart can read the 6m letters, his sight is recorded as 6/6, the upper figure denoting the distance from the chart, and the lower figure indicating the size of the line that has been read. This is recorded as normal vision.

If the subject can only read the 24m line when standing at the 6m distance from the chart, vision would be recorded as 6/24. (This subject would be reading from 6m the size of letter seen clearly by the normally sighted at 24m.) A subject only able to see the single large letters at the top of the chart (the 6/60 line) would be able only to discriminate at 6m what the normally sighted person would see clearly at 60m. Such vision would be recorded as 6/60 and would indicate severely reduced visual acuity. The procedure is followed with each eye being separately tested, with and without corrective glasses.

In measuring visual acuity in this way, a figure which looks like a fraction is recorded. The top figure denotes the distance from the chart (6m) and the lower figure the distance at which the subject with normal vision can see the letters. This information is significant for the teacher as blackboard and wall-mounted work may be difficult or impossible to discriminate for a pupil with poor visual acuity. (It is interesting to note that in order to pass a driving test a motorist needs a visual acuity of 6/15, that is, a standard between the 6/12 and 6/18 line.)

For accurate measurement of distance vision, when the Snellen chart is used, lighting must be good but not dazzling, the test administered singly, and the distance at which the child stands exactly measured. Consistent standards are essential if visual anomalies are to be recorded accurately.

Pre-school children, or those who are developmentally delayed may be tested with the Sheridan vision test for young children and retardates. This is known as the STYCAR test and was devised by

Mary Sheridan using the Snellen standard but with a smaller selection of letters and with the possibility of using a 3m distance, more suitable for younger children than the standard 6m distance.

NEAR VISION

In addition to the Snellen test for distance vision, all school-aged children should be screened to assess their levels of near vision. This again is relevent to school tasks since it is near vision that is used for close work such as reading and writing. The subject is given examples of print of decreasing size to discriminate, or single letters of measured and decreasing size. There are several versions of the near vision test, but in each case there is a standard number preceded by N for each print size. The larger the number, the larger the print size. These graduate from N36 to N5 which is the size of print found in the standard telephone directory; the first books in the 'Ladybird' series of readers are in N36 print. If a child's vision report gives a figure of distance vision as 6/24 and near vision as N8 with corrective glasses, this would indicate that the pupil should be able to read quite small print, but has a lowered visual acuity in terms of distance vision. For such a pupil blackboard work with small writing could well cause difficulty.

COLOUR VISION

Colour vision should also be tested. Although defective colour perception does not usually have significant effect in many class activities, there are some careers for which absolute perception is needed (armed forces, electrical trades). Defective colour perception has a high incidence among males (one in ten) and teachers should be aware of the fact that some of the coloured materials that they present will not be normally discriminated by a proportion of their pupils. One six year old painted a picture of a strawberry in a murky green in spite of the bright red of the original fruit, and it is usually the red/green part of the spectrum that is affected, although blue/yellow deficiency may occur or there may even be a total loss of colour perception. There are various tests for colour perception, some using plates of solid colour, but the most usual one is the Ishihara Test which presents a symbol or number depicted in coloured dots against a background of dots of another colour. These presentations are referred to as pseudoisochromatic or confusion plates and set a task in which the normal eye can discriminate figures composed of coloured dots, whilst the eye with abnormal colour vision cannot do so.

If there are reasons to indicate that the child has visual defects, more detailed and sophisticated tests will be undertaken by an ophthalmologist to whom the child will be referred. These procedures are likely to include mapping out the field of vision in each eye, measuring the pressure within the eyeball, and testing for contrast sensitivity. Difficulties in contrast sensitivity may not become apparent when the Snellen Test is used, but a child scoring medium or low levels on a contrast sensitivity test could have problems in discriminating print unless it was presented in strong contrast in a good light.

Further procedures which may be undertaken in cases where more detailed information is needed or where it is suspected that there may be serious problems with vision include the visually evaluated response (VER) and the electroretinogram (ERG).

As children grow there can be changes in their vision, and since screening tests may be infrequent, teachers should be aware of some of the physical signs and behaviours that may indicate that a child is having problems with sight. In both formal and informal activities within the classroom, children use their vision in different ways, and observant teachers can help to identify visual difficulties by being alert to the ways in which such problems can manifest themselves. Because the recognition of defective sight is so significant in terms of the child's development and learning, it is not surprising that the importance of attention to presenting symptoms has been emphasised by experienced educators of visually handicapped children. Lists of significant indications of the possibility of sight difficulties on which Marshall (1969), Chapman (1978) and Mason (Fitt and Mason, 1986) lay stress are set out here with only minor variations or additions; the present writers confirm and extend these listings as a basis of cause for further investigation of the child's sight:

1. *Physical indications that may be caused by defective vision:*
   unusual head position while working (poking forward or held sideways);
   work held at an unusual distance or angle;
   frowning, squinting or facial grimaces when trying to read;
   complaints of headache or dizziness during visual activities;
   covering one eye with the hand, or closing it;
   aversion to bright light.
2. *Difficulties in managing school tasks:*
   confusion of letters which are similar in shape (o and a);
   unexplained delay in reading;
   short attention span in visual tasks;
   marking the place with the finger continuously when reading;

     reversing letters;
     poor hand–eye co-ordination;
     inability to copy work from blackboard.
3. *Indications of possible visual problems in play activities:*
     reluctance to take part in physical activities;
     clumsiness and tendency to bump into objects;
     hovering on the edge of the playground rather than actively playing;
     walking 'carefully';
     poor balance and fear of lights.
4. *Appearance of the eyes:*
     swollen, sore, crusted or drooping eyelids;
     continuous or uncontrolled eye movements (nystagmus);
     misshapen or irregular pupil;
     eyes that are not normally aligned and working in co-ordination.

Naturally, some of these indications are quite likely to be related to problems other than faulty vision, but since sight problems may be causing them, a screening test which is, after all, quick and easy to perform should help to confirm or rule out defective vision as a reason for concern.

PROCEDURES FOLLOWING VISION SCREENING

Children who do show difficulties in the screening test for vision must be referred for further examination. Vision screening procedures, even when administered regularly and appropriately, are useless if the results from them are not followed up. Although it is the responsibility of the Child Health Service to refer the child, the teacher will have an interest in knowing if a hospital appointment has been made and kept even though this is the prime responsibility of the parents. Co-operation between educational and medical services can minimise potential neglect of visual conditions in children.

Whilst vision screening for the school population as a whole is essential in order to identify pupils with sight defects so that they can have appropriate treatment and correction when this is applicable, there are implications for educators too, arising from the procedures used to identify children with visual handicap. The specialist teacher or adviser will need to discuss with the pupil's own teacher the information obtained from screening procedures that has a bearing on adaptations to learning materials or to the environment.

Such information will include the consideration of any problems that the child may have with near or distance vision, with colour perception, with reduction of the visual field, with discomfort in strong light (photophobia) or with monocular vision (sight in only one eye) which affects depth perception. The prognosis of the condition is highly relevant since it may indicate increasing difficulty in using printed material. It is also important for the teacher to know if any treatment is being given, such as eye drops, whether exercises have been prescribed and if there is any restriction on physical activities such as diving or lifting heavy weights. Spectacles or low vision aids may have been prescribed in some cases, and teachers should be informed about this.

Both screening and the observation of the child's visual behaviour will be used as a basis to determine the size of print to be used in individual cases, and will also indicate whether braille and tactile materials will need to be used instead. These measures will show the distance at which the child with defective vision can be expected to discriminate visually presented material.

FUNCTIONAL VISION

Whilst the clinical measurements of visual acuity and visual field yield key information for medical purposes of treatment and correction when possible, they also afford scientifically accurate data to be used as a basis for presenting learning materials that involve the use of vision.

But there are other factors involved in the way in which pupils use their sight that are of relevance to the teacher, especially since it may be found that pupils who have comparable recorded levels of visual acuity seem to use their sight differently. For instance, there are examples of children with very low levels of vision in terms of measured acuity who use what vision they have remarkably effectively for learning, whilst there are others, less motivated, who use a higher recorded level of acuity apparently to very little effect in day-to-day tasks.

Previous experience of using visually stimulating material, encouragement to do so, interest in the task in hand, curiosity and enjoyment seem to play a part in the way that some pupils use even low levels of vision to help them to find out the things they are interested in. Apathy, lack of confidence and previous discouragement to use sight actively for learning may contribute to the less effective use of the sight a child does possess. The negative effects of lack of stimulation on visual functioning and the potential for improved functioning are discussed in studies relating to visual perception by Hebb (1937), Gibson (1953), Vernon (1966) and Tobin, Chapman *et al.* (1978).

Clearly this is a much more subtle, fallible and variable aspect of the child's visual behaviour to attempt to measure than the clinical aspects of use of vision. But, for the educator, the extent to which a pupil uses vision in day-to-day tasks is a highly relevant factor to take into consideration when planning educational programmes.

Barraga (1976) offers a useful definition of functional vision in the following terms:

> Visual functioning is related in part to the condition of the eye. More explicitly, visual functioning is determined by the experiences, motivations, needs and expectation of each individual in relation to whatever visual capacity is available to satisfy curiosity and accomplish activities for personal satisfaction.

Incidental but careful observation of the way in which the pupil uses his vision in diverse activities can yield useful information about visual functioning, but structured observation with a planned method of recording data is more helpful to the teacher. One way of checking and recording information about the functional vision of pupils in the 5–11 year old age-group is given in the *Look and Think* programme (Tobin, Chapman *et al.*, 1978) and this also gives specific recommendations for programmes to encourage the use of vision in a range of tasks which tap different areas of visual activity.

The advantage of finding out about the pupil's present level of visual functioning is that it can be considered as a starting point. Appropriate materials and activities can help some pupils to function better in terms of visual competence. Naturally the physical bases that are the cause of defective sight remain unchanged; measured visual acuity is unlikely to be improved, but children can be positively helped to pay attention to visual stimuli, and can be given motivating visual tasks in optimum conditions that help them to enjoy the experience of using their vision as fully and effectively as possible.

Programmes which seek to do this are referred to as 'visual enhancement' and aim to give encouragement and motivation to pupils with defective vision to use this with maximum 'visual efficiency'. They are particularly relevant to the visually handicapped child in the first school years in an integrated setting.

REGISTRATION OF VISUAL HANDICAP

If screening procedures and subsequent medical investigations show the presence of significant visual handicap, it may be decided by the ophthalmologist that the child should be registered as blind or partially sighted. The BD8 (form of registration of blindness or partial sight) is completed by the consultant ophthalmologist and is designed primarily for medical and legal purposes. It defines the child as being blind or partially sighted, and contains information about the age of onset of the visual loss and the prognosis of the visual condition.

Bearing these criteria in mind, the ophthalmologist can also enter a recommendation of this form relating to the educational placement of the child concerned. Since the implementation of the 1981 Education Act such directives on the BD8 Registration Form are placed alongside other professional recommendations relating to the child's school placement. The BD8 Form is sent to the Social Services Department and a social worker will then visit the family to inform them about the services and allowances that may be available to them. The information contained on Form BD8 was previously the main criterion for deciding whether a pupil required education in a special school or an ordinary school, and whether the pupil should be referred to and educated as a blind or a partially sighted child.

There is now much greater flexibility with regard to educational placements for visually handicapped children and less adherence to the use of terms which define children in categories based on medical criteria.

TERMINOLOGY RELATING TO PUPILS WITH VISUAL HANDICAPS

Teachers may find that terminology which is intended to clarify is sometimes on the one hand, over-prescriptive or, on the other, so indefinite as to be confusing. They may question why the terms 'blind' and 'partially sighted', still used in the BD8 Form and defined in the Schools Health Services Regulations (1945), are not now used to give precise definition of the educational needs of pupils. Without these signposts, the terminology used to describe children without sight or with defective vision may seem unduly complex or even inexact. But the issue is indeed a complex and subtle one and the educational needs of children with visual problems do not fall neatly into two distinct compartments. Current educational thinking is moving away from the whole concept of labelling children by closely defined categories, and the emphasis is rather on the individual needs of children and on the shared aspects of their development and learning.

Nevertheless it is necessary to use some specialised terminology in order to define pupils who have little or no sight, so that their needs can be realistically exposed and appropriately met. To this end, the following commonly accepted terms are considered relevant. The term 'visually handicapped' is used to refer to those pupils who have difficulties in seeing which necessitate the use of special educational methods or adaptations to materials and who need to use special aids and equipment for learning. This is an umbrella term, used widely and well understood in an educational context. Barraga (1976) sums up the implications of its usage by stating that: 'A visually handicapped child is one whose impairment interferes with his optimum learning and achievement, unless adaptations are made in the methods of presenting learning experiences, the nature of the materials used, and/or in the learning environment.' She amplifies this in a way that is helpful to the teacher by explaining that the term is used to describe the total group of children whose vision is affected by impairments in seeing, irrespective of the nature or extent of these. It is used with reference to education, and does not divide the pupils sharply into two groups with totally different needs.

For these reasons the term has been chosen for use in the title of the present book and throughout the text to denote the whole range of children from those who are totally blind through to those who possess useful but impaired vision. It is not a term without some disadvantages, since it can justifiably be argued that the term 'handicapped' may have some negative overtones. But it is here presented to the teacher as the basic condition of the child, offering a challenge that the potentially handicapping effect of lack of vision or defective vision can be overcome or minimised through appropriate education, social opportunities and the provision of well-chosen aids and equipment.

The breadth of this term is useful, but it is necessary to use more specific reference to denote particular levels or types of visual problem in relation to the child's use of sight for learning. The term 'blind' should be used carefully to describe those pupils who are completely without vision, or who have light perception only. To use the term more widely may reduce the likelihood that the pupil will be encouraged to use any vision, however slight it may be.

Clearly, blind pupils will be those who depend on tactile and auditory means of learning, and they will require specialised equipment and additional elements in their curriculum such as braille, mobility and orientation, but other aspects of their educational needs will include careful consideration of language development, concept formation, social interaction and information processing. The age at which total sight loss has taken place is also highly relevant to the way in which pupils interpret their environment and the teacher whose class they attend should be aware of this.

Our emphasis on the desirability of using the term 'blind' carefully arises from the many positive developments that have taken place over the last two decades. Previously pupils with very little useful vision were referred to and treated all too often as if they were totally blind. Fear that the use of defective vision would make it deteriorate further has been replaced by positive encouragement and training to use even severely defective sight as effectively as possible in learning and in day-to-day living. Practice and definition have both progressed. Thus, the description 'low vision' used in the educational context is the generally accepted term for those children who are able to use their vision quite effectively in the near environment under suitable lighting conditions, in an appropriate working position and, in many cases, with the use of magnifiers or individually prescribed optical aids. Such children are the ones who have considerable problems with distance vision, and indeed their sight may not be adequate for the use of print as their means of literacy. Thus, although they may be braille readers, they are not totally blind children and should be encouraged to use what vision they have in the learning situation. The use of closed circuit television, the presentation of clear, highly contrasted learning materials and the implementation of visual enhancement programmes are all highly relevant to these pupils.

The term 'visually limited' is used frequently by writers in the United States (Barraga, 1976; Bishop, 1971) and refers to pupils who use their vision for all tasks including reading print, but who may need prescriptive lenses in order to do so. Some of these pupils will be helped by attention to task lighting and to a suitable position in which to work and view demonstrations. Clearly presented materials and a well-ordered environment can be helpful to them.

'Impaired' and 'defective' are also self-explanatory terms used in relation to vision, sometimes with the addition of 'severe' to emphasise the degree. It will be appreciated that the precise nature of the degree or defect in acuity or field of vision is highly individual.

The term 'partially sighted' has been used over the years to refer to pupils who have vision useful for all school tasks but require adaptations to teaching methods and materials in order to accomplish them. It is a broad term, with the appropriate emphasis on the child's potential, but has been used too often previously to contrast with 'blind' without consideration for the needs of pupils who have to use both tactile and visual methods for learning.

The simplified scale in Figure 1 gives an indication of the range of vision as described in terminology based on visual acuity. There may be individual differences in the way in which field defects as well as acuity affects vision and in the way in which children are motivated to use their vision for learning. These differences should be reflected in the descriptive terminology.

Terminology and acuities

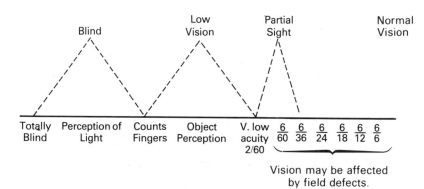

Figure 1 *Levels of visual functioning of pupils with impaired sight*

SIGHT IN LEARNING AND IN DAY-TO-DAY ACTIVITIES IN SCHOOL

Some of the consequences of vision screening will be in the area of correction or remediation as well as in identifying problems with sight and influencing educational placements. For example, refractive errors (those defects in the shape of the eye that prevent light rays from being brought sharply on to the retina in a single focus and which include short-sightedness, long-sightedness and astigmatism can often be at least partially corrected by the provision of appropriate lenses in eyeglasses. The effect of such correction can, in some instances, be dramatic, as in the case of a child who, after receiving his first pair of spectacles, spent several evenings looking at the stars as it was the first time he had ever been able to see them. Children may sometimes be unaware that their own sight is changing, or indeed of what people with normal vision can see. 'Can you really see leaves on the trees?' a nine-year-old girl who was severely short-sighted asked. She explained that the tree, to her, looked like a green fuzzy clump even at a distance of a few feet. Such anecdotes cannot be a basis for generalisation, but rather illustrated the response of particular children to their own improved or deteriorating vision. The way in which each child adapts to defective vision will be individual, and there are considerations both in the causes of defective sight and the effects of these on the way that children can use their vision. Indeed Adams (1985a) states that there is a need for further research into ways of obtaining 'realistic and objective' pictures of the way that visually handicapped people see. He suggests that many assumed effects of low vision, for example field loss, totally ignored the brain and the whole mechanics and chemistry of visual perception.

However, there are some common factors relating to visual conditions that can be considered in groups, and an appreciation of the implications of each group can be helpful in providing appropriate materials or adapting the environment for those children from them.

In broad and generalised terms, visual defects give rise to loss of clear vision, loss of central vision, or loss of peripheral vision; the visual field may be reduced or interrupted. A child may have a combination of these effects resulting from complex visual anomalies.

Loss of clear vision

The visual conditions that cause blurring and distortion of sight are also likely to result in the reduction of clear distance vision. In addition, the powerful lenses needed to correct severe refractive errors also reduce the extent of the field. (The enlargement, for example, of what is seen results in a smaller area being visible.) The result of this is likely to be that close work will present few difficulties, but more distant visual tasks such as reading sentences written up on the blackboard will give problems. Socially, children with unclear vision can seem slightly 'out of step'. They may, for instance, be unaware that they are being spoken to unless referred to by name, and they can miss out on humorous incidents which make the rest of the class laugh. Severe refractive errors can give rise to visual defects of this sort.

Loss of central vision

The central vision area of the retina needs to be intact for it to be possible to discriminate sharp, fine images. When vision is directed to an object immediately in front of the eyes, objects in the peripheral (outer) areas of the field of vision are not seen in sharp focus, so it is necessary to turn the head and direct the gaze on to these objects in order to see them clearly. If the central part of the retina is damaged, clear, acute vision will not be possible in any part of the visual field. In day-to-day activities a child will usually have no problems with mobility, but reading and fine visual tasks may prove to be very difficult. Misunderstandings can arise as a result of this, when, for example, teachers see children who are able to run about in the playground with confidence, but seem unable to discriminate printed letters in their reading books. Disease of and damage to the macula, the central area of the retina used to discriminate fine detail, can give rise to these effects and precise information about the child's eye condition is needed in order to understand the reason for these apparent anomalies.

Loss of peripheral vision

The loss of vision in the peripheral field is frequently referred to as tunnel vision as this describes the effect. Although it is sometimes simulated by looking through a peephole, this gives only a crude approximation of the condition.

The child's central acuity can be normal, giving detail that is sharp and clear, and there may be no difficulties in reading the Snellen Chart. However, the child may have problems in getting about easily without bumping into things, and stairs or badly lit corridors can be hazardous. Reading may be slow as the eyes are able to take in only one short word or a few letters at one glance. This can disturb the normal eye movements that would be used by a fluent reader, and visual scanning can be impaired. In the central area of the visual field distance vision can be surprisingly good, and this disparity can give rise to some particular problems in the use of vision in classroom activities.

Variable vision and the effects of fatigue

There are some children whose vision seems to vary from one situation to another, and there may be valid reasons for this. A pupil who is making a constant effort to use vision as fully as possible in school tasks may sometimes find this effort to be somewhat of an overload when his or her general level of well-being is low, for instance, when suffering from a cold or feeling particularly tired. Sometimes apparent laziness, or 'playing-up' can be the response to visual demands that the pupil is having difficulty in coping with. For example, the hands or even the figures on the dial of a wall-mounted clock may be clearly visible to the child with tunnel vision, but the problem could be that of locating the clock itself. Similarly, while a pupil with this type of visual condition might be able to read words up on the blackboard with little difficulty, locating the words themselves could be an initial problem. These apparent discrepancies in visual behaviour can easily be misunderstood. Physical activities can also sometimes cause difficulties since restricted visual fields can make it difficult for a child to catch a ball, wield a bat effectively or aim at a goal. Despite this, there are instances of visually handicapped pupils who do much for themselves in overcoming their limitations because they are really interested in taking part in sport.

Although intensive visual concentration can sometimes lead to fatigue it must be stressed that it does not damage vision. Some visually handicapped children will overcome their difficulties so well that they are indistinguishable from their fully sighted classmates, but the effort needed may have a cost for them that is not always appreciated. To illustrate this, it is relevant to remember that driving a car is possible for the fully sighted in foggy conditions, but it is a more tiring procedure than driving when visibility is good. Commuters read paperbacks as they sit in trains, but find that they may need to rest from this activity more frequently than when they are reading in a comfortable and well-lit place at home. Classroom tasks can make considerable demands on children with defective vision, but teachers can reduce the risk of fatigue by trying to ensure optimum learning conditions and offering clearly presented materials. Visual fatigue can sometimes be lessened if the pupil looks away from a task briefly, or closes the eyes for a minute or two. This will often be sufficient to relax the sense of pressure and ease tension.

Field loss

There are various ways in which the visual field can be reduced or interrupted, causing problems with some school tasks whilst apparently not affecting others. For example, one half of the function of the retina of each eye can be lost. The defective area may extend from the centre of the visual field to its outer perimeter, affecting the same side of the field in each eye. The condition (hemianopia) usually causes problems with visual tracking as in scanning along a line or print. Problems of this kind tend to be more pronounced if the left side of the visual field in each eye is affected.

Besides these main groups of effects arising from visual disabilities there are other, sometimes additional, factors which can influence visual behaviour. Nystagmus (spasmodic oscillation of the eye), for example, may present on its own, but sometimes accompanies visual defects that cause problems with focusing. Tasks involving fixation, that is, the ability to hold a steady visual image, can be considerably affected by the presence of nystagmus. Activities involving the close use of vision can be tiring for children with this condition, and stress or excitement seem in some cases to exacerbate it.

Children who are photophobic (sensitive to bright light) will find that dazzle on bright sunny days can be quite distressing, especially when they move from a shaded interior into bright sunlight outside. Conversely they may find it difficult to adapt to poor lighting conditions, and they may be nervous when coming indoors after being in brighter light outside. Varying light conditions, and the demands of either close or distance work will make different visual demands on children, and the nature of these visual tasks should be considered in terms of the child's visual capabilities.

Virtually every task in the ordinary school involves the use of sight, since the ordinary curriculum is designed for fully sighted pupils. It is usual to assume that the pupils will be able to use close-range materials on the desk or table in front of them, and then look up to the blackboard, perhaps to copy notes or diagrams displayed there, then quickly refocus on to their desk work. Visual discrimination is exercised in reading print, which can demand some fine visual tasks such as discriminating between letters of similar shape. The software programs for microcomputers demand visual concentration and sometimes tracking and scanning skills. Visual tracking skills are also needed for reading a line of writing, and searching and scanning skills will be brought into play in interpreting maps and diagrams or in reading mathematical tables; handwriting, crafts and other practical skills require competent hand–eye co-ordination.

In order to be able to understand the situation of the visually handicapped child in an ordinary class it is relevant to be reminded of the function of the eye and the visual system, since without such basic information the demands which such a child faces are unlikely to be understood. The following simplified description indicates the areas of the visual system that can be affected by disease or trauma.

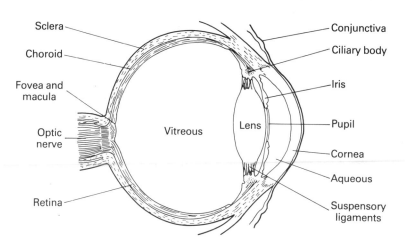

Figure 2 *Simplified diagram representing cross-section of the human eye*

THE VISUAL SYSTEM

A simplified diagram of the eye appears in Figure 2. An object cannot be seen unless light reflected from it passes through the eye on to the retina and the brain receives the impulses transmitted from the retina via the optic nerve. The reflected light first passes through the cornea (the curved transparent outer layer of the eyeball), thus beginning the refraction of light rays which will focus sharply on the retina. Behind the retina lies the anterior chamber, filled with the aqueous humour. Light passes through this to the pupil (the central hole in the iris), the iris itself being composed of circular muscles which are visible as the blue, brown or hazel colour of the eye. The iris reacts quickly to changes in light levels, dilating or contracting, enlarging or decreasing the size of the pupil. The lens lies immediately behind the pupil; it is a transparent solid body, elliptical in shape, enclosed in a capsule and attached to suspensory ligaments within the eye. It is the lens which completes the refraction of the rays of light as they pass through the posterior chamber (which is filled with a jelloid substance, the vitreous humour). The refracted rays then reach the retina. The retina consists of the inner lining at the back of the eye and is a delicate membrane, constructed of ten different layers, one of which contains the two types of light-sensitive cells, the rods and cones. The rods are situated mainly in the peripheral area of the retina and they are activated in lower levels of lighting. The cones are receptive to colour and to higher lighting levels. These cells are concentrated in the central area of the retina which is used in the discrimination of fine and sharp images. Visual impulses are transmitted to the visual cortex in the brain via the optic nerve. The impulses from the right field of vision of both eyes are received by the left side of the brain. Impulses from the left side of the field of vision are received by the right side of the brain. The process of seeing is thus a combination of factors, both physiological and psychological. Not only must the eye itself be functioning fully and normally, but the brain must be intact and visual perception possible, if vision is to be fully developed.

DEVELOPMENTAL ASPECTS OF VISION

The eye is easily discernible in the developing foetus and the development of the retina is complete between the 28th and 36th week of pregnancy, except for the macula area which continues to develop until the baby is four months old. The development of the eye is susceptible to disease and damage *in utero*; for example, rubella (German measles) can seriously damage the visual as well as other systems in the unborn baby. The visual system is complete at birth, although the eye continues to grow in size until adolescence. At birth the baby's vision is blurred and he cannot discriminate between foreground and background in the visual panorama. However, even at this early stage, the baby does respond to a source of light and attempt to follow the mother's face. Between one and three months of age the baby indulges in finger play, focusing the eye on the hands. At this stage there may be some long-sightedness which adjusts to the norm as the baby grows. By about four months of age the baby's visual acuity may be as exact as 6/6, but accurate perception of what is seen will normally still be developing. There seems to be a readiness in the baby to react keenly to visual stimuli during the first few months of life. It is sometimes found that operations to remove congenital cataracts (soft opacities in the lens) when a child is of school age are disappointing in that full vision is not effective because the appropriate stage in development of visual perception has been passed while the opacities were still present. Fortunately, with improved surgical and technical techniques it is now possible to operate on the cataracts of newborn children within the first ten days of life in some cases, and this is considered by some consultants to be advisable. However, teachers may encounter children at school who still have visual problems although cataracts have been removed.

DISEASES AND DEFECTS THAT MAY CAUSE VISUAL DISABILITY IN CHILDREN

In a book written by educators for educators, a description of some of the causes of visual disability that can be encountered in schoolchildren is given for the guidance of teachers in their work with pupils. A medical textbook has a different emphasis and purpose but can usefully be referred to when more detailed information about a specific condition is desired.

Albinism

This is an inherited condition, involving the loss of pigment in the hair, skin and eyes. One type of albino child is very easy to recognise because of his very fair hair, paler skin and the pinkish appearance of the eyes. But there is another form, known as 'ocular albinism', in which only the eyes are affected. Both types of albino child are photophobic, that is, they will be distressed and even suffer pain when in bright light and most will wear dark glasses to alleviate this.

They will find it extremely difficult going outside on a bright day and may see very little on a sunny day. Any form of glare will cause difficulty. Such children, therefore, should not be seated near a window and the classroom levels of lighting may have to be adapted. Albino children can be near-sighted or long-sighted and need glasses to help with their distance vision, which often is no higher than 6/36. The prescription of glasses may not help their reading distance, but they may be able to read adequately by holding their books at closer than the normal distance. Using a book-stand may help to prevent associated posture problems. Children with albinism may have a squint and nystagmus. The amount of pigmentation tends to increase slightly with age up to adolescence and brings with it a gradual improvement in visual acuity.

As albinism is of genetic origin, genetic counselling should be available to teenagers.

Aniridia

This means 'absence of the iris' and can run in families. The muscles which open and reduce the pupil are lacking. The pupil is very large and only a portion of the iris is present, so the eye appears dark in colour. Because the pupil is so large, the child is usually very photophobic. Other visual problems can be associated with aniridia. Amongst these are glaucoma and nystagmus.

Tinted glasses, contact lenses or painted contact lenses with only a small clear 'pupil' may make the child more comfortable and improve visual performance. Attention should be paid to environmental factors which will aid the child (details of which are suggested in Chapter 2).

Complaints of headaches should be taken seriously and genetic counselling made available at the appropriate time.

Cataract

The word 'cataract' comes from the Latin word for waterfall and describes the appearance of the eye when the lens becomes cloudy and opaque. There are many types and causes of cataract. If present at birth, they are referred to as congenital cataracts. These can be inherited with other members of the family also having them, but are sometimes caused by the rubella virus. The cloudy lens prevents the passage of the rays of light on to the retina.

Many children will need cataract surgery. Unfortunately the eye is then aphakic (loss of lens) and the children still have a visual problem. They will have to use strong spectacles or contact lenses. The aphakic eye is unable to change its focus, so bifocal spectacles are required even for those with contact lenses. Although some children see very well once their glasses are prescribed, many have vision which cannot be improved above 6/60. Some children may be better off with early cataracts than with aphakic eyes, so early surgery is not always advisable.

Levels of lighting should be assessed for each child and a good contrast of print on paper provided. The size of print should be checked and the use of low vision aids or closed circuit television may be appropriate.

The strong glasses needed will give an odd appearance to the eyes which may result in teasing and although the child may see well directly through the glasses, there may be difficulties with the peripheral vision and mobility will have to be watched.

Corneal ulcers and scars

These can be caused in many ways, from infection in another part of the eye such as the eyelids, the iris (iritis) or the ciliary body. Accidents, both from injuries or harmful substances entering the eye, can cause scarring and ulceration. These can be very painful at times and also cause photophobia and a deficiency in the vision. Many are a temporary condition but there are certain types which are difficult to treat and last for a long time.

Children with these conditions will be averse to glare and have severely reduced vision in bright sunlight. There may be ongoing treatment of which the teacher should be aware.

Dislocation of the lens

The lenses may be partially dislocated. This is usual in children who suffere from Marfans Syndrome. With this syndrome, the body is tall and thin, the limbs are elongated, as are the toes and fingers. There is often associated muscle weakness and sometimes heart problems can occur. A back corset may be needed to prevent curvature.

There will be blurred distance vision, but the near vision can be good, depending on the type of dislocation. Physical activities need to be monitored as sudden body contact or jarring of the head can bring about further dislocation. The advice of the ophthalmologist must be sought before physical activities are allowed.

Glaucoma (Buphthalmos)

Although this is one of the rarer conditions in children, it is included here because children with controlled glaucoma will be in the ordinary classroom. It is a condition in which the pressure within the eye is increased, due to faulty drainage of the aqueous (Figure 2). Children with glaucoma at birth often have below normal vision and may need continued operations to keep the pressure at a safe level. The infant's eye is elastic and so a raised intra-ocular pressure causes the eyeball to enlarge. The cornea may become cloudy. Refractive errors develop because of the altered shape of the eye and abnormal position of the lens.

Hemianopia

Damage to one side of the brain can cause visual handicap. Messages from the right-hand field of vision of both eyes are received by the left-hand side of the brain. Similarly, messages from the left-hand field of vision of both eyes are transmitted to the right side of the brain. A tumour or trauma in one side of the brain causes a loss in the field of vision on the other side.

The remaining vision will be good, but mobility and associated activities will be affected. Reading, too, will be difficult. Children with right-sided field loss will be looking ahead into a space; left-sided hemianopia causes difficulties in finding the beginning of a line of print. Glasses will not help this condition, nor will the enlargement of print. The children need to be taught to move head and eyes to compensate for the field loss.

Macular degeneration

As can be seen from Figure 2, the macula is a minute area in the centre of the retina. If the specialised cells in the macula area do not develop before birth or are damaged or destroyed by disease, then the fine central vision will be faulty or absent. There are many causes of macular degeneration and it may be progressive. Vision may be normal in early life but deteriorate suddenly, first in one eye and later in the other. The peripheral vision is good and children may manage well, except in the area of close work. If the defect is not recognised, the children may be thought to have behaviour problems. They will see in some situations and not in others. Close work can be helped with the use of a low vision aid or closed circuit television. Good contrast is essential and the use of extra lighting may be helpful. Young children may need large print but should be educated to use smaller print as their reading develops. Dark lines on paper can be a useful writing aid. Macular degeneration can be hereditary and genetic counselling appropriate.

Nystagmus

As noted above, nystagmus is an involuntary movement of the eyes which is very noticeable. The oscillations are usually from side to side but can be up and down. The condition is usually associated with other problems, such as albinism. Near vision may not be affected but distance vision will be reduced, possibly severely. Frequently, those with nystagmus find their vision more stable if the head is held on one side or slightly askew. A balance must be found between the child's ease of vision and the tension, fatigue and other possible effects of the bad posture. The class teacher should ask for advice on this. The child should sit near the blackboard and the teacher must remember that vision across the room may be lowered and the child unable to see demonstration or materials presented.

Optic nerve atrophy

This is a term which describes damage to or degeneration of the cable of nerve fibres that transmits the signals from the retina to the visual centre of the brain (Figure 2). In some cases the optic nerve fails to develop before birth. In others the optic nerve is damaged by illness, tumour or trauma. (In hydrocephalic children, where a drainage shunt is fitted, the faulty functioning or blockage of this shunt can lead to damage of the optic nerve.)

How the child's vision is affected will depend on how many nerve fibres are still intact. Vision may be good or there may be total blindness or one of any gradations in between. Central acuity and fields of vision can be affected. Assessment of the functioning vision is important. Prognosis is also important as it may be necessary for the child to learn braille sometime in the future.

Refractive errors

Myopia (short sight – near sight)

As can be seen from Figure 2, the normal eye is virtually round, which means that rays of light coming from outside the eye are focused on the retina. The myopic eye is longer from front to back (Figure 3) and the extra length prevents the image being in sharp focus. Most myopic children can be fitted with glasses with concave lenses which will bring their vision to normal. If the myopia is of high degree the vision may not be normal even with glasses. Contact lenses sometimes give better visual acuity in these cases

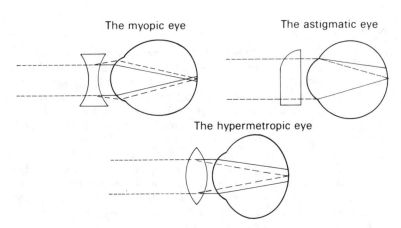

Figure 3   *Graphic representation of abnormality in eye shape*

and the field of vision is nearly always improved. Myopia tends to progress throughout the growing period and spectacles may have to be changed every six to twelve months. The child with high myopia is also at risk of further visual deterioration from muscular haemorrhage or retinal detachment. Books may have to be held very close to the eyes. Because of poor distance vision, children may miss much of what is going on in the classroom and seem 'out of step' with the rest of the class. Physical education and games will pose difficulties and myopic children will often 'opt out' of these activities, preferring to stay on the sidelines.

Hypermetropia (far sight – long sight)

It can be seen from Figure 3 that this is the opposite to myopia. In this case the eye is too short and the rays of light, were they able to do so, would fall behind the retina. However, light can be focused and distant objects seen clearly if the ciliary muscles contract (as if for near vision). Even more ciliary muscle contraction will be required for near vision and this may be uncomfortable. Hypermetropia commonly causes a squint. Long-sighted children are often reluctant to do much reading and writing and may also suffer from headaches. Convex lenses can help this condition.

Astigmatism

In this condition the eye has a misshapen curve and this produces a distorted image on the retina. Once identified it is correctable with glasses with cylindrical lenses. Astigmatism that is not discovered can result in a child confusing letters or copying incorrectly. Faulty concept development may result if appropriate lenses are not prescribed.

Retinitis pigmentosa

This term includes a group of diseases which affect the retina. They are usually progressive. It is a hereditary condition and different forms have different types of inheritance. Though some children are born with extremely poor vision, often the first signs occur in the teenage years and good vision is present until this time. The condition affects the peripheral area of the retina, including the rod cells which help vision in poor light, and can result in progressive 'tunnel vision' and 'night blindness', the inability to see in the dark. The latter is often the first symptom noticed by a young person. Visual acuity is often normal even when the field of vision is so poor that the child is registered as blind. Ultimately, however, all vision may be lost. Since the condition often occurs in the secondary-school years, the young person may not only be faced with the trauma of the diagnosis and the confusion of being still able to see clearly in some situations and not at all in others, but there may also have to be a decision to transfer the medium of communication from print to braille, all this taking place in the years leading up to important examinations.

The following points are important. A close watch must be kept by the teacher to note any changes in the vision. Sympathetic handling and understanding of behaviour problems that may arise may be necessary. The visual skills of scanning and reorientation, for example, from book to blackboard will be difficult. Mobility may be increasingly affected. Genetic counselling should be available.

Retinoblastoma

This is a malignant tumour of the retina. Surgery is often necessary to remove the affected eye and prevent the fatal spread of the tumour of the brain. In this case, an artifical eye (prosthesis) is fitted. The tumours can also be treated by radiation or photocoagulation. Unfortunately, this is often a bilateral condition so both eyes may have to be removed. Some cases are hereditary so genetic counselling should be given.

Retrolental fibroplasia

During the 1950s, retrolental fibroplasia was the most common reason for visual handicap in children. Premature babies, in need of oxygen, were given unlimited amounts. This caused the growth of deviant blood vessels in the retina. Once this was discovered, the amount of oxygen given to young babies was carefully monitored and a dramatic fall in the number of cases resulted.

Nowadays some cases do occur, almost always associated with prematurity, and the result can vary from light perception only to relatively good vision. How useful this vision is will depend on where the undamaged areas are on the retina. If the macula area remains clear, then reading should be possible. But the scattering of damage may mean the vision is fragmented. Scanning and the use of maps and diagrams may cause problems. There is a risk of further visual deterioration from retinal detachment or glaucoma.

Strabismus (squint)

A squint means that the eyes are not straight; one is directed inwards or outwards relative to the other. Causes include refractive errors, particularly hypermetropia, eye diseases such as cataracts or retinoblastoma, and ocular muscle paralysis. If the two eyes are not directed at the same object, double vision results. However, children rarely complain of double vision because their brains suppress the image from the squinting eye. If the squint is constantly present, the suppression quickly becomes permanent and the squinting eye becomes 'lazy' (amblyopia). An amblyopic may have vision below 6/60.

If a squint and amblyopia are detected early, the amblyopia may be treated by patching the good eye, so that the lazy one has to work. Patching is more effective if done in the pre-school years. After the age of seven, a lazy eye is unlikely to improve. Also patching the good eye of a child whose lazy eye has an acuity of 6/24 or less may make it impossible to manage normal school work.

Once amblyopia has been treated by patching, squint surgery may be necessary to straighten the eye and restore binocular vision, otherwise the problem may recur. Squint surgery is sometimes required for cosmetic reasons alone. Occasionally, correction of hypermetropia with glasses is sufficient to straighten the eye. Because a squint may be due to serious disease, its sudden appearance should always be taken seriously.

SPECTACLES AND CONTACT LENSES

The Warnock Report (Department of Education and Science, 1978) stresses that there are already in ordinary classes children with special educational needs whose difficulties are not evident as severe physical or sensory handicaps. These may include pupils who have visual impairments of a slight or moderate degree, including those who need to wear spectacles to correct refractive errors. Attention to the environment in terms of appropriate lighting, both overall and to meet individual needs, and the provision of clear, well-presented learning materials should be helpful to these pupils as well as to those who have more severe visual defects. It is important for the teacher to know which pupils should be wearing spectacles, since without the necessary correction provided by lenses these pupils can experience quite unnecessary difficulties with their work.

The hazards to which spectacles are prone include being lost, broken, ill-fitting, dirty, put on crookedly or rejected as an aid to better seeing. Both pupils and their parents need to know that spectacles will neither cure a visual condition, nor hasten its deterioration; they will simply give necessary correction to vision in appropriate cases whilst they are being worn. It is important that regular eye tests are given, and that any ophthalmic appointments are kept as levels of vision in the case of children using spectacles may alter.

It is helpful if a pupil who is totally dependent on the use of spectacles for schoolwork can have a reserve pair, since repairs can sometimes take time. Parents should be aware that vouchers from the DHSS intended to cover the cost of spectacles are available for children. The use of a spectacle-case for protection and the habit of keeping the lenses clean helps to ensure that these aids to sight are kept in a usable, effective condition. One may question whether drawing attention to such matters should be part of a teacher's role, but spectacles can be essential for some pupils who will not be able to use learning materials properly without them. Children can be notoriously careless with their glasses or obstinately refuse to wear them. Patient insistence is needed.

Contact lenses, now sometimes used with very young children as well as older pupils, provide optical correction in another form. Pupils should be able to take over increasingly from parents or from care staff in school the responsibility for the management and cleaning of the lenses. The whole question of eye care and hygiene and the use and proper maintenance of aids to vision needs to be included and discussed in the health education curriculum.

Spectacles

The prescription of glasses is an exact science, and they are made to fit correctly at a specific distance from the eyeball. They can be made with either plastic or glass lenses, with convex lenses prescribed for long-sightedness, concave for short-sightedness and cylindrical for astigmatism. Plastic lenses are lighter, an advantage if the lenses required are of high power, but with the disadvantage of scratching easily. Glass lenses are heavier, but are less likely to become scratched; they can be made shatterproof. Fitting must be precise, and in the case of young children who have not yet developed a firm bridge to the nose this can be difficult. The shafts can be tied on in the case of very young children, especially during active play.

Contact lenses

Contact lenses are less frequently prescribed for children than spectacles because physical growth is still taking place and because they are relatively more expensive. However there are some conditions in which they give more useful correction and they may therefore be provided for visually handicapped children. Adolescents conscious of personal appearance may prefer them to eyeglasses. There are two kinds of contact lenses, hard and soft. Hard lenses are generally well tolerated and are relatively easy to care for. Soft lenses are made of plastic with a high water content. They are soft and pliable and consequently comfortable. However, they are more expensive, require more complicated care procedure and are more likely to show signs of wear. All contact lenses must be very carefully fitted to allow the cornea to receive enough oxygen. The lenses will be as small and thin as possible and fit as loosely as appropriate in order to maintain the health of the eyes. Teachers should certainly know if any of the younger children are wearing contact lenses.

LOW VISION AIDS

There are specialised optical aids which can be helpful to some visually handicapped pupils. Low vision aids, as the term implies, are designed to facilitate the use of low vision, and range from the simple magnifier to the complex closed circuit television set. Optical aids prescribed by a low vision specialist will be described later in this section of the book. No aid, however beneficial, is totally without disadvantages and children often need positive encouragement in practising their use before they become aware of the advantages that they offer when adroitly used. Before low vision aids are prescribed, an assessment should be made both of the child's vision and of the varied classroom, home and leisure situation in which the aid will be used. Unfortunately this is not always done, lessening the chances of full and effective usage of the aid provided. Directions as to how to use the aid should also be given together with a discussion of the circumstances in which its use is likely to be helpful. Directions of this kind, given at the low vision clinic, should be communicated to the teacher who is working with the child at school, and this will usually be done through the specialist adviser for visually handicapped pupils. The child will need some training in the use of the low vision aid and detailed descriptions of training programmes are to be found in Faye (1984) *Clinical Low Vision* and Jose (1983) *Understanding Low Vision*.

Techniques will vary according to whether the aid is to be used for distance work, but the following elements should be included in training a child to use a low vision aid. Firstly, the aid should be demonstrated for correct holding, the parts named and some instructions given on its care. Secondly, the pupil will need training in fixation skills, including eccentric viewing (holding reading material in an unusual but visible position), spotting skills, tracing skills, tracking skills, and scanning skills. In order to master these skills with a low vision aid, it will be appreciated that the development of perceptual skills (visual memory, hand–eye co-ordination, spatial perception, matching and sorting visually) should receive attention prior to its use.

A re-assessment noting the effective use to which the child has put the low vision aid or the reasons for his inability to do so should be made at regular intervals, so that adjustments can be made or more intensive training given. In integrated settings, children are sometimes understandably reluctant to use aids which are unsightly or cumbersome. The teacher has a role in encouraging the pupil to use the aid and in reducing teasing by other pupils.

The most frequently prescribed optical aids are microscopes and telescopes with a power of magnification ranging from 1x to 20x. Microscopes can only be used for close work, telescopes for viewing objects from arm's length distance to infinity. Usually the microscope will provide a wider viewing field but a short working distance, whilst the telescope give a longer working distance but smaller field of view. The simplest form of microscope is the convex lens, the magnifying effect being caused by the curvature of the lens. Unfortunately, as power and therefore magnification increase the maximum working distance decreases also. The telescopic form of low vision aid can extend the working distance, but with the disadvantage that, as the working distance increases, the field of view decreases. The effect of this is, for instance, to reduce considerably the number of words, or even letters, visible within the field of the lens.

Both microscopic and telescopic aids can be hand-held, stand-mounted, or fitted into a pair of spectacles. Hand-held magnifiers do not leave both hands free and are therefore not suitable for some activities, especially practical work. In addition, when a hand-held instrument is used, any shake or movement of the hands will cause a tremor in viewing, and this will be particularly evident when high magnification is involved. A low vision aid must be held at the correct distance from the material to be viewed for maximum magnification to be effected, and it can be difficult to sustain this with a hand-held magnifier for any length of time. Stand magnifiers overcome this problem as they are mounted on supports that ensure the correct viewing distance, and some have built-in illumination to increase the luminosity on the working surface. However, with stand magnifiers, the restricted space under the lens does not permit activities such as writing or sewing to be undertaken while the lens is being held. If it is mounted instead in a flexible arm or frame, the working distance can be adjusted. Aids of this kind are useful but expensive and difficult to carry. A disadvantage of the microscope aid is that as the magnification increases the size of the lens has to decrease, owing to the weight and expense of high-powered lenses, and this results again in a smaller field of view. The child may discriminate printed letters with the higher-powered lens, but reading may be slow and laborious.

Telescopes also have a small field of view and are seldom made to magnify more than 2x or 3x, and even low-powered telescopes can create some difficulties of adjustment for the user. The compact telescope, which is very small and can be mounted on a ring that fits on the finger, is useful in activities which require mobility and can be helpful in identifying street names and bus numbers.

Magnification, however, is not useful for every visually handicapped child. Those with tunnel vision, for instance, would not find it so. For such pupils, the application of reduction can be more useful than magnification. It has the opposite effect from magnification, which reduces the field of vision. Reduction, while decreasing the size of the print, increases the area of the field being viewed. (The security 'peepholes' used in front doors are an example of this principle.) One use for an optical aid for pupils with tunnel vision that is designed on this principle is for mobility since it helps to increase the extent of the visual panorama.

Despite some of the disadvantages outlined, low vision aids can be immensely helpful to some visually handicapped pupils in classroom and more general situations, but they are of no use at all lying on a shelf gathering dust. Pupils do need encouragement and help in making the best of them, and these expensive items should be returned to the clinic if they are not being used. Teachers should enquire as to whether a low vision aid would be appropriate for an individual low vision child in their class. Consultation can be made with the advisory service for the visually handicapped and the ophthalmologist will then usually refer children to the low vision clinic in the region or to an ophthalmic optician who specialises in low vision aids. The prescription of an aid, however, is only the beginning of the potential improvement in learning for the pupil who uses it. Learning to use it fully and without embarrassment is a challenge, but one that many visually handicapped pupils have met with success.

QUESTIONS THAT TEACHERS ASK ABOUT VISUAL HANDICAPS

There may be aspects of day-to-day management of visually handicapped pupils that seem simple but require clarification. For example, teachers may pose the following questions:

Why don't all children with visual handicap wear glasses?

Although spectacle lenses will correct errors, they cannot replace vision that does not exist. For instance, a visual field loss resulting from a damaged retina will not be helped by wearing spectacles, and they will not be prescribed. Moreover, spectacles have uses other than for correcting refractive error. Photophobic children are often recommended to wear dark or tinted glasses to ease the discomfort caused by bright light.

Should children with defective vision be resting their eyes?

In the years before 1945 children with visual defects, especially high myopes (children with severe short sight), were admitted to 'sight-saving' classes, as it was then considered that restricting the use of vision would help to conserve it. Evidence from ophthalmologists, especially Mann and Pirie (1946), and observation of good practice by educational psychologists and teachers confirmed that this was not so, and that children with low levels of vision should be encouraged and trained to use their vision as effectively as possible and to enjoy using it. Although the concentration and effort required to do this may sometimes produce fatigue, this is temporary and in no way signifies that sight will 'wear out' with use.

Do the other senses automatically compensate for limited or non-existent vision?

Visually handicapped pupils can certainly be trained to use their other senses very effectively in listening, tactile, and haptic skills. Vision, however, is a unifying sense (Lowenfeld, 1974) and helps to integrate the partial or fragmented information transmitted, through the other senses. It is possible to hear that there are many people in a room, but without vision impossible to count them. People hear the sound of movement but look to see what has caused it. Some able and highly motivated visually handicapped people develop sophisticated levels of hearing and touch that astound the fully sighted, but these are not an automatic compensation for poor vision, and there is considerable individual variation in these areas of competence.

Should children attempt to read in poor light?

Any visual task is rendered more difficult and fatiguing if it is undertaken in poor lighting. Improving the quality of lighting is one of the most effective ways of increasing the effective use of vision, especially when there are problems with sight. Sometimes lighting levels will need to be reduced to avoid distracting dazzle for photophobic children. For other conditions such as retinal disease and macular degeneration, illumination must be good but without glare.

Does it matter how close children get to their work?

Proximity to the eye is one effective way of magnifying visual material. It is not harmful to vision, but attention needs to be given to lighting and position to prevent postural fatigue and the development of spinal curvature.

Management of the environment

THE PHYSICAL ENVIRONMENT

Access and safety

A teacher whose classes include visually handicapped pupils is unlikely to welcome the prospect of trying to engineer an elaborately contrived environment that will single them out unduly from their classmates, and yet may experience apprehension about their safety as they move about the school and within the classroom. 'But won't they fall over the milk-crates?' a teacher asked when it was proposed that two young children with severe visual problems should join the reception group.

Alterations to the environment required for safety and access to buildings and classroom by pupils with physical handicaps, especially if they are in wheelchairs, may be more easily foreseen, and their need for ramps or lifts instead of stairs, adaptations to toilet facilities may be readily recognised as essential. There are fewer generally accepted criteria about what environmental adaptations are necessary or desirable for pupils with problems in seeing and some debate as to whether any special attention needs to be given to them at all. There is, however, a consensus of opinion among experienced practitioners used to dealing with visually handicapped pupils and among writers concerned with the education of such children that competence in personal mobility and orientation is a prime source of safety and a great help in ensuring access to the whole campus and its various buildings and rooms.

In the case of pupils who are totally blind, or have little guiding sight, an orderly and reasonably predictable environment can help the pupil when he is still gaining confidence in independent mobility, but experience in purposeful movement and appropriate mobility training are even more essential. The basis of independent and safe personal mobility is best developed in skills established in the pre-school years and fostered in the early years at school. Purposeful movement results from body awareness and orientation in relation to fixed objects and furniture. A developmentally based programme of independence training such as that described by

Tooze (1981) is of prime importance in helping the severely visually handicapped pupil to move about safely and adventurously in his school environment. Early experience in exploring the environment at home should precede this, and will not only be stimulating as an activity in its own right but a helpful and positive preparation for coping with the wider and more varied situation of school. Although ideally basic competence in moving about independently should be developing by the time the pupil first comes to school, there is likely to be among visually handicapped children a range of levels of skill in independent mobility and in competence in using the environment fully and safely. These variations can arise from the nature of pre-school opportunities for active play and exploration, as well as from the amount of useful vision the child possesses. The extent to which the child has been encouraged to be physically independent, to develop spatial awareness, a sense of direction and response to sound and tactile cues and to use any vision he possesses positively will have a considerable influence on the extent to which he is able to meet the demands of his school environment.

The emphasis on helping the visually handicapped pupil to develop skills to cope with his school environment, rather than adapting the environment significantly to accommodate the visually handicapped child, may, however, be usefully tempered by an understanding of the way in which the developmental and experiential levels of the child can be affected by his school life. Ashcroft (1982) stresses that:

> Through our school programmes we alter the capabilities of the student so that environmental demands can be met. A good example is intensive work on physical development and mobility and orientation, so essential to increase healthy self-regarding attitudes, to increase capability to cope with the environment and to evoke positive attitudes.

Significantly, he recognises that the pupil with defective vision has a need for gradation in the extent to which his environment is adapted or supportive, the ultimate aim being to reduce the supportive and adapted elements so that the totally unmodified environment which the visually handicapped pupil will encounter on leaving school can be faced with safety and confidence. These recommendations would not preclude sensible attention to aspects of environmental safety particularly important to visually handicapped pupils, but rather they emphasise that the pupil should have the challenge of encountering 'a series of situations of just manageable difficulty'. In concrete terms this could involve gradually introducing incidental activities of fetching and returning materials and taking messages, until the pupil is finally able to take total responsibility for getting about unaided and coping with all aspects of the environment on the school campus.

It can be very helpful for the pupil with marked problems in seeing to have an opportunity to explore the school buildings and the particular class or specialist rooms as the library, gymnasium and science laboratories at a quiet time in order to gain an impression of their layout. Both tact and time are needed to effect this, and it may be that fully sighted friends are the best guides.

The statement of individual educational need in the case of a child with severe limitation or blindness should give an indication of levels of indoor and outdoor mobility and whther individual mobility instruction will be needed in order to cope with the ordinary school environment. The child's class teacher will then more confidently be able to encourage full use of the environment.

Barraga (1976) focuses on encouraging a positive and challenging approach to the visually handicapped child's encounter with everyday surroundings, considering that most mishaps and collisions are a part of learning for future independence, since 'Expanding knowledge through using the body, combined with interpretation is the key to continuous refinement in motor skills for blind children and youth throughout their lives.' Specialised help from an adviser for visually handicapped pupils or a specialist teacher or mobility officer will be needed for the blind or virtually blind child to use the environment safely and this should be sought. Halliday and Kurzhals (1976) describe the value of specialist techniques for the child who 'learns the simple travel techniques of trailing in unfamiliar places, squaring off directly to go to a designated place, using the cross bar techniques when away from other children on a playground and retrieving dropped objects. Orientation and mobility should be emphasised in every situation in the school programme.' The terminology used in mobility training sounds technical, but a trained mobility instructor who has experience in dealing with children or a specialist teacher or adviser trained in mobility and independence skills will be able to plan mobility and orientation activities together with the pupil's class teacher. These will be relevant to the child's present and future safety and independence. It is essential that the parents of a severely visually handicapped child know of and agree to the approach to be followed by the school in relation to the pupil's independent mobility, and it will be very helpful if they have seen the school environment and know what kind of tasks it will impose on the daily life of their child.

In attempting to meet the needs of individual pupils, it will be necessary to take into account aspects of the training of the child's visual loss or depreciation of sight which may cause a lack of confidence in moving about. A problem here for the responsible head or class teacher is to reduce the possibility of accident (of a different order than the odd bump or collision referred to by Barraga (1976)). Careless or unsafe elements in the physical environment are a threat to all pupils but especially to those who have poor vision or no sight. A balance needs to be struck between obtrusively over-protective vigilance and insufficient care for pupils' safety; simple orderliness and environmental awareness are needed.

The pupil's increasing familiarity with the campus and buildings will also increase confidence in their use. Teachers who are unused to the behaviour of pupils with severely defective sight can be surprised by the way in which such children can move about within a setting in which they feel secure, negotiating stairs and corridors and moving along at speed with the stream of pupils going from room to room; but unfamiliar settings and unexpected obstacles can cause difficulties or even be hazardous, and such hazards should be minimised.

If a sighted guide is needed at the stage when a blind pupil has not completely mastered independent mobility techniques or is in an unfamiliar environment, it is safer and more comfortable if the correct sighted guide technique, which is a very simple one, is adopted. It can otherwise be all too easy for the blind child to be pushed and pulled about. The guide should be slightly in front whilst the blind pupil holds the guide's arm lightly just above the elbow. Techniques for going up and down stairs, through doors and in narrow spaces should be properly demonstrated by a mobility expert so that pupils guiding a blind friend can do it in a safe, efficient way. The book on independence training by Tooze (op. cit.) illustrates sighted guide techniques clearly.

To consider the effect of the environment of the day-to-day life of the visually handicapped pupil only in terms of minimising hazard and ensuring reasonable safety is to underestimate its potential. The pupil's surroundings can be used as an aid to mobility by providing clues to help in orientation, and key points in a building or a room can be utilised as reference points in terms of location and direction.

Interesting work has been undertaken in Sweden by Braf (1984) relating to those aspects of the environment that can be of positive help to visually handicapped people. His work is geared towards the community of which the school is a part. Other studies which offer recommendations for buildings used by visually handicapped people in the community include those set out by the Royal Institute of British Architects (1981) which give a six-point plan to maximise safety and efficiency in the use of buildings, namely:

1.   orientation and simplicity of layout;

2.   good lighting and elimination of glare;
3.   use of colour and tone contrast;
4.   use of texture contrast and tactile clues;
5.   good acoustic conditions;
6.   clear, large graphics at eye level.

These recommendations are particularly significant in the case of pupils who have fallible and defective vision, and they are as relevant to a school environment as to any other. They range from fundamental principles to be incorporated in the building at the design and planning stage, to relatively simple but specific attention to decor, illumination and room arrangement. A positive benefit arising from such specific attention to what is best for visually handicapped pupils can be that there is increased attention to environmental factors that are advantageous to all the pupils in the school.

Since the majority of heads of schools and teachers inherit the school and the class or specialist rooms in which they work with their pupils, they are seldom in the happy position of being able to contribute to the initial planning of buildings, and consequently their interest may well be centred on adaptations or changes that they can realistically effect, although an appreciation of the more fundamental issues of design and planning may concern them too. Relatively small changes in the layout of a room or in its lighting and furniture may seem insignificant when considered separately, but the sum total of such adaptations can result in safer, more pleasing and efficient surroundings for pupils with sight problems.

Common-sense measures likely to minimise problems for children with visual impairments can increase safety awareness for all pupils. For instance, low-level objects can be dangerous for any pupil, but are especially so for one with little or no sight. Trailing cords from televisions or projectors, loose mats or badly fitting floor-covering can be hazardous, especially if lighting is poor. The floor is the worst place of all to store equipment such as typewriters, braillers or even piles of books, especially if they are put down on thoroughfares between desks or tables. Doors, cupboards and hatch windows should be fully opened and fastened back or else closed. Any window that opens outwards and is at head level is particularly dangerous for those without sight. Some visually handicapped pupils have good central vision and seem to have little difficulty in reading, but poor peripheral vision can give them problems in managing their environment. Adams (1985b) illustrates this kind of difficulty in showing how a subject with good vision in the right eye, but perception of light only in the left eye, could easily bump into a half-open door before realising it was there. Pupils with field defects who therefore do not have a complete visual panorama may have difficulties of this kind.

Although pupils with little or no sight will, with training, be able to cope with a variety of environmental situations and even obstacles such as odd chairs, waste-paper baskets or sharp-cornered pieces of furniture scattered or left about in unexpected places, these are an unnecessary and possibly harmful source of trouble for those with visual problems. Simply remembering to put such objects in accustomed places avoids this.

Décor can be used imaginatively and helpfully as an aid to location for visually handicapped pupils. The use of strong colour contrast as an aid to orientation is shown graphically in the Welsh Office Package (1984). Doors painted in a strong, dark colour are shown clearly against light matt walls, or bands of strong colour are used to outline door window frames to emphasise focal points in a room. The effect of this in an ordinary classroom is interesting and attractive, as well as being useful to pupils who are visually handicapped. It can be helpful to put contrast paint along the noses of stair treads; yellow is especially visible when used for stairs that are situated in dark places. Levels of lighting on stairs and in corridors may need boosting.

Whilst specific lighting recommmendations for study are discussed later in this chapter, in general terms good overall lighting is needed in an environment where there are visually handicapped pupils. Illumination can often be improved quite simply by ensuring that windows, lightbulbs and fittings are kept clean; light matt coloured walls can also give measurably greater light reflection than darker colours used for overall décor, and this should be borne in mind when redecoration is undertaken. The benefit of giving attention to décor in terms of improving overall light levels is shown by Gazeley (1968) and can be verified by the simple use of a light meter.

The outdoor as well as the indoor environment of the school campus may need to be reviewed when we are considering the needs of visually handicapped pupils. The surface of an ordinary playground can contain particles of strengthening materials that may, in strong sunlight, make it dazzling for children with photophobia. Surfacing such as 'Playscreed' has the advantage of a non-reflective surface and also a shock-absorbing quality which makes it especially useful for playgrounds for children with sensory or physical disabilities. Strong, well-constructed playground equipment is available from various firms who have given particular attention to safety factors for children with special needs. A soft play area is desirable for pupils with little or no sight as it can encourage them to move and play adventurously. Incorporating such facilities when possible does not constitute over-protection if it encourages visually handicapped children to move about freely and with reasonable safety and to make use of standard facilities with increased confidence and independence.

Classroom organisation

The classroom that offers a pleasant and interesting environment for all the pupils working in it is likely to be well suited to the visually handicapped pupil as it will be to his fully sighted classmates. For instance, first-school classrooms with colourful montages of the children's own work and collections of objects that are interesting to touch and fun to look at provide a stimulating background for pupils whether they have defective vision or not.

At the present time teachers may be working with limited resources whilst seeking to meet the varying demands of children with special educational needs. Such pressures can lead to lack of environmental awareness or at least an understandable questioning of whether spending time or money or both on improving classroom ecology justifies the effort involved. However, an overcrowded room with either poor lighting or too much glare from unshaded windows and haphazard storage of materials adds to the daily problems of self-organisation and comfortable study habits that can be particularly important for children with visual problems. Good classroom planning and organisation and an awareness of the way in which children relate to and use their surroundings can help to reduce at least some of the stresses and confusion that can arise in day-to-day work for children with sight problems.

Pupils with little or no sight need the opportunity to explore the classroom, not only for reasons of access and safety but also to find out where the key activities take place and where the objects needed for their work and play are kept. Encouragement to use sight effectively in daily classroom situations can be reinforced by a working environment that facilitates this exploration. Barraga (1976) claims that 'In order to stimulate interest in visual development, and in learning to see more things, many children may need to spend some time visually investigating objects in the classroom or in the natural environment to broaden their visual experiences.' Personal independence can also be encouraged if the visually handicapped pupil can find, fetch and return materials from known locations rather than wasting time trying to investigate muddled cupboards, or asking or expecting the fully sighted to undertake the searching.

Materials and equipment kept in a particular classroom or specialist room should be clearly labelled in large print or braille (such as labelling with Dymotape, for example). Cupboards and drawers used for storage should also be labelled and can be colour coded according to contents. Involving pupils in these tasks as a project can increase interest and emphasise the need for good personal organisation, which will be invaluable for pupils with poor sight both at school and after leaving it. Confusion and muddle resulting from mislaid books and materials involve a waste of time for any pupil, but are even more of a nuisance for one who sees poorly.

Specialised equipment and materials required for visually handicapped pupils can pose a storage problem. Braille and large print materials are bulky; braillers, typewriters, tape recorders and closed circuit television sets are both heavy and demanding of space. The need to store and maintain specialised equipment in good condition is a problem that has to be faced by schools accepting pupils who need to use these in order to fulfil their special educational needs. A central storage and resource room reduces pressure for space in individual teaching rooms, but needs pre-planning and co-opera-tion in order to have equipment available for specific lessons. In preparing particular sections or blocks of work for classes or groups of pupils which include visually handicapped children it can be useful to code in a mark when drafting the programme to indicate the need for a piece of specific equipment to be available, and check this quickly on a daily basis (for example, closed circuit television □ tape recorder ⌒⌒; overhead projector △).

Materials and equipment less frequently used or too heavy for pupils to handle easily should be stored on upper shelves. Keeping braillers, typewriters and even magnifiers in their cases, or at least under covers when not in use, helps to maintain them in good condition, since dust and grime can cause damaged surfaces. Insistence on this in the early stages of use helps to make it become simply a good habit.

In describing stimulating environments for children who are visually handicapped, Halliday (1971) recommends that 'materials and equipment should be organised and placed in different areas to implement the kind of learning and teaching done in each space'. She is referring particularly to work with younger children, and suggests not only an area for creative play but, in more structured situations, a library with low cupboards containing a variety of books (some homemade) and 'in another part of the room ... low cupboards containing many kinds of commercial materials, such as peg boards, nesting toys, puzzles, discs for the development of discrimination and hand and finger dexterity'. Materials of this kind, and strategies to deal neatly with their storage, are typical of many ordinary well-equipped classrooms, but it is the emphasis on the visually handicapped child's special need to learn to master the environment and locate and use the objects in it without too much difficulty that warrants attention. The layout and organisation of the classroom should enable the visually handicapped pupil to develop a facility to understand and use the equipment and material in it 'so that he can feel at ease in the setting, and can respond freely and accurately about what he is doing'. Reorganisation of both storage and seating arrangements in the class or specialist teaching room may be constrained by the size of the room itself and the size of the class in it, but even so it may be possible to improve the present situation by looking at it purely in terms of its current, rather than traditional, use.

Seating arrangements will, of course, depend on the nature of the activities being undertaken and the extent to which the work is taking place in informal groups or in a more structured teaching situation. Pupils often want to sit next to their particular friend and many classroom activities involve moving about, but even relatively small alterations can make a difference to the visual comfort of pupils with sight defects. A major factor here is that the pupils who have useful sight should be able to work in a position that enables them to use it more easily and effectively. For desk work the pupils should be in a place from which they can most clearly and easily see any demonstration or illustration work that is being shown. For instance, a pupil with hemianopia or a diminished visual field may have to sit at an angle rather than square to the blackboard in order to use remaining vision usefully to discriminate what is on it.

Over the last twenty years a number of publications concerned with the education of visually handicapped children have given very prescriptive advice on the most suitable seating arrangements for classes which include visually handicapped children. Both Bishop (1971) and Hathaway (1959) give carefully worked out guidelines of suggested seating in relation to classroom lighting, blackboard and fixed furniture. These suggestions may be considered dated in that they seem to presuppose a somewhat static teaching situation with pupils amenable to being told where to sit, rather than the modern classroom with its active learning, and mobile, enquiring pupils. Nevertheless, the basic guidelines are sound and pupils with visual handicap will for the most part be pleased to co-operate in working out their own best visual environment.

There may be pupils whose eye condition makes it difficult to tolerate bright light and who suffer to some extent from photophobia (for instance those who are albinos or who have coloboma). Such children should not be working in conditions where there is glare, such as bright light from an unshaded window streaming on to a child's face. A better working position results from arranging the seating with light from the window coming from behind the pupils and on to the work surface. It is helpful for pupils not to have to look into bright light. For instance, when a teacher is speaking or demonstrating it is better not to stand in front of windows. Bishop (op. cit.) even recommends that spaces between windows are inappropriate places to mount visual materials, again in order to avoid the likelihood of photophobic pupils gazing into bright light.

Visual displays

When visual displays are wall mounted, whether they are instructional, such as graphs, charts and diagrams, or examples of pictures and samples of the pupil's own work, they form part of the informational and aesthetic environment of the classroom. They should be displayed in a way that enables them to be appreciated by all the children in the class, whatever their visual capabilities. Just as it is sensible to place notices in braille at hand level or just above so that they can be easily read with the fingers, so visual material needs to be put up near to eye level if it is to be seen or read without difficulty by all the pupils. Notices should be in clear, good-sized print and they are best removed when they are no longer relevant. A noticeboard bearing a multitude of papers half pinned over each other, or with yellowing papers curling up at corners, is not an attractive or useful sight. The use of white wallpaper mounted on dark backing paper gives good constrast and helps to draw attention to the material displayed. A room that is visually stimulating and interesting is an encouraging environment in which to use vision for learning. Wall-mounted material that has both visual and tactile interest is intriguing and can, in the form of collages and friezes, incorporate designs or figures made by the pupils. Rather than overcrowding the wallspace with closely packed displays which can result in visual muddle, it is more striking to have fewer, more defined displays that are changed quite frequently to stimulate and maintain interest.

Displays of three-dimensional materials can give opportunities to handle and explore interesting objects which pupils would not otherwise have the chance to examine, as well as more commonly found ones. Pupils have a good deal of two-dimensional material presented to them, on the television screen, in software programs run on visual display units, in books and illustrations. Pupils with defective sight are especially in need of the opportunity to look at objects at close range, holding them near to the eye and having time to gaze. Common objects, a marble or pebble, a shell or a shiny conker can be part of a nature table collection and more unusual objects may be borrowed from museums. Careful exploratory touching and examination of objects by both sight and touch should be encouraged to help all pupils, but specially those who are visually handicapped, to form concepts relating to solid objects.

Sound in the environment

The environment does not only consist of what we can see and touch, it encompasses sound too. A reasonably low level of background noise means that the pupil with little or no sight can pick up sound cues without undue difficulty and strain. Hard surfaces against which objects clatter are no help in reducing environmental noise. Carpets, carpet tiles or rubberised floors help to keep background noise low, allowing meaningful sounds to be more audible. Such refinements may seem to be out of reach, but any practical approaches to reducing environmental noise will be helpful to pupils who need to rely more on their hearing as a channel for information.

THE PRESENTATION OF EDUCATIONAL MATERIALS TO VISUALLY HANDICAPPED PUPILS

Visually handicapped pupils are likely to need adaptations to the educational materials that are in the ordinary classroom if they have severe sight defects that prevent them from discriminating the size of print being used by the class. They may not have become skilled in using aids to vision such as magnifiers or telescopic aids, or the material that they need to read may be finely or densely printed, visually complex, or difficult to decipher. Even so, the pupil's motivation to use sight purposefully, his interest in the task in hand, the appropriateness of task lighting and position of work can sometimes enable material to be used with surprisingly little adaptation. The ultimate aim must be to help pupils with defective vision to use as much standard material as possible in common with their classmates. It will help all of them if the learning materials that they use are clearly presented and legible. When there is a need for modification beyond this, individual needs must be carefully assessed.

Materials to use for learning through play

Like fully sighted children, pupils who have sight problems will need experience in manipulating and examining three-dimensional materials before they start to interpret two-dimensional representation and later begin to read. Learning through play gives enjoyable opportunities for the child with defective vision to handle, explore and build with colourful and attractive three-dimensional material alongside fully sighted children and in interactive play with them. There is plenty of ordinary play material available commercially that is perfectly suitable for use in shared play by children with a range of levels of vision; simple shapes, bright colours, strong construction and surfaces that are not too shiny are particularly suitable. Visually stimulating objects, such as Christmas tree decorations and toys with sound effects are recommended for pre-school and playgroup activities. When these are outgrown and more complex activities and materials are needed, the clear visibility of the item chosen can be enhanced if they are used against a contrasting background. A good example is the placement of bright-yellow bricks and matching shapes on a table covered with a dark cloth or piece of material. Play materials should be used in a situation where there is good lighting directed on to the toys and objects being used. It is useful to have trays with a non-skid surface and a raised rim, so that small objects do not slip on to the floor or out of reach. Near vision tasks need to be presented in a way that ensures that materials can be easily accessible to handle.

Assessing the need for adaptations in presenting materials

An assessment of how the child is able to use his sight in day-to-day situations of work and play can be helpful in indicating the kind of activities involving vision that will be possible, and the kinds of learning and play materials that will be particularly appropriate for each child. The *Look and Think* Checklist (Tobin, Chapman *et al.*, 1978) administered in the early stages of the visually handicapped child's schooling is a useful predictor of areas of visual perception that may be a source of problems when the child is using ordinary play materials, pictures and toys. The Checklist enables the teacher or adviser for visually handicapped children to draw up a profile which shows the child's strengths and weaknesses in managing day-to-day visual tasks, and also outlines activities and suggests materials helpful in remediating areas shown to pose problems. It offers no magic formula to improve the sight but describes activities and materials shown to be motivating in helping pupils to pay attention to visual stimuli. The companion book which is a sequel to the Checklist is referred to as the 'Teacher's File' and recommends appropriate commercially available materials. It also gives instructions and illustrations of teacher-made materials which have been used effectively with visually handicapped children in the 5–7 year age-group. The programmes concentrate on such visual tasks as pattern making and matching, perception of symmetry, perspective and discrimination of detail and describe materials to use in each area, besides suggesting activities involving the interpretation of communication through facial expression and body gesture. These are all aspects of learning that have been shown to present difficulties to some visually handicapped children, but which may be amenable to remediation.

Although this material was devised nearly a decade ago, it remains a very useful guideline to activities involving visual perception that are tailored to meet the needs of individual children with defective vision. However, some of the activities suggested can be incorporated into group-work with pupils of differing levels of visual competence. The visually handicapped pupils in the group will tend to need more extended opportunities to practise such activities as naming and describing drawings and photographs, understanding the concept of perspective in pictures, and matching objects to sample.

The process of discriminating likeness and differences in shapes and patterns, first in three-dimensional and then in two-dimensional form, can be a precursor to discriminating differences in the shape of letters. Linear search and scan, another *Look and Think* activity, can lead on to the visual scanning technique required in discriminating the different shapes of words and letters in a line of print. Tasks of this kind may need extensive practice by children with defective vision, since using their vision for learning may present difficulties in terms of blurring and distortion or a reduced or interrupted visual field.

Choice of books and modifications to print

The books that children use when they begin pre-reading activities and progress to reading itself offer much less fine and complex visual tasks than the textbooks used later on, especially at secondary level. Small print, dense layout, footnotes and detailed diagrams can be very demanding for some pupils with defective vision. In addition, as they go up through the school, pupils, whether visually handicapped or not, will increasingly be required to undertake independent study involving looking up references and using graphic information such as charts and diagrams. If such materials are clear in their visual presentation and able to be used in appropriate environmental conditions, the pupils' task will be that much easier. The need to build up effective study habits is also essential. The pupil with sight defects should be encouraged to contribute to discussion about the best presentation of material for his individual needs, as well as the most useful visual aids to use for independent study.

As reading material progresses in difficulty, presentation as well as content should be considered, especially when pupils have difficulty in seeing. For initial and early readers, books of a manageable size with clear print giving a good dark contrast against a light background and attractive colourful pictures are readily available. These are usually well accepted by children with a wide range of vision competence. Shiny pages can reflect uncomfortable dazzle for photophobic children, and books whose pages combine printed text interwoven with illustrations or print set against varying coloured backgrounds are generally less easy to decipher than simply set out and clearly constrasted displays.

Although a comprehensive study by Shaw (1969) has shown that increased boldness of print increases legibility for some readers, differences in typography were found to be considerably less significant for younger than for older readers with partial sight. Bold print, clear layout of the page and adequate margin and spacing between words and letters, however, may well mean that at least in deciphering print, the pupil with sight difficulties is not having to deal with unnecessary complexities to compound existing problems.

If the blackboard is used for notes, these should be written in large, clear print. If the class contains pupils with very low levels of vision, it is also very helpful for the teacher to read out what is being written. It is difficult to get a good clear contrast with chalk and an overhead projector, or white board with thick black felt pens for writing, can give better constrast. Whatever the method used, the pupil's position in relation to displayed work should be considered. Sitting close to the blackboard seems like an old-fashioned solution, but remains useful for some pupils. Advanced planning is needed if 'desk copies' of blackboard work are to be used by pupils with defective vision or if the whole class is going to receive them. In order to justify the time spent on producing them, the copies should be consistently clear and legible. Older methods of producing duplicated material can be defective in this regard. The photocopying of typed sheets, although relatively expensive, gives clear and reliably consistent copies. These can be made even more legible for visually handicapped pupils by turning up the print contrast setting to 'dark'. Material produced on a word processor is clear, but can be made even more so by being photocopied on a high-contrast setting. The provision of copied material is expensive in resources and in time, but can facilitate work for pupils who have problems with distance vision, and a bank of basic material can be built up for future as well as current usage. Such material is not helpful if it is on sheets that have become dirty or faded; shortages of text material are disadvantageous for all pupils, but especially so for pupils with poor vision. Sharing books, or using material that is virtually illegible because it is faint in colour or soiled, increases problems of deciphering. All our children need adequate resources in order to learn, and while working with such inadequate materials is difficult for the fully sighted, for the visually handicapped it is daunting.

Using materials in the near environment

However clear and well presented reading material may be, there can still be problems in its use, particularly for pupils who need to use it at a very close distance from the eye. A spontaneous way to effect magnification is to bring reading material close to the eye. As Lindstedt (1986) explains, 'there is a simple correspondence between the distance of a focused object from the eye and the size of its image on the retina. If the distance is reduced to the half, the image will become twice as large, if the distance is reduced to a third, the image becomes three times larger and so on.' When visually investigating objects for details, the visually impaired child as a rule 'peers close', that is, brings the object close to the eye, or the eye close to the object. By this method the detail of the object will be seen in a wider visual angle and the retinal image will be magnified, a greater part of the retina thus being activated. This in turn might compensate for a reduced number of active cones and visual neurons per unit of retinal area.

However, Lindstedt cautions that such visual behaviour as peering closely at the work being undertaken by no means offers a complete solution to the problems arising from the need to work at close range.

'"Peering close" is often looked upon as a sign of excellent accommodation capacity. Nothing could be more wrong. On the contrary, as stated above, the ability to accommodate properly is often inadequate, imprecise or totally lacking in the visually impaired child. The child "peers close" in order to magnify the retinal image.' The child prefers a large, somewhat blurred image to a small, sharp one. Lindstedt refers to the possibility of providing reading glasses or magnifying lenses for near work, of a power corresponding to the degree of failing.

In addition to such correction, attention needs to be given to the position in which the pupil is using reading materials. If the material is being used on a table or flat surface, it means that in order to use it at a close distance from the eye, the head is bent low over the book in order to try to discriminate the print. This position means that a shadow is inevitably thrown on to the working surface. The reader's neck and shoulders are bent and tense, postural faults easily develop, and the whole process of reading is made tiring and uncomfortable. These are not trivial discomforts. It is interesting to try reading in this position oneself for a minimum of ten minutes in order to appreciate its inefficiency, and to experience the uncomfortable and tiring effects of doing so. Close work is not in itself detrimental to sight and need not be discouraged, but it should be undertaken in a comfortable position and with appropriate task lighting. An adjustable reading stand is an essential piece of equipment for pupils who need to work at a close range. This needs to be placed at the angle which gives the best support for the material being used in relation to the pupil's vision, and some initial experimenting with different angles of work may be needed in order to settle on this. A desk with an adjustable sloping top is useful as it provides storage space too, but probably the most practical aid, especially as the pupil progresses into secondary school, is a light, portable reading stand that can be easily taken from room to room as required. It will need to have a ledge to support the reading material and strong clamps to hold pages in place are useful. The earlier a pupil is able to find and keep to a comfortable and efficient working position, the better.

Another factor in the pupil's near environment that can affect the comfortable use of vision for work is the 'fit' of the furniture (chair, desk, table) in terms of individual requirements. School furniture usually comes in three standard sizes; pupils do not. It may be possible to exchange chairs and tables within or between classes, however, to get a better match of furniture to the individual pupil. Having work at an appropriate height in relation to distance from the eye makes a real difference to avoiding unnecessary fatigue, and this can only be effected by a comfortable working position. It is well worth checking that the pupil's chair and desk or table make this possible.

The question of enlarged print

The value of using enlarged print for pupils with visual impairments is controversial. It can be expensive to provide and difficult to obtain at short notice, and has the disadvantage of not being readily available in ordinary schools. Some special schools for visually handicapped pupils which have facilities for producing their own enlarged print use this for lesson notes and for enlarging finely printed text and reference work, finding this helpful to their pupils. 24 point print, or even 18 point print, gives a very clear distinction of letter shapes, especially if a bold, dark type is used. However, as with the magnification of print by lenses or low vision aids, enlarged print has the disadvantage of reducing the number of words or even letters that can be glimpsed at one time, and therefore may reduce speed and fluency in reading. It is, of course, necessary to check carefully and individually the size of type that a visually impaired pupil can discriminate. The *McClure reading types for children* gives examples of type in decreasing size which can be used to test this.

A more complex but useful measure can be obtained by using the Lindstedt BUST playing cards which depict two-dimensional forms in specific sizes on cards which can be given to pupils to discriminate in the form of a game. The size of figure represented on the card which an individual child can discriminate is then set against the information in the conversion table which indicates the correct text size usable by the child, as well as indicating the visual aid needed when reading certain print sizes at specific distances. It needs skill and experience to use this comparison table, and the advice of a specialist teacher for visually handicapped pupils should be sought if there are problems in deciding the size of print that should be used in individual cases.

There is, however, a stage in the pupil's progress through school when offering print in an enlarged form may be particularly helpful. This is when the pupil is still coming to terms with using a low vision aid and is not yet skilful in its use, but needs to read text and notes that are too advanced in content to be available in the large print of junior and early reading books. In addition secondary-aged pupils find it relaxing to use enlarged print for leisure-time reading at home.

There is no evidence to show that a particular typeface is generally more legible for pupils with visual impairments than any other; it is the layout and contrast that require attention. Checking printed material for legibility, adapting where necessary and helping pupils to use appropriate aids with well-presented standard material are essential aspects of the presentation of material to visually-handicapped pupils in any educational setting.

Writing

When a pupil who is visually impaired is writing or drawing, his work position is as important as when he is reading. A comfortable position for writing when work needs to be undertaken at close range is in some respects more difficult to achieve than it is for reading. The arm can be in a very cramped position and the movement of the hand rather restricted if a flat surface such as a table is used; a desk with an adjustable sloping top gives a much better angle whilst also providing storage for books. If it is not possible to provide this, a firm, adjustable stand can be used on a table. An architect's drawing-board makes an excellent piece of furniture to use for close-range work, but it is too large to be accommodated in the classroom. Even if it is not feasible to provide a slanting surface for all writing activities, the possibilities of doing so whenever possible should be explored; an inexpensive custom-made board can sometimes provide the answer.

Utensils used for writing need to provide as much contrast as possible with the background against which they are used. Felt-tips or fibre-tipped pens that give a strong, dark line are useful for children in the first classes, the disadvantage being that pressure can cause the tips to splay or split. Brightly coloured, non-smudge crayons are suitable for drawing and letter outlines, while if pencils are used, those with thick, dark lead should be chosen. If they are cut in half they will be easier for younger pupils to wield.

When progress is being made to finer handwriting tasks, a black-coloured ball pen is usually the best choice. Some experimenting may be needed to find a brand whose ink does not fade and which does not skid on the surface of the paper.

Matt white paper is the most suitable to use and lined paper is helpful for those who have difficulty with hand–eye co-ordination and keeping the line of writing straight. As the process of copying the shape of a letter can be difficult for some visually handicapped pupils when they begin to learn writing, there will need to be close one-to-one demonstration, or demonstration on a closed circuit television. Paper which has dark ruled lines alternating with a light pencil line to act as a guide for mid-letter levels may also be employed. It is the darkness, not the thickness, of the ruled lines that makes it helpful as a guide for writing. To achieve this, ruled paper can be run off on a photocopier on a high contrast setting. Squared and lined paper with good contrast can also be obtained in bulk from the Partially Sighted Society. (See 'Useful Addresses' section.) Both these sources provide suitable but expensive paper; it may be possible instead for a teacher's aid to produce appropriately ruled paper as required. As writing skills become well established the need to use specially provided paper of this kind will diminish.

THE ROLE OF THE TEACHER IN THE MANAGEMENT OF THE ENVIRONMENT

Often it is a combination of adaptations to the classroom environment and to materials used for learning that will be most helpful in terms of giving pupils with defective vision the opportunity to have access to the full curriculum followed in the class. With attempts being made to meet the requirements of pupils with a diversity of special needs in the ordinary school whenever possible, teachers are facing a considerable challenge. There may be pupils in the class who require adapted materials or curriculum because of social or cultural factors, or as a result of physical or sensory disabilities and learning difficulties. The teacher will want to seek ways of meeting diverse needs through the individualisation of programmes, but will also look for solutions to problems of providing appropriate materials in the face of additional complications in class management. An acceptance of the fact that some pupils will require adaptations to learning materials or specialised equipment such as braillers or magnifying aids as necessary rather than remarkable is a good pragmatic basis on which to work. Experience in teaching children with special needs helps to reduce apprehensions about their singularity.

Theoretically, the recommendations in this and other chapters which describe adaptations that can usefully be made in order to give pupils with defective vision the most suitable environment and materials for work may seem complex. In practice, implementing these suggestions is likely to simplify the day-to-day class situation, since the visually handicapped pupils will be in a better position to manage themselves and their belongings and to work independently and effectively. They will not be struggling with defective sight in a confused environment in which they are using materials that are hard to decipher and presented without sufficient clarity. In addition, attention to the special needs of the pupil with poor sight in terms of good lighting, classroom arrangement and clear presentation of materials can raise the teacher's awareness of the way in which these aspects of classroom ecology are helpful for all pupils.

There will be classrooms where it is evident that these factors are already borne in mind, and which will need only minor additions such as the clear labelling of cupboards in print or braille, or a rearrangement of seating in relation to light sources from windows and to ensure clear visibility of blackboard or overhead projector. More specific adaptations and special equipment may be needed in the case of some severely visually impaired pupils in terms of task lighting, position of work or modified learning materials. These additional changes to the ordinary working environment should be effected as a result of the recommendations in the pupil's statement of special needs. However, the recommendations here are sometimes generalised, and more detailed and precise help in working with the pupil's exact requirements can be achieved by consultation with an adviser or specialist teacher of visually handicapped children. Recommendations arising from assessments carried out by an educational psychologist, or from medical records containing information from ophthalmological examination, or from an ophthalmic optician prescribing low vision aids, will need to be translated into practice in the day-to-day classroom situation, and specialist help from an advisory teacher is invaluable here. The class teacher will also gain a good deal of useful information by observing how the visually handicapped pupils handle and attempt to use visual material. Do they try to hold it close to the eyes? Do they hold it in an unusual position – to the side rather than full-square to the eyes? Do they seem to be dazzled by strong light, or flounder in less well-lit places? Such observations should also be discussed with the adviser or specialist teacher as they can be very helpful in working out the optimum visual environment for the pupil.

THE CONTRIBUTION OF THE TEACHER'S AID

The teacher will be part of a team concerned with the educational support of the severely visually impaired pupil and will be the person responsible for implementing the recommendations of other professionals in day-to-day terms. Teachers in first schools are often more used to working in the classroom alongside other profession-als than those who are subject specialists at the secondary school level. Ideally consultation with advisory or special teachers should be started before a pupil is accepted into the class, or at least at the very beginning of term, so that the provision of special equipment and materials can be organised. Subsequently it will be necessary to review the nature of the support regularly, since co-operation between professional and ancillaries in terms of provision of materials and the need for individual help in some curriculum areas will need to be continuous. The class or specialist subject teacher will be able to contribute a great deal to the discussion of the pupil's special needs as a result of daily or frequent observation of the pupil's visual behaviour.

However, it is the setting up and initial implementation in practical day-to-day terms of recommendations from other profes-sionals about the nature and extent of specialised equipment, materials and support that is the most demanding phase for the teacher in the ordinary school whose class contains visually handicapped pupils. Once changes in the classroom have been made and special items of furniture and equipment have been introduced, they usually come to be accepted as a matter of course and are regarded by pupils as 'how things are'. It is the initial sorting out of requirements that must be done on an individual basis for the pupil with severe visual defect. Obtaining the necessary, sometimes expensive, special equipment such as closed circuit television takes time and persistence. Then there is the need for the nature of any adaptation to learning material to be understood by the teacher and the teacher's aid. Again, once this has been clarified, custom is likely to work in favour of continuing use.

Teachers who have a severely handicapped pupil in an ordinary class can be greatly helped by a teacher's aid, especially in first-school work and in those areas of the curriculum in the secondary school that involve practical processes such as science and geography. The teacher's aid can give valuable assistance in producing specialised materials under guidance of the teacher or adviser. Help which involves working directly with the pupil in class or specialist subject room must be geared towards increasing, not reducing, the level of personal independence of the visually handicapped pupil; this aim needs to be discussed by the teacher and teacher's aid and to be understood and accepted. The aim will be fulfilled if the teacher's aid encourages self-help skills and good personal organisation by the pupil rather than doing everything for him in the way of fetching and returning materials. It can be all too easy for a severely visually handicapped pupil to be physically inactive and desk-bound, or dependent on the adult helper. The teacher's aid can help, however, by ensuring that equipment that is difficult for a child to handle is available when needed and properly stored when not in use. A skilful teacher's aid, with the teacher's guidance, can be very helpful in adapting materials, perhaps by making a large, hand-made copy of a detailed map or diagram, photocopying material, producing darkly ruled paper, and reproducing lesson notes in large, clear handwriting. Sitting beside the pupil with severe sight problems in some learning situations, the teacher's aid can describe visual demonstrations and oversee the handling of objects in practical work.

THE NEED FOR CLEAR EXPLANATION

The valuable contribution of the teacher's aid is, as the name implies, a help to the teacher, but it is the teacher who takes the main responsibility for preparing work in a clear way for all pupils, including those who are visually handicapped. Since there are pupils in the class with defective vision, however, there will need to be an additional emphasis on some aspects of teaching. The pupil with poor sight may not be able to see facial expression and body gesture clearly, and these forms of non-verbal communication reinforce meaning and intent. Because of this, verbal explanations and instructions must be particularly clear, and sometimes include more precise detail or directions in words than would ordinarily be necessary for fully sighted pupils. Vague or inexact directions can be mystifying for pupils with poor vision. For instance, the instruction 'Put it over there' is far less useful to them than the more precise directive 'Put that back on the table by the door.' In the teaching situation, verbal descriptions should draw on aspects of the pupil's experience, and it will be necessary to ensure that there are opportunities for individual and small-group demonstrations supported by relevant verbal descriptions. Even simple activities, such as the right way to hold and use a pair of scissors, may need to be shown to a pupil with very poor vision, not because it is beyond the child's capacity, but because defective vision may make it difficult to see exactly how to manipulate utensils and objects without precise demonstration on how to do so. It is easy to assume that such skills will be picked up incidentally, as they will usually be by fully sighted children, who often copy what they see other children doing, especially if a teacher's directions are unclear to them. Such useful solutions to confusing situations are difficult to adapt by children who have visual disabilities.

Any additional support or special tuition that a pupil needs as a result of defective sight must be given tactfully by the teacher or teacher's aid, with an emphasis on what the pupil can do rather than on difficulties. Reducing possible misunderstanding or confusion by ensuring that tasks requiring vision are presented as clearly as possible both in terms of the materials themselves and the way in which explanations and directions are given will be a great help not only to pupils with defective vision but also to their classmates.

LIGHTING

The importance of good lighting for people who are visually handicapped has already been stressed, as has the need for each child's requirements in levels of lighting to be stressed. Classroom teachers who look at the lighting in their classroom may question whether they are able to do anything positive to help. However, understanding what good lighting means is the first step; assessing what the ideal situation would be, then working towards it follow after. Requests for adaptations to classroom lighting or for individual lamps cannot sensibly be made until the principles are understood.

Requirements for lighting fall into two groups – firstly, environmental, and secondly, task lighting. Environmental lighting is generally concerned with mobility in the environment. Is there sufficient light to be able to move around safely? Task lighting usually entails higher levels of illumination needed for reading and other close work. Shops mainly concentrate on environmental lighting which is cleverly designed to make the environs and merchandise attractive visually, often with extra lighting at service points and cash tills.

There are three main sources of light, the first of which is the sun which provides natural daylight. In the United Kingdom, there is, to say the least, variable illumination with different levels being present in winter and summer and in varying weather conditions. Modern school buildings make as much use as possible of natural light, incorporating as they do large windows. Natural light, though a good-quality light, does produce problems. Often the light is too bright, which can cause difficulties for all children. Window glass can produce glare and the sun can cause harsh shadows.

The other two sources of light are the ordinary, filament light bulb and fluorescent tubes. Although in common use, the tungsten light bulb has several disadvantages, and the preferred source of light for public buildings, and increasingly for homes, is the fluorescent tube. This makes efficient use of electricity and provides more light. There is now a wide variety of hues available, but the deluxe warm white is considered to be more appropriate for people who are visually handicapped than lighting which is blue-white (Jay, 1978). As fluorescent light comes from a larger area the light is more diffuse and therefore produces less glare, and the flickering that was associated with the early form of fluorescent lighting should not be experienced now.

For desk lighting, provision of an individual lamp can be most helpful for those who are visually handicapped, although the availability of power points in the classroom may cause problems. However, if an individual lamp will help a child to succeed in an integrated setting, every effort should be made to provide one. The L80 asymmetric light is particularly suitable. It contains a fluorescent tube and can be set at different angles and at varying distances from the working surface. The shade has a double skin so that it remains cool and the light is well diffused, thus reducing glare and shadows. Another suitable lamp is the Waldmann light, but this is slightly more expensive. (Addresses where these can be obtained are at the end of the book.)

Levels of lighting are measured in lux, which is the amount of light landing on a surface, not the light emitted from a source. Recommended levels of lighting are given in the *Code for Interior Lighting* (Illuminating Engineering Society, 1977). For instance, an operating theatre would need a level of over 10,000 lux, a boxing ring 2,000 lux, kitchens 300 lux and bathroom 100. It is suggested that the lighting of blackboards should be 500 lux, and general teaching areas 300 lux. A light meter can be used to assess the level of lighting present.

It is vitally important to remember that the lighting source is only one factor. Just as important is the amount of light reflected from walls, ceilings and floors. Light is absorbed by dark surfaces and reflected by lighter surfaces. The level of lighting can be increased greatly by paying attention to the décor and state of cleanliness.

For some visually handicapped children the amount of glare caused by various forms of lighting adds considerably to their difficulties. Discomfort glare, experienced by the normally sighted when looking at something in bright light, causes no special difficulties. Disability glare is rarer and affects some low vision or partially sighted people. This is where the lighting is excessive, such as in bright sunlight, or where glare is caused by badly sited lighting or unsuitable décor, so that the person is unable to function visually. What may be discomfort glare to the normally sighted may well be disability glare to the visually handicapped.

In order to assess the children's lighting needs, teachers must look at the tasks that are to be performed, such as moving around, close and distance work, and see how each child performs in different lighting conditions, then adapt accordingly. Once the ideal conditions have been decided, every effort must be made to attain them. Although some expense may be involved, much can be done by the class teacher in the day-to-day management of the classroom.

Whilst considering lighting levels, the problems of open spaces should be appreciated. These cause special problems for many partially sighted people who must be shown how to negotiate them. Any dangerous elements in large halls and playgrounds should be pointed out, as should the changing effect of shadows which may create false edges and hide certain landmarks. Ways in which mobility can be made easier for visually handicapped pupils are discussed in the section on mobility in Chapter 6. Suffice it here to remind the teacher that areas which are well and appropriately lit in the morning may be dark or over-bright in the afternoon and vice versa. Children who perform differently at different times of day may be reacting to a changed quantity or quality of lighting level.

Figure 4 summarises the recommendations given in this chapter for

1. The Physical Environment in the Classroom

Seating	– suitably arranged in relation to light sources (windows), blackboard and demonstrations
Blackboard and overhead projector	– clear background; large, clear letters
General décor	– light, matt surfaces and use of strong colour contrast
Visual displays	– selected; strong contrast; mounted material at eye level
Storage areas	– accessible, consistently used, clearly labelled and sufficient

Lighting	– good overall level, but avoid dazzle and reflected light
2. The near environment of the pupil	
Working position	– reading stands, drawing boards, sloping desk tops, chair and table right size for individual
Task lighting	– check on cause of visual impairment; direct lighting on to task, not into pupil's eyes
Play and practical tasks	– non-slip trays to contain materials
3. Learning materials	
Toys and games	– robust and colourful; look for tactile and sound interest
Books and printed materials	– good contrast; dark letters, lines or figures against light, matt background
	– well-spaced layout
	– clear delineation
	– consider need for enlargement
'Desk copies' or duplicated notes	– clear and legible (as above)
Writing materials	– consider ruled and squared paper
	– writing utensils that give strong contrast and are easy to hold
4. Aids to vision	
Spectacles, magnifiers, low vision aids	– encourage appropriate use, proper care and cleanliness
5. Special emphasis in teaching	
	– audible and clear verbal descriptions and directions
	– provision of individual or small-group demonstrations and explanations
	– allow sufficient time to complete tasks
	– measures to counteract reduced experience (handling objects)
	– visual enhancement programmes
	– attention to listening skills
	– self-help skills and personal organisation
	– keyboard skills
	– special methods and adaptations for blind pupils
6. Specialised equipment	
	– discuss with adviser or specialist teacher the appropriate use of:
	– closed circuit television
	– tape recorders
	– typewriters
	– special software
	– braillers
	– adapted materials for maths and science

Figure 4 *Recommended measures to help visually handicapped pupils in the school environment*

the organisation of the physical environments. A teacher who has visually handicapped pupils in the class will need to consider these recommendations and implement them as necessary. Pupils with mild or moderate levels of visual problems are likely to need only some of the adaptations listed (for example, closed circuit television will not be needed), but they will benefit from an environment and materials that are clear in visual terms. Pupils who need to work in a tactile mode will also be helped by a well-organised physical environment and their special needs are described in Chapter 6.

It can be helpful to check the environment and materials used in the classroom in terms of the functional vision of the pupils. The following checklist (Figure 5) is an example of the way in which useful information about the child's needs in this regard can be compiled.

THE SOCIAL ENVIRONMENT

There is an emphasis in educational thinking today which stresses the common and shared aspects of children's schooling. Classes in ordinary schools are increasingly composed of pupils of different ethnic origin, cultural and religious persuasion, pupils who may have physical or sensory impairments, learning difficulties or social and emotional problems, since the neighbourhood school rather than the special school is seen to be the first choice for children's education. Emphasis is laid on trying to meet the special needs of pupils on an individual basis, rather than choosing educational placements with regard to a category. In order to be able to meet the diverse needs of individual children, the social climate within the class must be an accepting one, and resources in material and human terms sufficient to be able to accept these special children without neglecting the others. There will be pupils who need to work at a different pace from most of their classmates, and who require specialised equipment and materials in order to have access to the curriculum. Such pupils are likely to flourish in a class where the ambience is not competitive, pupils' achievements are not ranked against each other, and individual progress and achievement are encouraged in their own right. Competition can be a spur to some pupils and fun in some activities, but the individual's improvement of his own levels of attainment should be seen to be what really matters and be the most evident cause of encouragement.

Theoretically, in today's educational environment, the disabled pupil has the right to be different, to be accepted in the ordinary class, encouraged to participate in it fully and in his own way and to

Tick boxes as appropriate

NAME:... DATE OF ASSESSMENT ....

DOE .... SEX...

CAUSE OF VISUAL IMPAIRMENT
GLASSES PRESCRIBED ☐
LOW VISION AIDS PRESCRIBED FOR   NEAR VISION ☐
DISTANCE VISION ☐

MONOCULAR VISION ☐
BINOCULAR VISION ☐
PREFERRED EYE   L ☐   R ☐
PHOTOPHOBIA ☐
NYSTAGMUS ☐

USE OF DISTANCE VISION
Pupil uses:
BLACKBOARD ☐
WHITEBOARD ☐
OHP ☐
CCTV ☐
Pupil needs to sit in class
Left front ☐   Right front ☐   Other ☐
Pupil requires additional time for copying from board etc. ☐
Requires specific help with mobility/orientation ☐
Requires individual demonstration of practical tasks ☐

USE OF NEAR VISION
Pupil appears to be helped by:
   Use of marker when reading ☐
   Use of finger when reading ☐
   Uses low vision aid for reading ☐
   Requires additional task lighting ☐
   Suffers from glare from light or windows ☐
   Requires reading stand ☐
   or
Can use:
Standard reading books ☐
Standard mathematical materials ☐
Standard dictionary ☐
Standard atlas ☐
Standard examination papers ☐
Requires additional time for reading ☐
Requires special paper for writing ☐
Requires special writing tools ☐
                colour ☐
Requires additional auditory work ☐
Uses tape recorder ☐
Uses computer monitor ☐
Requires additional time for writing ☐

Additional comments on pupil's functional vision:

Figure 5 *Classroom checklist for functional vision*

be considered as an individual, a totality with assets and strengths in addition to those disadvantages or difficulties which arise from his disability. The de-categorising of pupils with special needs does not automatically lead them to full social integration in an ordinary class. A pupil whose difficulties in learning and in social interaction are connected with difficulties in seeing and the way that these difficulties are regarded by others will require both understanding and knowledge of the nature of the problems from the teacher. To put the case simply, such a pupil may not be able to undertake a task such as cutting out a paper figure, not because of not understanding how to do so, but because of being unable to see properly how it is done.

There are risks of misjudging the nature of a visually handicapped pupil's problems both in learning and in social situations. In a class buzzing with activity a child with severely defective vision can get left behind or left out because he cannot see clearly how to perform the tasks involved. It is easy in this situation for classmates to consider such a child a bit stupid and for the teacher to consider the problem to be a cognitive one. It needs to be appreciated that pupils with defective vision may respond inappropriately as a result of missing visual detail, for instance the facial expression and body gestures of others.

Other day-to-day situations that may not be attributed to visual difficulties include the extended time the children may need to complete tasks, their need to come close to the blackboard or to demonstrations, and their apparent clumsiness in certain practical activities and sports such as ball games. These are not inevitable problems for visually handicapped children and where they occur can sometimes be improved, but they do not tend to be considered assets by other pupils and may contribute to low self-concept. That these may be continuing problems is evident by a study by Bauman (1964) who found partially sighted pupils to be particularly insecure and with a greater sense of loneliness when they were integrated into open education systems. The anxieties for these pupils centred around areas of social competence, personal appearance and adjustment to handicap. Ironically, some of the aids to vision which can be helpful in assisting the pupil to see more clearly, and thus perform tasks more adroitly and effectively, may be rejected by the pupil because of a dislike of looking different. These fears are not always groundless. Even an aid as commonly encountered as a pair of spectacles can be a focus for teasing. Madge and Fassam (1982) examined some of the social interactions of physically disabled pupils in a range of educational situations including integration into ordinary schools. In this study a 13 year old, when asked about being teased in his comprehensive school, replied, 'I should think that in my first week or so there was a fair bit. Because when I first got my glasses they all went "Ha, ha, four eyes" for about a week or so, and then they all shut up because they forgot about it.'

Also in this study another pupil's comment was 'But in this school they see you're different from them – like you would wear glasses – and they'll be calling you names.' These disabled children some-times showed resilience and determination, calling names back or, better still, ignoring unkind comments. Although the findings relate to physically rather than visually handicapped pupils, there are implication for teachers with disabled pupils in their classes and an indication of a special need to be aware of potential problems for secondary school pupils. The study concludes that 'teasing of disabled children does occur both in and out of school ... older pupils and those in integrated schooling are particularly likely to come across such behaviour.' More hearteningly it showed that teasing seemed to decrease as pupils got to know each other better as classmates, and despite the possibility of teasing most of the children interviewed welcomed the social breadth of the integrated setting.

In the case of visually handicapped pupils in an ordinary school, there will be spectacle wearers and pupils with mild visual handicaps. Even those few with more severe visual handicaps will operate as sighted people. Because of the low incidence of blindness among school-aged children in the UK there will be only a few pupils who are totally blind. Among the visually handicapped pupils there will, of course, be as many heterogeneous characteris-tics as among children in any class, some being immediately attractive and outgoing, others timid or aggressive, just as one finds among their classmates. Visual handicap is not going to elicit a common response to situations although it can impose some shared problems. Jones (1970) observes that:

> ...the child with a severe visual handicap may be diffident, or at the other extreme, amazingly precocious. These different conditions can arise from over-protection or lack of understanding of visual handicap. This shows failure to provide an environment conducive to normal growth, where initiative and independence will develop.

The need to give attention to the social aspects of the school environment for the integrated visually handicapped pupil should not be underestimated. It is significant that currently in Sweden, where resources to support visually handicapped pupils in main-stream schools are considerable and of high level and where the integration of handicapped pupils is particularly well supported and virtually universal, there are still problems for a significant

number of visually handicapped pupils in terms of social adjustment (Svenson, 1986).

Besides opening up and retaining choice of educational placement for pupils with severe visual handicaps, evidence of this kind
calls for continuing research into the social aspects of integration for
such pupils. The teacher with less severely visually impaired pupils
already in the class who faces the prospect of receiving pupils with
more severe visual disabilities will want to consider practical and
immediate strategies to mitigate problems of social acceptance and
to reduce or eliminate cruel teasing or isolation of the pupils who
have defective vision. It may not occur; pupils may be resilient
enough to deal with negative social encounters themselves, or may
have the kind of personality that makes them unlikely to arise. Good
practice such as that described by Hegarty *et al.* (1981) also shows
how positive measures to meet the needs of visually handicapped
pupils can help them to flourish in a happy community atmosphere.

Where poor social acceptance does occur it can be useful to look at
ways in which this problem has been tackled, possibly with children
who have other educational disadvantages. Strategies used to help
mildly academically handicapped pupils to remedy situations of
social rejection include co-operative learning and working together
to achieve common goals; both strategies can be used with visually
handicapped pupils. Less easy to implement is the suggested
'coaching' in social skills, in which the poorly accepted child has
specific instruction on how to interact with peers in a positive way.
It is conceded in this study (Hegarty *et al.*, op. cit.) that the class
teacher is unlikely to have time or training to do this, but that an adviser or social education teacher may be able to do so. One turns
here to child guidance and the role of the educational psychologist.
Further work with such pupils which has shown success has included structuring games in which poorly accepted pupils were paired
with moderately accepted pupils; modelling with guided examples
on film and video was also found to be helpful in terms of social
acceptance. A more modest role model is offered in *Suzy* (Chapman,
1982) which illustrates in a simple way some of the practicalities of
coping with poor sight in day-to-day situations on the ways that
friends can help. 'Suzy', an imaginary character in a small book for
and about children, is a 10-year-old partially sighted pupil going to
an ordinary school. The incidents related in her story, however, are
drawn from actual experiences of visually handicapped pupils.

The use of specialised equipment, telescopic aids, reading stands
and closed circuit television may make a pupil feel singled out from
others because of having to use such devices. Fortunately the
introduction of microcomputers into schools and their use by pupils
in individualised programmes, makes the use of sophisticated

equipment less remarkable in the classroom than was the case some years ago, and some software is specially designed or particularly useful for visually handicapped pupils. One positive approach to the acceptance of other special equipment is to explain its use to fully sighted pupils, let them see it and use it so that it is regarded as something of interest to everyone. The skilful use of a piece of interesting technology by a visually handicapped pupil can become a source of pride rather than embarrassment.

For all that the teacher can do to promote acceptance, it will ultimately be the shared interest and enthusiasm of pupils that help them to form and maintain friendship. Encouraging the visually handicapped pupil to improve self-help skills and personal organ-isation can help to reduce the 'nuisance level' of visual impairment and enable the pupil more confidently to 'have a go' at enjoyable activities with friends. The 'buddy' system, whereby a fully sighted pupil is paired with a visually handicapped peer, can sometimes be enjoyable and lead to lasting friendship, but care must be taken that the visually handicapped pupil is not always dependent.

Lukoff and Whiteman (1960) found that blind pupils make blind friends when they have the opportunity to do so, and it may be that they need as they grow up to have some shared experience with children and young people who face similar challenges. These authors state that 'For events of monumental signifi-cance for one's life's chances, such as blindness, there are important experiences in addition to the direction of the norms for independence.'

They caution, however, against a situation which can occur in the special school when the organisation of the entire curriculum is adapted to the vision problems of the students. The entire education of these children in these schools, then, is attuned to their handicap.

Raefnaeskol in Kalundberg in Denmark is able to offer holiday summer schools for visually handicapped pupils who are otherwise in ordinary schools but who apparently welcome the social interaction with other visually disabled pupils, whilst enjoying integrated schooling at other times. Teachers in ordinary schools need to be aware that some visually handicapped pupils may have these social needs while at the same time encouraging positive and enjoyable social interaction between pupils within the full range of vision.

The visually handicapped pupils attending an ordinary school may be greatly helped by a physical and social environment that has been planned with some sensitivity to their special needs while retaining a challenging or 'normal' character. Specific steps may need to be taken. 'Buddies', for example, can be briefed about particular environmental hazards for their classmates with sight defects, and shown how to help them when necessary by using correct sighted guide techniques. Environmental awareness and friendly helpfulness are important aspects of daily life at school for pupils who have sight problems.

Some developmental implications of visual handicap

Every child's development is individual and visually handicapped children are likely to show differences in their understanding of concepts and in the acquisition of skills, just as all children do. Despite this generalisation, it is relevant for the teacher whose class includes children with little or no sight to know whether the development of a child has been delayed, disturbed or impeded, and whether defective vision has been a factor in this. The class may well include children who have other and different challenges to their development: for instance, the pupil who needs to learn English for the first time in order to take part fully in school work; the child who cannot hear clearly, or whose physical disabilities hinder participation in play activities. Whilst considering each child as an individual, not as a member of a category, the teacher will nevertheless need to be aware of the potential effect on development of a factor as significant as visual handicap in order to be able to meet the child's educational needs effectively. The presence of visual handicap can affect some aspects of a child's development, but the extent to which this is so is likely to be variable and may be influenced by other factors such as appropriate visual stimulation. In any case, shared activities with other children should not be left out of the growing child's experience. Compensatory and specific teaching strategies can help to promote and maintain the interaction with classmates and participation in a range of activities that are vital to healthy development.

MOTOR DEVELOPMENT

Lack of sight and severe visual impairment can influence both movement and independent mobility, but much can be done during the pre-school years especially to mitigate the negative effects that difficulties in seeing may have on the child's motor development. During the school years physical activities, an appropriate working environment and in some cases specific mobility and orientation skills will be needed, and there may be a case for remedial measures if the early stages of motor development have not been successfully completed. A developmentally based programme with well-tried practical activities has been set out by Tooze (1981) whose book on independence training for visually handicapped pupils is an invaluable guide for teachers and parents.

Movement in the early years

Problems with independent mobility can be significantly reduced by specific training in appropriate techniques, but it will be difficult for such training to be fully successful unless body-awareness, spatial orientation and directionality have been developed in the first years of life. Being aware of physical separateness, of the position of the body, limbs and head in space, and awareness of the different parts of the body are aspects of motor development that may be delayed or may be difficult to master by severely visually handicapped infants, especially those who are totally blind or who are under stimulated. Even in the first few weeks after birth, control of the body and exploratory and purposeful movement can be encouraged. Bathing and dressing give good opportunities for stroking the baby's trunk and limbs, back, fingers and toes. Touch must be substituted for vision in helping to develop an awareness of the different parts of the body.

There are a number of useful procedures for helping to develop body-awareness and spatial orientation in the RNIB *Guidelines for teachers and parents of visually handicapped children with additional handicaps*. These suggestions relate to the first weeks and months of life up to infant level and are particularly helpful in instances in which retardation and additional handicap have further complicated motor development. Even without such complicating factors, some visually handicapped infants show delays or differences in their motor development from that usually encountered in fully sighted children. There are, of course, considerable individual differences among all children with regard to the age of accomplishing particular motor skills, but Tooze (op. cit.) notes that there is a tendency for visually handicapped infants to have little motivation to crawl, with the result that this stage of motor development is missed out. It is an important stage in developing co-ordination and should be encouraged. Visual motivation to move towards an object may have to be replaced by sound motivation, and specific encouragement given in crawling patterns, for example, by rolling a ball containing a bell or pellets in front of the child.

The services of a physiotherapist can be helpful to the visually handicapped infant. These professionals have an expert knowledge of normal motor development and their firm and confident handling can be a positive encouragement to both parents and children, while they can give specific suggestions for activities to promote purposeful movement. The physiotherapist's understanding of the way in which visual impairment can affect movement will be enhanced by co-operation with an advisory teacher for the visually handicapped and make her contribution to early intervention particularly valuable.

Once the patterns of movement are established, the baby's activities become more goal-directed and internal movement patterns and control of external movement begins to be learned. Sheridan (1975) observed that sighted babies do not reach towards sources of sound until they are nine to ten months old, and children with visual handicaps would be unlikely to do so earlier. They can, however, be encouraged to sit, supported against cushions, and given rattles and toys to hold and explore. Fraiberg (1977) stresses the significance of bringing the hands together at the midline, necessary for the manipulation of objects; this movement is more likely to occur in the sitting position. Tactual searching for dropped objects can be encouraged in the immediate environment. Hand and body-part games such as 'pat a cake' can be played, as can pointing games touching the ears or knees of both child and carer. More active play with adults, swinging the child, jumping up and down and catching, can help to give the experience and later the understanding of the body's orientation in space and begin to develop the trust in the environment and in other humans needed as the basis for later training in mobility. Further activities including playing on the floor, being rolled over one way and then back, climbing over safe obstacles can help to develop body awareness and strengthen movement. Infants with severe visual handicap may not be able to see and copy some movements, such as lifting a spoon, and these may need to be established through a 'patterning' sequence given by parents or carers.

The activities of standing alone and walking can be accomplished by visually handicapped children at ages comparable to those of sighted children, although more specific encouragement may be needed. These are activities which require balance and confidence in moving into an environment without the reassurance of visible goals, such as the waiting hands or the familiar chair.

Cratty and Sams (1968) stress the necessity of developing a sound body-image as a basis for all movement-related learning. Play which includes crawling, walking, running, climbing, rolling and turning somersaults can help to promote this, and safe, interesting 'obstacle' courses can be devised in almost any room for children to experience movement over and under objects, through hoops, thus gaining a knowledge of the size, shape and limits of their bodies.

'Free' walking, with good posture and rhythm, is the best basis for independent mobility. Here again there is good advice from Tooze (op. cit.) who considers that physical activities should finish with walking, skipping or running. When a child has developed enough strength and confidence, visual handicap should not be a barrier to free running if safe areas can be ensured. A guide rope can be useful in this case.

For all children, gross motor activities precede fine ones, and the small, fine movements of the hands needed for tactile discrimination of braille by visually handicapped children can be developed later. However, strong, useful hands are a great asset for these children, and they are not always developed. Jan *et al.* (1977) describe the 'floppy hands of the blind' as being hands that are weak and unused to manipulating objects. They suggest that early training in feeding, dressing and undressing should be encouraged, but since these activities involve hand movements, play activities involving pushing, pulling, twisting and rotating toys and small objects should be undertaken. The children may not initiate such activities themselves, they may show reluctance even to use their hands, but they may be encouraged to do so by engaging in activities that have a reward. Some commercially produced games, for instance, have a rewarding sound, but simple activities of crumpling paper or playing with toy bricks can be incorporated into games as well.

An understanding of the early activities helpful in promoting motor development is relevant to teachers as well as to parents, since, as Cratty and Sams (op. cit.) point out, not all children who are visually handicapped enter school with established patterns of motor development. There can be a number of reasons for this, including lack of parental access to appropriate guidance and advice on the management of young visually handicapped children and parental over-protectiveness and anxiety about the child's physical safety. Guidance on encouraging activity within a safe environment is therefore needed, especially as exploration of the environment is essential in order to learn about space through moving about in it. A child who has toys constantly fetched and retrieved for him will have such experience limited.

Moving about at school

It can be possible, therefore, for teachers to find that some children who are visually handicapped come into school with poorly developed body-image and spatial awareness and little confidence in moving about, whereas often the young fully sighted child has a 'hunger for sheer activity'. Usually children are building up their strength, suppleness and stamina during the primary school years, with the exhilaration of using their bodies to the fullest extent. These are the years when they practise all forms of movement, running, climbing, kicking or throwing a ball, gradually refining these movements into more sophisticated skills. There is an enjoyment in exploring and extending the limits of physical abilities as far as possible, and there must also be every encouragement for children with visual handicap to be energetic and adventurous. Some physical skills involve visual information which must be replaced whenever feasible by physical demonstration often in an individual or small-group situation.

Posture

Throughout the school years it may be necessary to give particular attention to the posture of the visually handicapped pupil. Late or poorly developed body-awareness may be further affected by lack of visual reinforcement. Fully sighted people catch sight of themselves in mirrors, shop windows, and tend to straighten themselves up, while they also see good alignment in others. Small variations in posture can be seen rather than felt; a head slightly dropped can affect posture significantly. The need to peer closely at work, to hold the head in an unusual position because of a visual condition such as nystagmus or a reduced field can accentuate postural fatigue. Physical activity can be a useful release for tension and fatigue of this kind and there need to be opportunities for this as well as, and not instead of, specific mobility training which will in itself be demanding of fitness and stamina.

By adolescence visually handicapped young people may have developed a low self-concept (Chapman, 1978) and this is unlikely to be helped by low levels of physical fitness, poor co-ordination and dependent mobility. Remediation at this stage is likely to be difficult, time consuming and possibly resented. Therefore early and continuing attention to physical development and activity is vital for visually handicapped children.

DEVELOPING CONCEPTS

Since some of the crucial stages of motor, language and concept development would normally have been passed in the infant and pre-school years, it is necessary to give some attention to these if developmental delay has occurred. There is a consensus of opinion among practitioners and researchers that concept development and motor skills can be affected by visual handicap. Fraiberg (op. cit.)

suggests that while development may be subject to delay, children with significant visual handicap may make detours in development, eventually reaching levels comparable to those of fully sighted children. Wills (1965) is convinced by her observation of young visually handicapped children that they reach their development goals and understand their world later and in a different way.

Clearly, some of the possible delay, especially in concept development, will be caused by lack of vision itself, or by the severely reduced quality and quantity of visual experience which the child receives. Other factors influencing development can arise from indirect influences (Lowenfeld, 1974). The child with little or no sight may be discouraged from making meaningful discoveries because of over-protection and lack of encouragement to engage in independent exploration. It is particularly in the management of the consequences of visual handicap that ameliorating and compensatory strategies can be effectively brought into play. Tobin (1979) shows in his longitudinal study of blind and visually handicapped children that whilst there is a significant tendency for their development to lag behind that of fully sighted children, effective teaching programmes can ameliorate such delay and encourage levels that are comparable to those more usually encountered among fully sighted pupils.

Fraiberg's reference (op. cit.) to 'experiential poverty' sums up the fragmented and reduced experience that the child with severe visual handicap receives from the earliest years. Whilst always seeking to reduce the consequences of impairment and emphasise the shared aspects of development among children, it is unrealistic to ignore the influence of blindness and severe handicap in the first years of life. Vision integrates, unifies and is a vehicle for the understanding of cause and effect. Fortunately, intervention can be helpful. There is a particular need for visually handicapped children to interact through touch with those who care for them and with the objects in the near environment in which they live. They need to find out about the nature and qualities of things by being able to handle, explore and touch toys and objects as hand control develops. Experience will be limited by the impossibility of handling some things that the fully sighted child can see in reality or at least in picture form. Some things are too large, or too small, or too fragile for tactile exploration, for instance, an elephant, a fly or a moth. Such restriction may affect concept formation and Tobin (1972c) again notes some delay in levels of concept formation among blind children who were unable to conceptualise conservation of substance at an age comparable to that of sighted children. The fact that a child with severe visual handicap cannot see milk poured from a jug into a glass of different shape deprives him of an example of conservation which could help to clarify this concept. Despite such experiential deprivation, encouragement to explore tactually and to develop kinaesthetic experience can be fruitful. The demonstration through touch of examples of conservation and the verbal support of tactile discovery may over a period of learning result in the possibility of pupils with severe sight loss being able to function comparably with their fully sighted peers by the time they reach adolescence (Barraga, 1974). Elsewhere, however, Barraga (1976) suggests that without vision many concepts cannot be fully developed without the intervention of carefully planned teaching strategies which emphasise a combination of first-hand experience in handling and exploring objects with the reinforcement of verbal explanations of cause and effect in processes that cannot be visually observed.

Scott (1982) describes the gaps in concept formation that visually handicapped children can experience as 'unexpected black holes'. This phrase illustrates well the sometimes bizarre impressions that children with severely defective vision may have developed with regard to common objects and situations that would normally be clear to the fully sighted. Such misunderstandings of the nature or function of common objects can be encountered in the school years as well as in infancy. Teachers who have considerable experience of children with significantly defective vision have much anecdotal evidence of this. Whilst it is unscientific to generalise from particular examples drawn from experience, the following instance exemplifies a typical misunderstanding. The idea that the position in which a bird flies is on its back with its feet in the air was seriously entertained by a pupil who had helped to cook a chicken placed on an oven tray and had felt the bird in this position.

Teachers of infant and primary school children are particularly aware of the importance of establishing learning through discovery and practical experience, but verbal instruction becomes more marked as the pupil progresses through to the secondary school and work hardens into curriculum areas. Visually handicapped pupils are in particular need of continuing experience in the first-hand exploration and investigation of objects and in the clarification of verbal references by concrete and practical demonstration. Models may sometimes be used to clarify concepts, but they are at best imperfect replicas and need to be used with the support of verbal description or misconceptions may occur. Ducks and giraffes, for example, were thought to be of a similar size and possessed of hard skins by a blind child who had been handling a set of model zoo animals.

The concept of reduction of size can present considerable difficulties for children with little or no vision. Ideally, a real object and a small model of it can be presented for investigation in order to help the child to appreciate the concept of miniaturisation. Models do have the advantage of helping a child to feel and hopefully to understand connections and the relationship of the different parts of a whole object. Later, with careful introduction, tactile diagrams or simple clear diagrammatic examples in well-contrasted format can be used to help to clarify concepts of inaccessible objects or processes.

Pupils with visual handicap will benefit considerably from encouragement to use their hearing, touch and sense of smell in order to gain information and form concepts. Learning and playing with fully sighted children, the discussion of shared discoveries and enjoyment of shared activities is an informative and natural way of helping to build concepts.

LANGUAGE DEVELOPMENT

Teachers will find a range of language development in their visually handicapped pupils, just as they will among all the pupils in their classes. Factors which affect the acquisition and expressive use of language, such as home influence and different ethnic origins, will mean that all pupils have varied exposure to different language usage. Their pre-school experience will be significant in terms of the encouragement and opportunities that they have had to talk, to listen, ask and communicate needs and feelings through words. There are, though, questions which are likely to be posed by those whose classes include children with little or no sight, such as, 'Should I refer to colour?', 'How can I help the pupil to imagine things that cannot be felt – a cloud, a star?', 'Should I try to leave visual imagery out of my teaching?'

There has been considerable interest among research workers in the development of language in visually handicapped children, but this has been largely focused on the blind and concentrated on the infant and pre-school years. Although the practising teacher may rightly consider these findings academic, the discussions which they engender are relevant to the practical situation, since they increase awareness of the particular difficulties that children without sight may have in the different aspects of language development. This aspect of a child's development is in any case a complex one and research appears to support this impression of complexity, since different findings may sometimes seem contradictory, but are nevertheless illuminating.

Communication between parent and infant

Clearly some of the most significant work in exploring the language development of visually handicapped children, especially those who are blind, focuses attention on the early stages of verbal communication which take place well before the child comes to school and are centred round parent/child interaction. Some illuminative studies result from observing and recording the verbal communication of individuals and of small groups of blind infants and young children (Urwin, 1983; Kitzinger, 1984). Differences in the way that communication takes place between blind infants and their mothers compared with such interactions in the sighted are of interest, not only because of the nature of the responses from the infant, but because of the nature of the input from the parent. This was shown by Kakelis and Andersen (1984) to be highly directive but with few descriptions. It would be interesting to have evidence as to whether this bias in communication extends to other adults with blind children as they grow up. Attention to the nature and aptness of verbal communication between blind children and their parents in the early stages of language development is crucial in the view of Matsuda (1985), who contends that language acquisition should begin at the same age for blind as for sighted children, with parents using words to help put the blind child in touch with the environment and all it contains.

Vocabulary of blind children

There are two themes that run through much of the research relating to language development in blind children, especially as most observations are made of children in the pre-school and early school years. In introducing his *Vocabulary of the Young Blind Schoolchild* (1972), Tobin examines these themes in relation to his own study. On the one hand, visual handicap is seen as in some way retarding the full elaboration of language (for example, Tillman, 1967); on the other, language is seen as 'an important, eagerly used tool for defining the child and his world'. Tobin does not consider these to be necessarily incompatible views, since he considers that within a restricted range of use the blind child may in fact be manipulating language effectively although he may, at the same time, be having difficulty in extending it.

Later studies continue to show this dichotomy and also to reveal that straightforward comparisons between the communication of blind children and of sighted children leave a number of questions unanswered. This fact complicates educational aims by raising the issue of whether blind children should be encouraged to communicate in ways primarily arising from sighted contexts or concentrate on language that has direct relevance to their own ways of finding out about their world.

Perspectives from research studies

The richly divergent research findings put forward in an international symposium on the language development of blind children and published under the title of *Language Acquisition in the Blind Child* (Mills, 1983a), were drawn together in a chapter by McGurk (1983) who affirms that much of the evidence from these studies showed that in the case of otherwise normal blind children there is a 'delayed rather than deviant communication'. There are some exceptions to this conclusion, in that Mills (1983) and Dodd (1983) showed in separate studies in the same book that the psychological development of blind and sighted children differed in a number of aspects. Even so McGurk holds to his affirmation that in terms of verbal communication the blind child 'follows the same route but takes longer' than the sighted peer. The blind child misses out on a whole range of opportunities for self- and other-initiated contingent exchanges and this is likely to have a generally delaying effect on language acquisition. This view gives positive encouragement to educators, since it holds out the expectation that delay can be overcome, thus reinforcing the experience of practitioners who find the language of the blind children that they teach in the later primary and the secondary school years shows little, if anything, to distinguish it from that used by their classmates. In their book *Beginning Reading/Writing for Braille/Print Users*, Danielson and Lamb (1983) look at studies of the language development of blind children from the educator's point of view. They emphasise that a number of writers have underlined the importance of experience in the language development of these children. Citing Fraiberg (op. cit.) and Urwin (1983) as being among those who observe that developmental delays and differences in the development of linguistic concepts in such children are related rather to the absence of experience than to vision, they stress the importance of maximising the experiences and language environment of blind children.

Communication between teacher and pupil

However, as in the case of infant/parent communication, pupil/teacher communication is composed of two-way traffic and the educators may wonder about their own choice of words when teaching a class containing blind or severely visually handicapped pupils working alongside the fully sighted. The question of whether or not to use words and phrases with visual reference is sometimes posed – for example, 'Let's look at this.' Should words relating to or naming colours be avoided? What can a blind child gather from a reference to a 'blue sky'? Such questions are part of the most subtle but controversial issues concerned with communications with blind children, whether in connection with what they hear or read. A strong opponent of the use of visual reference for and by blind people themselves is Cutsforth (1951). A blind man himself, he rejected many of the experiences of his own education, regarding them as inappropriate. The use of visual reference, he considers, devalues the communication of blind people if it is used simply to conform to the expectation of the sighted. Warren (1984) questions the use of visual reference in communication with the blind, and Tobin (1972b) finds evidence of the relative paucity of colour words in the language use of five- and six-year-old blind children in the compilation of his vocabulary used by young blind children. After two or three years at school the pupils in this study were showing more awareness of the language used by their peers, teachers and others and their language repertoire was increasing. Therefore, Tobin urges the educator not to avoid using visually orientated terms, stressing that the blind child grows up in a sighted world and must communicate with the sighted. Even for those with full vision, all verbal references are not based on first-hand experience.

Landau (1983) takes up a similar challenge, rebutting the implication that where visual experience is lacking, concepts cannot develop, and setting out to dismiss the argument that blindness can impair concepts 'standing behind word meanings', rendering the language of blind children 'meaningless'. Affirming that language need not be diminished by blindness, her hypothesis also bears the possible implication that the teacher's own use of language does not need to be diminished as the result of having blind pupils in the class. The claim is that the use of visual terms by blind people is a semantic activity. When a blind child is asked to 'look', the expression signifies 'explore it with your hands'. There are immediately evident implications here for the educator, namely the provision of interesting and relevant materials that are accessible for the blind to explore and handle and of opportunities for the perceptual experience of real objects using the unimpaired senses of touch, smell and sound. However, whilst the teacher should in no sense diminish language in communicating with blind children, sometimes it will be helpful to them to have a different emphasis with a more precise and descriptive use of words than would usually be necessary for pupils with full sight. In addition, time can be taken to give the blind child opportunities to verify verbal reference whenever possible and to talk about words with a visual connotation, not simply to omit or to ignore them.

Another aspect of the child's use of language which can be of concern to teachers is the evidence of verbalism and echoing. Von Tetzchner *et al.* (1980) confirm earlier claims that verbalism characterises blind children, but they were also able to show that sighted children, when blindfolded and examining household objects for recognition, showed a surprisingly high incidence of verbalism as, more predictably, did blind children undertaking the same activities. The researchers thought that the lack of visual clues rather than lack of visual experience was a factor here. When verbalism is markedly evident, language needs guiding into more purposeful channels – language games, language-related activities, rhymes and singing.

The extent to which partial rather than total visual impairment might influence language is another area of debate. McGurk (op. cit.) notes that some studies show little or no difference between the language used by totally blind, partially sighted and fully sighted children. He considers these to be generalised comments and informal discussion of these issues may support a different experience. There must be recognition of individual differences among children with defective vision, with age of onset of visual impairment and the extent and quality of visual experience being some of the variables, as well as the way in which the child with visual handicap is regarded by adults and peers and talked to by them. The child with defective vision may look and behave as a sighted child and it may not be appreciated that his blurred and interrupted vision may make it difficult to see details, separate leaves on a tree or separate bricks in a wall. Such a child will need the encouragement to describe things in his own way and, like the totally blind child, should have enhanced opportunities to handle and explore objects using his intact senses to enrich experience and provide contact for descriptive and expressive language.

SOCIAL AND EMOTIONAL DEVELOPMENT

Since the integration of visually handicapped pupils into classes in ordinary schools has particular significance in terms of social interactions, aspects of social and emotional development warrant particular attention.

In considering the development of blind infants, Warren (op. cit.) asserts that the establishment of emotional bonds constitutes one of the most crucial processes of infancy and early childhood, forming the basis of the security from which positive concepts can grow. When a child is born with a significant visual handicap, circumstances can conspire against the easy and natural parent/child bonding. Parents are likely to experience distress and anxiety arising from a sense of insecurity with regard to their own ability to manage the baby and to predict needs. They can be without a role model of parenting of a handicapped child and be apprehensive about the extent and implications of their child's visual impairment. Jan *et al.* (1977) even consider that in the early months after the baby's birth the crucial problem is vested in the parents rather than in the child.

The challenges of parental acceptance of the child's disability and their attempted adjustment to it have been well discussed in relevant literature over a considerable period of time. Indeed, as early as 1944 Sommers suggested that acceptance of the visually handicapped child has really begun when there is a shift from the questioning of 'Why did this happen?' to 'How can we help?' and 'What should we expect?' Lowenfeld (1971) describes denial of the handicap, over-protection, disguised or open rejection as being possible responses to the situation. The necessity of providing parent guidance programmes and the value of these is another strong thread running through the literature relating to the responses of parents to the discovery of visual handicap in their baby. Langdon (1968), in putting forward the case for services of this kind, describes the experience of parents who at that time had to cope not only with their own feelings, but also with the trauma of facing the reactions and sometimes the uninformed advice and apocryphal stories about blind children that friends and neighbours might offer. Since Langdon's survey, parent support groups and self-help groups have been formed, sometimes using a special school as a base. The RNIB and some local education authorities have developed advisory services for the parents of pre-school visually handicapped children, but there is a continuation of the situation noted by Chapman (1978) in which 'The parents of visually handicapped children may, as individuals or as a group, almost unwillingly adopt the role of advisers.' The extent to which parents can and do come to terms with some of their earlier doubts and apprehensions, and develop in their place strong but realistic aspirations for their visually handicapped children by the time they reach school age, is evident in the findings of a Scottish survey (Budge *et al.*, 1986). This is concerned with parental choice of educational placement and reflects the view of the majority of parents that they would choose an integrated placement with their child living at home wherever this was feasible. They were prepared to accept special school including residential placement only if this appeared to be in the interest of the child's education.

Parent/child interactions

In the pre-school years and the early stages of child rearing the demands on the parents of a visually handicapped child are considerable even when positive supportive services are available. Parent/child interaction can be disturbed; the eye contact and the smiling response that are normally a channel of communication between the baby and parent may be reduced or absent and need to be replaced as far as possible, or augmented, by caring and handling, tickling and cuddling and talking to the baby. Fraiberg *et al.* (1969) noted that the blind baby can recognise the presence of the parent, as the sighted baby does, through sound alone. Nevertheless there is evidence of 'separation anxiety' at a later stage in the case of blind infants. Seemingly, without clear vision, infants can have difficulty in establishing a concept of the mother as a separate entity. Convincing developmental delay has been observed by Reynell (1978) who records evidence of social independence normally evident at three years of age delayed until five years in the case of significantly visually handicapped children. The extent to which the disability itself, or the more protective child rearing often practised, is causative of later attainment of skills remains problematic.

Problems in the management of young visually handicapped children can arise if parents are so anxious to compensate for their child's disability that no attempt is made to foster socially acceptable behaviour. As the infant begins to move about, the minimum restriction should be imposed and exploration and discovery encouraged. Opportunities for choice and decision making within a sensible framework of discipline can be increasingly given. Dependence on adults will need to be reduced as the child develops, just as in the case of all children, but a perceptive understanding of when to give help and support is needed. As a result of parental apprehensions there may understandably be a shadow of anxiety or depression in the household of a child who has severe visual handicap, but the enjoyment of ordinary childhood activities, the sharing of fun and laughter are important for the happy development of all children, and not to be missed because a child has a visual disability.

A cause of parental distress can be found sometimes in the unusual appearance or behaviour of a blind or severely visually handicapped infant. Some visual conditions are disfiguring as in the case of buphthalmos in which the eye appears swollen and enlarged. Parents should have the opportunity of discussing frankly their reactions to distressing or disfiguring conditions in their children. Self-stimulating behaviours, often described as 'mannerisms', can be a cause of disquiet too. Children who have little or no visual activity sometimes indulge in eye probing, rocking or hand flapping. These mannerisms are by no means an inevitable consequence of visual handicap, although they are sometimes unfortunately referred to as 'blindisms'. Such behaviours can also be encountered among some sighted children who have severe deprivations in other areas of their development.

The task of managing and hopefully diminishing such behaviours presents quite a complex problem, since there is a danger of giving the child too many negative messages. Solutions range from the devising of a custom-made behavioural programme built on rewards for abstaining from the activity, to ignoring the whole question in the hope that the child will 'grow out of it', a hope that is sometimes realised.

Mannerisms

It is suggested that 'eye poking' can produce some visual response in the form of 'sparks' when pressure is induced by pressing the knuckles against the eyeball. From every point of view this particular mannerism should be discouraged. It looks unpleasant and can cause damage to the eye socket. This and other self-stimulating activities can decrease when more active and purposeful use is made of the hands for play activities or in handling interesting objects, perhaps with texture or sound appeal. Boredom and understimulation may underlie the manifestation of mannerisms in some visually handicapped children, but over-stimulated children may show evidence of them too, withdrawing from a world that they are unable to control and retreating into their solitary world of rocking and hand flapping. The gradual introduction of simple activities that they can master, presented to them within a regular and predictable framework, may be helpful to children in engendering a greater sense of control of themselves and their environment. It can be inimical to early acceptance into an integrated environment for mannerisms of this kind to persist and they can become established habits which are hard to eradicate. Parents, together with a specialist adviser, can, on the other hand, try to work out a simple programme to mitigate them.

Social communication

As visually handicapped children grow up, the incidental learning that normally takes place as a result of receiving visual information will need to be replaced or boosted by direct teaching and informative interaction. Children normally learn a great deal about social behaviour as a result of what they see and subsequently copy from others. Sighted children learn, without knowing it, the significance of facial expression and body gestures that play a large part in social interaction; much communication between parents and children takes place through gesture. For instance, a mother may see her child looking or pointing at an object and may then explain or enlarge on the experience, parent and child both smiling and laughing with each other at seeing something unusual or amusing. This incidental sharing of a visually initiated interaction is less readily available or not available at all to a child who sees little or nothing. Later, as verbal communication grows, a situation or a conversation may be prone to misunderstanding because the facial expression or body language that extends or supports verbal messages can be absent or reduced. Both communication and relationships may be affected. Visually handicapped children themselves may have difficulty in communicating meaning through facial expression and body language, since these can be channels of communication that are not significant for them. Attentive listening and encouragement to take part in the give and take of conversation can be fostered, but some features of social interaction do remain challenges for those children and young people who suffer pronounced visual impairments.

Children with full vision are in a position to learn more easily about the social mores of their culture and to copy, practise and explore these in play situations. Social graces such as mealtime behaviour, including the management of utensils, will have in many cases to be quite specifically taught to a child who is not able to see clearly, or perhaps at all, the way in which a fork is held and a knife used for cutting. If these mundane aspects of accepted social behaviour are neglected when the child is ready to learn to master them, then difficulties of social acceptance can be compounded and the potential for later problems increased. However, the attainment of basic levels of competence in the management of self-help activities, such as feeding and dressing, can be significant for easy acceptance into school.

The readiness of the visually handicapped child to take part in learning and play activities with sighted classmates must be gauged and encouraged. Both parents and teachers in the reception class will need to be aware that the visually handicapped child requires both time and individual attention if his particular needs in terms of social development are to be met adequately. To ignore this will be both unrealistic and inimical to the child's chances of optimum development. Parmalee (1966) suggested that over-protectiveness by parents could make it difficult for blind children to handle infant programmes on first coming into school, and it has long been well understood that security within the family and an understanding of the child's special needs have been factors in both the educational success and personality development of the visually handicapped child (Norris *et al.*, 1957).

Play

The role of visual function in the development of skills incorporated in play activities is described by Parsons (1986), who in reviewing the literature on this topic refers to the conclusions of Warren (op. cit.) which show evidence of 'qualitative as well as quantitive differences between the play of sighted and blind children' with the blind showing far less creativity and imagination in their play. In Parsons's own study (op. cit.) children with low vision and fully sighted children in groups of two, three and four year olds are compared in the play situation, and in each of these groups significant differences were evident in the level and nature of the play, with delay shown in the play activities of the low vision children. The significance of these findings for the social development of visually handicapped children is important, since not only cognitive development but social development is needed for play.

Appropriate early activities can follow the play patterns of normal development, but will require more adult intervention. Playgroup leaders will be aware of the stages of social play, graduating from solitary play, through parallel play to partner play and finally group play. When a visually handicapped child is in the playgroup it must be ensured that activities are structured in such a way that each child can make a contribution and experience enjoyment. Sometimes even young children can be 'over-helpful' to their visually handicapped playmate and take over all the decision making, the fetching and carrying and choosing in group activities. Attention to the level of demand in a play activity can help to ensure that all members of the group including the visually handicapped can make an active contribution. Sound and texture incorporated in the materials used in games, games based on word usage, and the use of bright and visible playthings for those with reduced vision can all be useful in involving children with different visual capacities in shared play activities. Such activities are a basis for experiencing inter-personal relationships and social development.

Social integration

When a visually handicapped child first joins it may be necessary for teachers to face their own attitudes and apprehensions with regard to visual handicaps. There can be complex reactions, for instance, to the idea of blindness, ranging from a wish to protect to a wish to avoid. In order to foster a positive and open relationship with all pupils including those who are visually handicapped, teachers may need to examine their own responses to the differing needs of their pupils. Classes are likely to contain children with a variety of social and developmental competences and challenges. Those presented by visually handicapped pupils may not be greater but can be different in nature from those manifested by other children. Teachers may themselves have doubts in the face of such demands, and may experience feelings of resentment at having been asked to receive a visually handicapped pupil in the class. There may be a feeling of frustration arising from a sense of insufficient time to meet the needs of individual pupils who have specific requirements while resources and specialist support may not be considered sufficient to give the teacher confidence in meeting unfamiliar demands such as learning through tactile means. Dissatisfaction or apprehension can be all too easily communicated to pupils. Visually handicapped pupils will, in addition, need more positive encouragement than most in the ordinary classroom situation. An approving smile or an affirmative nod may not be visible to them and must be replaced by positive verbal reinforcement, or a pat on the shoulder. Teachers themselves will need appropriate support services if they are to create with confidence an ethos in their classrooms conducive to the good social development of all their pupils, including those with special needs.

It cannot be assumed simply by wishful thinking that social interaction will take place between children whatever their individual assets or disadvantages. There can be some adjuncts to visual handicap, particularly in the management of specialised equipment or materials, that can be inimical to an easy and trouble-free atmosphere in the classroom unless arrangements to accommodate these materials are handled with sensitivity. For instance, the visually handicapped pupil is likely to need a larger working space than that usually required by the fully sighted, since braillers, typewriters, large print and brailled books are bulky. Giving room for these can lead to a physical separation of the visually handicapped from other pupils. Lack of clear vision can also reduce the possibility of incidental social interaction, especially if the pupil concerned sits apart from others in the room in order to be surrounded by special equipment. A friend sitting nearby can be a reassurance and a link with others in the classroom.

Because of the relatively small numbers of children with severe visual handicaps in the total school population, some people in integrated provision, especially those attending units, will have to travel to school from a distance, possibly using a taxi service. In such instances parents and teachers need to encourage out-of-school contacts, and to foster situations in which friendship can flourish through shared activities. Imamura (1965) indicated that visually handicapped children have a tendency to have less motivation and opportunity for social contact than is the case for those who are fully sighted. It is to be hoped that effective integration, in reducing these differences in social opportunities and helping to make the presence of visual handicaps among pupils a less remarkable occurrence, will therefore make it a less intimidating one.

Social and emotional challenges in adolescence

There may be a tendency to consider that the specific problems and challenges of the totally blind adolescent demand particular understanding and sympathy. Bauman (1964) demonstrates, however, that young people with defective sight showed significantly higher levels of anxiety and insecurity than those who were totally blind, finding that the former could be 'misdiagnosed, misunderstood, undereducated and socially ostracised'. The role of the totally blind, as assigned by society, is clearly defined, even if on occasion incorrectly so. Variable sight, an undefined role, giving the impression of being a sighted person but at the same time experiencing considerable problems in seeing make development more complex for pupils who have defective vision. They will, in the ordinary classroom, be learning and growing up alongside pupils with varied and different problems of their own. All these difficulties must be balanced by positive experiences with every opportunity for all individuals to be valued in their own way.

Adolescence with its transition from childhood to adulthood is a challenging period for all young people, especially with the uncertain future created by the current lack of employment prospects. Acceptable levels of personal competence and of maturity will be important factors when the possibility of further education, vocational training or employment is considered. The progression towards personal independence away from the confines of home, parents and school may heighten anxieties about later lifestyle and relationships, but do these anticipations present particular stresses for visually handicapped pupils as they reach adolescence? Responses to such challenges will be individual, but there is some evidence of a low self-concept in the case of visually handicapped adolescents. Whilst it is by no means inevitable that the presence of visual handicap will in itself affect self-concept, teachers and counsellors will need to be aware of its potential effect on how young people regard themselves. Research evidence and the observations of teachers give some indication that young people with visual handicap experience anxiety about acceptance by peers and success in future lifestyle (Chapman, 1978). Particular stress may be experienced by visually handicapped adolescents who need to ask for assistance with day-to-day management. The social skills of requesting, accepting or declining help can pose problems especially at a time when personal independence is particularly desirable. Opportunities must be made for the visually handicapped young person to give as well as to receive help. There are certain frustrations affecting self-image that the visually handicapped adolescent must inevitably face. One frequently mentioned by these young people is the inability ever to drive a motor vehicle, a prospective limitation to which even primary school children have referred. Compensatory activities can be sought, such as playing with model cars, investigating and understanding the working of a car engine, but the fact that possibilities are limited is apt to be fully realised at adolescence. This makes it all the more important to give maximum opportunities to make choices and decisions on personal matters, such as clothes and food.

There is a particular need for a well-informed sex education programme to be offered that visually handicapped pupils can fully understand. One approach to meet this need, which has been voiced by visually handicapped adolescents themselves, is represented by a series of tape-recorded informational and discussion programmes made by the Kent Association for the Blind (see 'Useful Addresses' section). These can be used to supplement the topics considered in human biology and social science classes. The body image of visually handicapped pupils may be poorly developed and they may have less well founded information about bodily functions than the fully sighted. Discussion of problems such as the spread of Aids and the abuse of drugs needs to be explicit so that visually handicapped pupils, like all others, are in no doubt about the facts being referred to.

There are some visual conditions that become evident or show marked deterioration during adolescence, for example retinitis pigmentosa. Whilst the rapid and serious reduction of sight is traumatic at any stage of life, its occurrence at adolescence can be particularly devastating at a stage when a young person is struggling to establish an adult identity. Even when the visual condition is relatively stable, it can be at adolescence that the grieving period over defective sight is most marked.

These potential problems point up the need that visually handicapped pupils may have for counselling, especially as they reach adolescence in the ordinary school. Pastoral care is usually available to adolescents, but staff may feel that they need further information themselves in order to give appropriate support.

Occasional courses in the counselling of young people with visual handicap are offered by voluntary bodies such as the RNIB and the Spastics Society. Opportunities for visually handicapped adolescents to discuss and share problems with each other can be helpful (see Chapter 2).

—4—

The developing needs of the pupil at school

PRE-SCHOOL PROGRAMMES

Since the pre-school years are so significant in terms of development, the importance of parental access to counselling and the availability of playgroups and nursery provision that include children with special educational needs must not be underestimated. Visually handicapped children and their parents should have access to these services, and it is necessary for the professionals providing them to have an understanding of the implications of visual handicap in the development of the young child. A mismatch of provision to need at this stage can be particularly unfortunate, as when, for example, a blind three year old interacts in a playgroup only with three non-communicating physically handicapped children. This is not a felicitous placement, predictably fuelling frustration and disturbed behaviour. It can be difficult to fulfil the diverse needs of small children, but levels of communication must be considered just as fully as opportunities to share facilities.

The value of enriching the early experience of the visually handicapped child is well understood by practitioners and researchers experienced in understanding the needs of these children. There is a wealth of literature towards which the teacher can be directed for detailed examples of appropriate activities. The sensitive observation of Fraiberg (op. cit.) and the practical suggestions of the RNIB guidelines for teachers and parents (op. cit.) are informative, the one illuminating the understanding of the child's development, the latter offering well-tried activities. A useful example of a programme for visually handicapped children is the Oregon Project from the Country Education Department in Medford, Oregon.

Such programmes address themselves to the fact that the common features in early childhood development, including concept development, risk being affected by delayed or fragmented information, but that early and continuing compensatory experiences are possible, mitigating the effect of reduced incidental learning arising from defective vision.

THE FIRST YEARS AT SCHOOL

The infant class in a mainstream school, catering for the needs of young children along developmental lines, also offers an appropriate placement in many instances for children who are visually handicapped. Here, too, the variety of available activities, the concrete experiential approach, the availability of brightly coloured, simple learning and play materials can be appropriate and stimulating. There will be children in the reception class who have a diversity of backgrounds and needs. The nature of their early experience, their potential ability and their stage of development will be varied. As part of their social development they will be encouraged to conform to group rules, but their learning will largely be individually planned and based on practical activities. Such approaches are generally well suited to the needs of the visually handicapped child. The young pupil with little or no sight may need to explore the layout of the classroom on an individual basis and verify from experience the location of book and toy cupboards, the nature table and the position of the chairs and tables.

The teacher who has a visually handicapped child in the class will, at this stage particularly, need to give attention to supportive language and guiding operations during discovery activities. For example, at the water table it will not be sufficient to watch the child attempting play. Directive questioning will show whether concepts are developing and relationships becoming increasingly understood: for example, 'Is this full or empty?', 'Will it float or sink?', 'Why do you think so?' Such specific and directive questioning may well be needed for other children in the group, and perceptive guidance to encourage concept formation is a natural part of the expertise of the infant teacher. However, individual children, including those with sight problems, may need verbal prompting and explanation of even simple phenomena.

Children with defective vision are likely to have been deprived of much of the incidental, pre-reading experience which is normally available to the fully sighted child. The words on poster hoardings, labels on food packets, or television advertising features are often accompanied by pictures which illustrate meaning. It is difficult to quantify how much is learned in this way, but the teacher should be aware that these experiences will be diminished and should attempt to offer enriching compensatory ones. It will be important to be aware, too, that lack of visual experience rather than lack of ability or potential may pose initial difficulties when print is begun. Structured pre-reading activities and the application of the principles of clear presentation of materials will be helpful at this stage of the child's schooling (see Chapter 2).

The early stages of numeracy may also be affected by reduced visual experience. An outstanding international expert who devised a tactile mathematical code has shown awareness of the problems of basic number work for young visually handicapped children. Nemeth (1959) stressed that these pupils have much less opportunity for gaining pre-mathematical experience than is commonly the case for fully sighted children. There are fewer chances to see objects as a whole, yet with separate parts and features. There can be difficulties in appreciating classification and seriation, and in understanding basic concepts of shape, size, form and pattern. Tobin (1972c) also reveals delay in the understanding of conservation of volume in the case of visually handicapped children. In addition, the language of numeracy may be poorly understood, for example, terms such as 'large', 'small', 'different', 'more', and 'less'; such epithets have meaning primarily as a result of understanding what is seen. It can be difficult for a visually handicapped child to understand that the number 'one' can refer to one boy, one cup, one house, because early sensory experience has been limited. Children who suffer from such experiential gaps will need to be guided through a structured set of experiences, and early attempts at computation will need support and clarification by the use of concrete examples demonstrating the concepts involved. The need for such guidance may not be confined to those children who have defective vision but will be particularly necessary for them.

Practical approaches to classroom activities

Some learning and play materials such as pegs, cubes and beads can be difficult for children with poor vision to control, easily skidding on to the floor, or being dropped. Trays with a well-defined rim and a non-skid surface are useful as a working base that also keeps such small pieces of material contained within arm's reach. For children with no sight, or with near vision, the accessibility and control of materials in the near environment is essential. Lack of sight or defective vision can be a factor in poor hand co-ordination, or in hand–eye co-ordination, with consequent difficulties in the management of manipulative tasks. It may be necessary to demonstrate at close range exactly how to hold scissors or crayons, a skill that it can be easy to assume that a child will pick up from copying what he sees other people doing. The early school years include many new activities which involve the need to master new skills and manage equipment, materials and processes. Many of these will require the teacher to show and sometimes guide the child's hands into the appropriate grasp of movement. Although such individual tactile and kinaesthetic learning is time consuming for both pupil and teacher, it is essential to undertake this kind of learning in the first few years at school. The inability to manage practical skills at an appropriate stage can lead to problems that are more difficult to remediate later, when more complex and sophisticated levels of manual dexterity are necessary in science, home economics, craft and other curriculum areas which include practical activities.

The infant class is likely to have learning and play materials that are well suited to use in training functional vision. There are structured programmes which give guidelines as to how such materials can be effectively used to encourage visual search and scan, hand–eye co-ordination and more complex visual activities (e.g., the *Look and Think* Handbook and Teachers' File (Tobin, Chapman *et al.*, 1978)). It can be helpful to discuss the use of such procedures with the specialist adviser, particularly in terms of using readily available and commercially produced materials in specific and appropriate ways to enhance visual skills. Children should be encouraged in general ways to use any sight they have as actively as possible. Class teachers can help the children to want to look attentively, by pointing out details in pictures and posters and drawing their interest to search visually for different features in objects and in pictures. A simple invitation to 'Come and look at this' will inform the child that there is something outside his immediate visual panorama that deserves investigation. Interesting displays and materials should be placed where children can get near to them, and when stories are being read it can be helpful for a child with poor vision to sit near the teacher and have the chance to gaze at pictures in the book for a few seconds. It is the teacher who is constantly perceptive and aware who will often be able to find spontaneous solutions to situations which can be difficult for a child with defective vision.

Social interaction in the early school years

By the time they come into the infant class most children will have progressed from the early stages of play in which they take part in playgroups, though some children, including those with visual handicap, may not have had playgroup experience and the first term at school may be their first 'social' experience. Any teasing or bullying focusing on the wearing of thick lensed glasses or using low vision aids is less likely to occur at the infant stage than in the later school years. However, it can be helpful if any special aids are discussed and explained in simple terms when they are first used at school and perhaps remarked upon by other children. Teachers soon get to know their class and to judge the best approach to use in helping individual children to join in shared activities. They can help to promote situations in which children with special needs including visual handicap are seen in positive situations. There will be occasions when visually handicapped pupils can offer help to others, as well as receiving it.

Dinnertime and other breaks in the school day can be important times for children. These are the occasions when non-teaching staff will be involved and they will need to be told about the children with special needs, including the visually handicapped, so that a consistent approach can be both developed and maintained. Welfare assistants, catering staff and caretakers should be told that children with special needs are in school, and informed about the way in which their management is envisaged. The class teacher and specialist teacher may be encouraging mobility skills and personal independence which can be negated if an over-protective approach is used by other members of staff.

Real, not simply nominal, integration of visually handicapped children can be fostered by shared games and activities at playtime. Sometimes a temporary measure to differentiate the severely visually handicapped child can help to facilitate safety and thus encourage play participation. An instance of this approach was when a blind child, integrated into an ordinary school, wore an armband when in the playground until such time as the other children learned that it was they who had to take evasive action when they were running about together. In principle this could be criticised in that an intentional differentiation was made between children, though the outcome was that the child enjoyed the situation. This incident does highlight the fact that in many cases visually handicapped children are virtually indistinguishable from their classmates in appearance, integrating well and needing only manageable adaptations in order to take part in most school activities. Temporary adaptation can sometimes help to facilitate full participation in the curriculum and full access to the campus. For instance, landmarks can be emphasised by having audible mobiles at key places, such as the school entrance. Such audible cueing can be discontinued after a few weeks when orientation in the school grounds has been established. The balance between special adaptations and the ordinary provision of the school needs to be flexible and designed to meet real situations as well as theoretical principles. The range of activities in the school day, the availability of varied learning materials and the opportunities to offer individual programmes can mean that infant classes in the ordinary school are well suited to meet the diverse needs of both visually handicapped and fully sighted pupils.

THE JUNIOR SCHOOL YEARS

The transition into the junior department or school is usually associated with an increasingly structured timetable and more formal methods of working. A visually handicapped child who has happily settled into the infant classes will probably, along with other children, accept this change with little or no difficulty. Children will still be working individually in literacy, while being introduced at other times to a wider curriculum that will include environmental studies, history and science.

Learning through activity

Teaching approaches well suited to meet the needs of visually handicapped pupils will continue to be based on experiential activities. Reading and writing will form part of the total language programme which is being continuously and perceptively monitored by the teacher. New and initially difficult vocabulary is often carefully introduced and explained, but in these years the visually handicapped child may still have a poorly understood impression even of everyday concepts that have been firmly grasped by fully sighted classmates. The opportunity to relate words to actuality, and to learn through first-hand experience, continues to be necessary throughout the junior years.

Reading will present new challenges, even in the form in which it is presented. The quality and size of print will change as more advanced reading material is presented, and this may mean that additional aids to vision such as magnifiers may be required at this stage. Reading, as part of the reading experience programme, will encourage the development of imagination and creative oral and written work. Restricted visual experience can result in difficulties for some children in this area of their expression, and it may be helpful to them to augment their experience with additional material in auditory form, such as tape-recorded stories, short poems and descriptions. There may be other children in the class for whom this would be beneficial and so small group as well as individual listening activities can be organised. The consequences of the slower rate of informational processing which has been shown to be evident among visually handicapped pupils will need to be taken into consideration when assignments are given (Mason and Tobin, 1986). The quantity of work expected may need to be adjusted, without reducing expectations with regard to content.

Reading and recording work

In the junior school, children are gradually introduced to the activity of understanding their own research into topics by referring to books in the classroom, school library and public library. These activities make increasing demands on the use of vision. Scanning bookshelves in order to locate the right book can be difficult, and the books themselves may be produced in a variety of print size and style. The class or specialist teacher may need to help with the search for particular books and with reading out or enlarging footnotes or small print passages that are hard to decipher.

As more formal work is undertaken, the learning situation for pupils with defective vision will need to be appraised. Are the children working in a suitable position in terms of their visual functioning? Are the seating arrangements appropriate in relation to the lighting in the room? Is the blackboard surface in good condition, or would a coat of blackboard paint improve visibility? Are the necessary books, low vision aids and other materials and equipment readily accessible? If the pupil is using duplicated worksheets, are they clearly presented and in well displayed format? The recommendations on environment outlined in Chapter 2 are relevant at this stage as well as during the secondary years.

Special attention to handwriting skills may be needed for visually handicapped pupils during the junior years. Sometimes myopic children produce extremely small writing, but other children with visual defects may write large, poorly formed letters and have difficulty in keeping a straight line. If handwriting is taught as a class lesson it should be remembered that a child with defective vision can experience difficulty in seeing how a letter is formed, so that individual demonstration of this will be necessary. Perceptual skills are involved here, and large shapes drawn in the air or in sand trays can help to give the kinaesthetic 'feel' of letter shapes before smaller letters are written on paper. The use of cursive writing from the start is sometimes recommended for visually handicapped children (Chapman, 1978). This is particularly helpful for those who develop handwriting skills with a heavy dependence on kinaesthetic rather than visual sense. Some children can be taught to work in a perfectly legible way without needing continuous visual reference to what they are writing. This is a very useful skill to develop at the junior stage, especially for pupils whose visual condition makes it difficult for them to refocus from blackboard to book as they copy notes. Handwriting may give problems for the pupil who has to peer closely at the work being written, since a cramped and uncomfortable position can result. The provision of a stable, sloping surface can be helpful and short rest times can relax tense muscles.

The introduction of typing lessons in the later junior years may be necessary for some pupils for whom handwriting is extremely slow and difficult, or who cannot use print. It is very useful if this has begun to be a reliable skill by the time the pupil meets the curricular demands of the secondary school. Typing is a useful means of presenting work in the integrated setting, where few teachers will be able to read the brailled work of blind pupils. It is also helpful for those visually handicapped pupils for whom the sheer writing of an assignment is demanding, not necessarily in terms of content, but because of the physical effort involved in producing several pages of legible handwriting whilst working at close range, or using low vision aids. Typing involves manual dexterity, and this may need remedial activities before, or during, the early stages of learning to type by the 'touch' method. Keys can be shielded to prevent 'peering' and to encourage reliance on touch not sight. Typing can be an enjoyable skill to master if a comfortable seating position is arranged and encouragement given to produce a page of well-typed material that is pleasing to pupils and a boon to their teachers!

The Research Centre for the Visually Handicapped has, as part of its project on microcomputer systems, produced both 'talking' and large-print typewriter programmes which form an exciting basis for instruction. The centre also offers a copy-typing programme, available in large print or synthetic speech (Blenkhorn, 1986).

Beginning mathematics

During the junior years work in mathematics will need to continue to have a practical basis to ensure the understanding of increasingly complex concepts and relationships. Relevant language referring to shape, size and quantity will still need verification by practical examples, and individual demonstration of processes is likely to continue to be necessary. Mental computation is not likely to cause any particular difficulties, and some visually handicapped children become adept at this since they are used to relying on their memories rather than referring to books for prompting. Pupils with defective sight, however, may need additional time for recording their work in mathematics because of the visual tasks involved. For instance, the setting out of long multiplication and long division will involve the visual skills of scanning and searching which can be time consuming, especially for children who have visual field defects. The teacher will need to be aware that the pupil with severe visual limitations may not be able to produce such work quickly although able to cope with the thinking involved.

The mathematics scheme will need to be carefully chosen bearing in mind the requirements of visually handicapped pupils. Some schemes are highly visual in design, with full-page diagrams and graphs which involve a daunting amount of pictorial material for pupils with low vision to deal with. The visual difficulties that such material can present are compounded if text is printed on a coloured background which may look pretty but reduces legibility. Text may be scattered irregularly over the page with illustrations embedded in it. A lack of clear definition and contrast can make such material difficult to discriminate and visually handicapped pupils in particular can miss pieces of text set in unexpected places on the page. Mathematical schemes can also sometimes incorporate a large amount of text, and this imposes a heavy load in terms of information processing on the visually handicapped pupil who is able to cope with it only at a slower rate (Mason and Tobin, op. cit.). It must be considered carefully, therefore, whether the mathematical concepts learned or practised in such schemes warrant the time and effort that would be demanded from a visually handicapped pupil in reading them. One interesting solution has again come from the Research Centre for the Visually Handicapped in its project involving the modification of thirty maths programmes from the SMILE maths scheme developed by the Inner London Education Authority. These schemes cover a wide range of topics in the secondary mathematics curriculum, but some of the topics are appropriate for the upper classes of the junior school. The modifications of the programme are such that the display of information is adapted to suit either pupils who have defective sight or those who are totally blind by the provision of an optical synthetic speech output (Blenkhorn, op. cit.).

Thematic approaches to learning

The thematic approach to the curriculum normally followed in many junior schools is well suited to visually handicapped pupils. Topics are explored and discussed in groups and pupils contribute individually to the recording of information in a form that is appropriate for them. This approach helps to ensure that work in literacy and numeracy is based on experience and understanding, not simply on the reproduction of information. The visually handicapped children in the group may need extra time to handle and explore the materials relating to the theme, and things that can easily be handled should be chosen when possible. For instance, in nature study if flowers are being studied a careful choice of plant, that is, one not too fragile to handle, can make the task much easier for an individual child.

Class outings are a usual part of junior school life and are particularly valuable for visually handicapped children in giving them the opportunities for discovery that might otherwise not come their way. Both safety and mobility factors must be considered and there may be a need for additional explanation and directive questioning for these pupils. It can be an education in social interactions too. Halliday and Kurzhals (1976) draw attention to the value of sharing, helping others, listening as well as talking, and accepting majority decisions. Such interactions can be particularly beneficial when over protection or solitary activities have been the consequences of visual handicap. It is wise to notify those receiving the children that the group includes pupils with visual handicap, since it may be possible to arrange for them to handle or have a close look at displayed material if prior notice is given. Museums are usually very helpful if they receive such requests, but any special arrangements must be perceptively managed. On a visit to a refinery, a group of children included a blind pupil who was allowed to climb all over the equipment and explore it in detail. He learned much, and showed this in his classroom work after the visit. Although the other children understood his difficulties they were envious and became more so in the face of his boasting about the experience. Some opportunities for exploration by the other children in small groups would have reduced such evident 'singling out' and might have been a happier compromise. As always the balance between the special needs of an individual and the well-being of the whole group may be exacting to maintain.

Special curricular needs

The burgeoning of educational technology gives increasing opportunities for visually handicapped pupils to have maximum access to the curriculum in the ordinary school, and it is in the final junior years and the secondary school that its value becomes most apparent. Closed circuit television, tape recorders and specially adapted calculators can be used to present learning material in a way that visually handicapped pupils can use effectively, though the use of such devices needs to be considered in the context of the pupils' total educational needs. Further information on such equipment appears in Chapter 7. The effective use of any piece of equipment will involve some training and this can involve taking time out of other areas of the curriculum, so that the different demands will need to be carefully assessed. Storage space will be needed to keep equipment, which is often expensive, in good condition, but it must be in a place that is easily accessible for use when needed.

Concentration on making the full curriculum available to visually handicapped pupils must not neglect the fact that they may also have curricular needs that are additional to those of fully sighted children. It is in the junior years that the development of independence skills both in self-help and in mobility needs to be firmly established. By the time adolescence is reached such skills will be more difficult to master and remediation may not be easily accepted. The adviser for visually handicapped children or the mobility specialist in the area will be able to give expert and necessary help. The statement of special educational need, or annual review, should include an assessment of the pupil's needs in mobility, with recommendations as to how these can be met. A teacher who observes that the visually handicapped pupil is having problems with mobility should draw the adviser's attention to this. The ability to travel confidently within both the school locality and home locality will need to be considered, and in the case of a child with no sight or with very little guiding sight, mobility training based on the use of the long cane should be considered. This training involves quite specific techniques in the use of a cane which is the length of the drop from the breastbone to the ground. Its adroit use is an excellent aid both to independent mobility and to safety and is an essential skill for those with severe visual handicap. If training sessions can be arranged out of school times this is helpful in preventing the erosion of time needed for school activities, but the pupil should be encouraged to use the techniques learned in the day-to-day life of school.

5

Curriculum access and adaptation for visually handicapped pupils in ordinary schools

'Meeting the curriculum needs of pupils with visual handicap is like trying to get a quart of water into a pint pot.' This comment arose in a planning meeting in which teachers were trying to fit mobility training sessions and braille teaching into the already full timetable of a visually handicapped pupil in the first year of a comprehensive school.

Since one of the aims of integration is to give pupils shared opportunities to enjoy a broad curriculum, a difficult equation has to be worked out in terms of aiming for this, whilst not, in the words of Wilson (1981), attempting to 'stretch handicapped children on the Procrustean bed of normal standards'. In order to avoid the danger of this, each pupil with special needs will have to have these evaluated carefully in terms of curriculum requirements and access, and in the case of the visually handicapped this will include recognition that there are special curriculum elements such as learning braille and mobility that are 'core' in terms of their essential value to the pupil, not 'optional extras'.

In real terms these are challenges that are being faced with workable if not always ideal solutions. For example, Hughes (1984), in describing the approach taken to curriculum planning by the staff of a visual handicap department in a secondary school where such pupils are integrated, emphasises that 'the individual child is the unit of consideration rather than the general curriculum'. The team of teachers here recognise that the visually handicapped pupil may need more time for academic areas than is the case for some other pupils. Time will also be needed for learning techniques relating to personal management, as well as adaptive skills such as typewriting and possibly braille. It was decided in the case of two pupils to reduce the academic load by one subject after thorough consultation with colleagues. Dropping French released five periods a week for training in adaptive skills and completing other academic work for which additional time was needed. Withdrawal for mobility training was organised on a fortnightly rotational basis and special help with spelling and handwriting was undertaken occasionally instead of the class lesson in English.

Break and lunchtimes were also used for additional skill training, and although this sounds like a rigorous schedule, Hughes (op. cit.) claims that the 'braille' club, to which parents were also invited and which took place out of class hours, had a relaxed 'club' atmosphere that was enjoyed. The BBC Computer *Transcribe* braille instruction program (available from the Research Centre for the Education of the Visually Handicapped) was used effectively and with interest by the participants.

Realistic and flexible curriculum planning will help to support the 'forgotten' visually handicapped pupil who may be struggling to keep pace with the fully sighted. In such a case, the curriculum load and need for remedial work will require examination in the light of the implications of visual handicap for learning.

Because teachers in ordinary schools may be unfamiliar with the specific ways of training and with the kinaesthetic approaches to the teaching of self-help skills to visually handicapped pupils, it can be easy to be dismissive about the necessity for these to be incorporated as an essential part of the curriculum for the individual pupil needing such training. The mastery of these skills is likely to make day-to-day school life much easier for pupils with defective vision, and incidentally for their teacher as well, as a result of the increased independence and competence of pupils that result from such acquired skills.

A team approach to solve the problem of making appropriate training available to integrated visually handicapped pupils is suggested by Fagan *et al.* (1985) who contend that specific skills in habilitation, or in some cases in rehabilitation, are not necessarily included in the mainstream curriculum for these pupils, some of whom have not had their need for mobility training assessed. They also stress the importance of good liaison between the school and the Social Services Department in the area where the child lives, stating that Technical and Mobility Officers for the Blind should be specifically employed in order to provide such a service. This, of course, would necessitate extra training for these professionals, who would require increased knowledge of educational and developmental issues, as well as joint funding by local education authorities and social services. The concept of a multi-disciplinary team contributing to the specialist curriculum areas which the pupil needs has much to recommend it and would be welcomed by many teachers, especially as the present opportunities for such co-opera-tion tend to be unacceptably haphazard. Nevertheless, contact with these services may well be helpful and if the pupil's home situation is supportive those areas of the curriculum involving training and self-help skills can be largely home-based, with parental involvement being a positive asset. Where the home situation does not make this feasible it must be ensured that school-based programmes are given if the pupil is to achieve true independence.

Some pupils will need visual enhancement programmes which will be a recorded part of the curriculum, especially in the first years of primary school. Here again, initial assessment of the pupil's individual needs by means of the *Look and Think* Checklist (Tobin, Chapman *et al.*, 1978) will pave the way to remedial activities that can be incorporated into activity sessions, art and handwork.

Although referring to the special school situation, the analysis of curriculum for pupils with special needs by Wilson (op. cit.) has relevance for teachers planning curricula in ordinary schools. The normal curriculum is designed for the fully sighted, but it may be largely appropriate for the visually handicapped pupil if access to it is improved by adapted presentation and by clarification of the concepts involved, so that learning by means of experience and not simply transferred information is possible for all pupils. The balance of the curriculum needs to be maintained in the face of adjustment to individual needs so that areas relating to intellectual development, personal development, social and practical skills are all considered. Usually the headteacher in consultation with class and special subject teachers will plan the curriculum, but the class teacher and special adviser will need to put forward the case and suggest the means for adaptations or additional areas in the curriculum that the individual visually handicapped pupil may require. It is important that all teaching colleagues understand the need for these so that a consistent but flexible approach to curriculum planning is achieved.

There will be some areas of the curriculum that require adaptation in the way in which they are presented to pupils on account of their blindness or restricted vision. Figure 6 draws attention to some of the solutions that can be offered to problems arising in these areas. It also lists the areas of learning that will need to be specifically included in the curriculum for pupils with little or no sight.

The underlying principles of curriculum access for visually handicapped pupils which involve clarity of exposition, clear demonstration of processes and appropriately presented learning materials will be relevant across the different curriculum areas. There will be some subject areas which involve in addition to these criteria some other special considerations of which examples are given in the following pages.

(a) Blindness	(b) Restricted Vision
Communication	
use of tactile codes, audio presentation, and appropriate equipment (typewriter etc.)	adaptations in presentation of materials, e.g. enlargement of print and diagrams, magnifiers, photo-copying
Practical processes	
tactile presentation; time to complete tasks	close visual demonstration use of CCTV etc.
Social situations	
measures to counteract reduced experience (drama, role play etc.)	
Independent mobility and travel	
mobility training	
Self-help skills	
systematic training and organisation	
Concept development and theoretical learning	
first-hand experience in handling objects;	opportunity to develop visual memories
language development personal independence stimulation of curiosity auditory skills	visual enhancement activities

Figure 6 *Some suggestions for the management of school activities affected by visual handicap*

THE DEVELOPMENT OF LITERACY

Meeting individual needs

It is understandable that teachers may approach the teaching of reading to visually handicapped children with some apprehension. After all, the odds seem to be set against the chances of such pupils reading fluently and easily since they will be dealing with visually presented material which they may need to use at a very close distance from the eye. Task lighting may be required, or the use of magnifiers, and low vision aids which will drastically reduce the span of letters or words visible at one glance. Such encumbrances to the speed of reading may also inhibit motivation to read. Teachers need not have negative expectations with regard to the reading attainment of their visually handicapped pupils. Although research findings in some cases indicate reduced reading rates, these are not inevitable, and much can be done to help these pupils to master and enjoy reading.

The challenges will be interesting and will demand attention to the individual needs of pupils. For example, a group of pupils beginning to use print included David, who had problems with distance vision and found blackboard work difficult; Tony, whose soft cataracts caused blurring of vision; and Jill, an albino, whose photophobia required careful monitoring of light; Ahmed had a reduced visual field and slight hearing problem. The effects on visual functioning arising from physical causes cannot be neglected, but it is unlikely to be the only factor involved in potential reading difficulty. David had a deprived social background with little conversation at home; Tony's school attendance was frequently interrupted because of hospital treatment, and Ahmed spoke no English at home.

In order to use printed reading material, all these pupils needed to master skills in visual perception, in movement and in language. There are diverse theories on the teaching of reading, but distinguishing figure from background, discriminating shape, and visual search and scan are essential aspects of reading. Fortunately, dismembering words and looking at letters as single informational units have become outdated. Pre-reading activities involving the commonly accepted areas of visual perception can be individually tailored to meet the needs of individual children. A *Look and Think* profile (Tobin, Chapman *et al.*, 1978) should be drawn up and followed by the appropriate teaching activities suggested in the scheme.

The reading scheme that the teacher has found useful as a basis for the whole class is likely to be equally well suited to the needs of the visually handicapped pupils within it. Fully sighted pupils and those with defective vision learn to read in the same way; it is in the presentation and management of the reading material itself that special attention may have to be given to some pupils with sight problems. There is no sole method of teaching reading to pupils with defective vision that has been categorically shown to be better than any other.

The variables that exist among pupils with defective sight, the nature and extent of their visual disabilities, levels of language development and their motivation to want to read preclude the possibility of a single solution to reading problems. A flexible approach is required in order to meet individual needs, as there are some problems in the management of print that arise from either the defect in vision itself, or as a result of the use of low vision aids used for optical correction and magnification.

Effects of restriction on reading strategies

For the fully sighted reader, one aim is to promote the ability to see words and phrases as a whole, rather than concentrating on individual letters in succession. Here words and groups of words are treated as informational units by the visual reader. Usually the maximum amount of time that is needed in order to identify whole words or even phrases is no longer than that required to identify single letters. For some visually handicapped pupils with a restricted visual field, however, or for those using high magnification that reduces the area visible at one glance, the capacity to perceive whole words and phrases as patterns instantaneously and to search and scan along a line in order to predict will be difficult. The pupil using closed circuit television to project an enlarged image of print on to the monitor is also in this position. 'Look and say' methods may present some difficulties, and a period of analysis with some phonic work followed by synthesis may be needed by individual readers. Problems of this kind underline a tendency for low reading rates to be associated with poor vision, although research findings do not show this consistently. Chapman (1978) cites a range of studies including Birch *et al.* (1966) and Vernon (1971) which indicate delay in reading attainment among visually handicapped pupils, but Lansdown (1975) does not. Speed of information processing is prone to be affected by defective vision (Mason and Tobin, op. cit.). This should not, however, be considered inevitable, nor need it prevent visually handicapped pupils from enjoying reading and gaining information from it. Much can be done to reduce difficulties by presenting legible material, encouraging search strategies and motivation. On an individual basis this is best effected by the combined skills of a competent teacher of reading and a specialist teacher or adviser for visually handicapped children.

Increasingly complex visual tasks

It is not only in the beginning stages that visually handicapped pupils may show some problems in reading. Tobin (1979) records that in the results of his longitudinal study of 99 visually handicapped pupils, most of whom attended special schools, these pupils, assessed on the Neale Analysis of Reading Test, showed increasingly a slower rate of reading than their sighted peers. Further work was undertaken with pupils at a school for partially sighted children which indicated 'an ever growing disparity between the partially sighted and the normally sighted in the speed at which they can process visually presented material'. These conclusions are not in some ways surprising, since visual tasks become more demanding as texts harden into curriculum areas and as a greater density of information is presented on each page of reading material.

Some causes of failure in literacy

Despite such evidence from research, it is interesting to note that visually handicapped pupils take public examinations alongside the fully sighted, with successful candidates going on to further and higher education. The Special Colleges of Further Education for visually handicapped students offer high-level vocational and further education courses, but in some cases also provide courses for those students who have not been successful in achieving competent levels of literacy. The reasons for such failure are considered by those teaching the students to result from:

the presence of handicaps additional to defective vision;
poor general levels of communication;
low motivation caused by inadequate reading material;
interrupted studies;
unsupportive social environment;
changes of educational placement.

Clearly some of these causes of reading failure are beyond the immediate control of the teacher. Unsupportive social environments, changes of educational placement and interrupted studies point to the need for such pupils to have effective interdisciplinary support involving social, medical and advisory services. The presence of additional handicaps requires thorough assessment of the pupil's individual needs, especially in terms of communication and perceptual areas. Poor levels of communication, low motivation because of inadequate reading material, and difficulties in managing printed material remain challenges for the teacher.

Providing a literate environment

For the visually handicapped as for any pupil, an environment that encourages communication and the purposeful imaginative use of language offers the most encouraging background for the development of the first stages of literacy. If the teaching emphasis is unduly biased towards skills training at the expense of motivation, or centred on the pupil's problems rather than potential, the visually handicapped pupil may be discouraged. Many of the stimuli to use language to communicate and to externalise thinking will be visual.

Pictures, games and toys that are attractive to look at and activities and outings that include interesting sights can generate verbal responses. So that these stimuli can be accessible and enjoyed by the visually handicapped children together with their classmates, any materials used should be bright and colourful and able to be handled. Activities will need to be supported by discussion at the level of the children's competence and understanding.

Pupils will enjoy story telling and the associated activities that happily go with it, including word and action games. Rhymes and jingles are especially valuable for visually handicapped pupils, and play can help them to use and listen for words that extent their expression. These pupils, like all others, need opportunities to talk about their own concerns, to describe incidents, pets and other favourite things, the common and shared experiences of these being more significant than differences of visual competence. Activities that stimulate and encourage oral expression need to precede recorded language whether it be in print or braille, while the perceptual skills involving tactile or visual competences will need to be encouraged with appropriate pre-reading activities alongside developing language.

An approach which stresses the enjoyment of communication has been examplified in the work that Danielson and Lamb (op. cit.) have undertaken successfully with visually handicapped children. These experienced practitioners advocate a psycholinguistic approach which they use with pupils whose vision ranges from blindness, through varied levels of defective vision, to normal sight. Reading and writing are developed and practised together and examples of pupils' work and activities are included in the publication *Beginning Reading/Writing for Braille/Print Users*. This teacher's guide not only sets out suggested activities, but is a heartening revelation of the way in which visually handicapped pupils can enjoy reading and writing. The approach taken here is to emphasise that language is a central issue in the reading process and that not all information needs to be processed visually for the reader to extract meaning from the text. The psycholinguistic emphasis is on the process by which the reader samples from the array of words on the page, predicting and anticipating on the basis of information that has already been taken up. The teacher who is perceptive of the needs of visually handicapped pupils would nevertheless stress that this graphic array should be clearly presented and able to be scrutinised in a comfortable position so that such sampling can be undertaken as easily and effectively as possible by the reader.

This approach has much to offer visually handicapped pupils since its emphasis is on what the pupil can do rather than on his or her difficulties. It also gives attention to what can be shared among all pupils whatever their levels of visual competence.

The literate environment advocated here encourages children to talk, to listen, to explain their ideas to others – in short to use language to express thoughts and ideas and to give and receive information. Visually handicapped pupils have the need and the capacity to do this just as other children do. As oral communication increases, familiar language patterns can be harnessed to encourage prediction in the early stages of reading, and Danielson and Lamb stress that their visually handicapped and fully sighted pupils 'learn to read by reading and being read to'. Reading aloud to children, silent reading, shared reading, and activities involving directed reading are advocated. Most teachers will be familiar with the 'Cloze' techniques which aim at encouraging effective prediction, and these are particularly well suited to pupils with defective vision since they focus on meaning and help to strengthen prediction strategies. Further recommendations include listening to pre-recorded stories on tape with written text simultaneously available. This activity is useful for visually handicapped pupils, since it gives them the chance to experience pace in reading and maintains and increases interest in content which can flag for the slow reader.

All the factors relevant to an effective reading scheme for fully sighted pupils will also apply to those who are visually handicapped, but will also need to include encouragement to use vision, even though it is defective, to get meaning from the text. A consistent approach to the teaching of reading throughout the school is important for all pupils, but for those who are visually handicapped it is especially so, since discouragement to continue a challenging task can so easily arise.

Literacy is unlikely to be encouraged by the use of material that is not adequately legible since this will compound the problems of discrimination for visually handicapped pupils. The recommendations on the presentation of materials in Chapter 2 give guidance that is directly applicable to reading materials.

Management of printed materials

In addition to the general recommendations of appropriate task lighting, position of work and well-contrasted text, there are some useful techniques which can become a habit and which can facilitate the management of printed material when it is being read by pupils who have a specific visual problem.

Pupils whose central vision is impaired by macular degeneration can often be helped by trailing a pencil or marker just below the line of print. This technique helps them to direct the gaze slightly beneath the letters, and means that the upper and most easily recognisable part of the letter shape is more clearly visible to them. Good lighting and magnification may well be helpful.

The use of an exposure device can help some visually handicapped readers to give attention to word shapes, and to minimise losing the place on a printed page. It is not helpful in encouraging speed of reading, but as a temporary aid it can help to concentrate visual attention. Dark cardboard or paper with an oblong 'window' is the most useful format. Good lighting and use of a reading stand will be helpful.

Pupils with a peripheral field loss (tunnel vision) may be helped by a 'reducer' which reduces the size of print seen in the central areas of vision. Good task lighting is essential.

If a pupil is using enlarged print, he or she should be encouraged to try to reduce to standard print gradually once reading skills have been mastered. It is possible that using enlarged or magnified print may become a habit.

Not only should reading material be appropriately lit and supported in a position at a comfortable distance from the eye, but 'eccentric viewing' may be attempted. This means placing the work at an angle which allows the reader to make maximum use of any residual vision to discriminate print. Such a working position must be discussed with the reader, not simply imposed. Pupils with nystagmus may find that when reading for a length of time, moving the book slightly from side to side reduces fatigue.

Visually handicapped pupils should be given enough time to complete reading assignments and the length and presentation of the material that they are given should be modified if necessary.

Writing skills and content

Visually handicapped pupils will need something to read and write about if their literacy is to develop. Writing and reading are parallel activities, drawing on the same need for oral communication and for visual perceptual skills, but additional pre-writing activities will also include hand–eye co-ordination, directionality and copying shapes. Drawing, colouring and pattern making will involve learning how to hold and control pencils and crayons later used for writing. It can be difficult for some visually handicapped children to see how a letter is formed, although the shape of the final character may be clear to them. Individual demonstration or the use of the closed circuit television monitor to show up the exact movement involved can clarify this, but plenty of opportunities to scribble should precede this. Crayons that contrast strongly with background paper should be chosen.

Partner and group work involving pupils of different visual levels can be encouraged, but it must be ensured that the visually handicapped pupil has access to visual materials and the chance to talk about unclear concepts. Short and frequent opportunities to write can emerge from daily work, and in the initial stages incorrect spelling, reversed letters and other mistakes can be contained rather than discouraged. Individual folders of children's work will show progress in areas of continuing difficulty. In the case of children with defective vision, these may arise from difficulty in copying processes (for example, letter formation), inability to see correct forms of spelling (less access to displayed materials) and difficulties with directionality and co-ordination.

Writing patterns which flow help to give a kinaesthetic impression of letter shapes, and cursive writing is sometimes recommended as being easier for children with defective vision to manage. It is likely to be the management of writing itself rather than the content of what is written that gives problems to visually handicapped pupils who should be encouraged to express their own thoughts, feelings and experiences in their own way. There is no reason why they should not share the same approach to creative writing as their fully sighted classmates, writing to give information and to draw conclusions.

Appropriate materials can help the pupil's own work to be legible (Chapter 2), and as with reading activities, sufficient time to complete tasks is essential.

MATHEMATICS

Children with defective vision can have difficulties with mathematics that make them poor attainers although, as Clamp (1981) points out, this is likely to be due to underdeveloped mathematical concepts and not to an inability to achieve. Despite the potential delay in concept formation that relates to problems in mathematical thinking, visually handicapped children can respond well in the integrated situation to appropriate teaching with an emphasis on concrete experience.

Development of mathematical concepts

Other factors which may require specific attention are poor manipulative skills and limited experience of the environment which may compound difficulties in learning through discovery for children whose concept development is already affected by the reduced visual input of information. Many of the crucial early mathematical concepts may be developed at least partly by fully sighted children as a result of what they see incidentally in everyday situations. They see the table being laid for a meal; the rectangular table is set with circular plates, and with sets of cutlery – knives, forks and spoons – one set for each person. Normally a concept such as that of conservation develops as they see examples of it occurring in day-to-day situations. They see mother pouring liquid from one large container (a teapot) into several smaller one (cups) or stacking up plates, which when laid out cover a wide area but when piled up form a tall shape instead. Sighted children can learn from such daily situations concepts that are incompletely evident to those who cannot see them happening.

It is likely, then, that visually handicapped children may enter school with some of the concepts that underpin mathematical thinking substantially delayed. Consequently their opportunities for discovery need to be increased, their manual skills developed, and the level of their concepts assessed so that appropriate activities can be planned. These considerations will not be unique to visually handicapped children but are likely to be more frequently encountered in those whose experience has been limited by defective vision. In the same way that teachers expose children to literacy through incidental activities in the classroom, so children can be exposed to a numerate environment with its opportunities for incidental learning throughout the school day. In physical activity times, the balls and hoops that have been used can be counted as they are put away; spatial awareness and the estimation of distance can be counted out in strides. In practical activities, shape discrimination and the qualities of three-dimensional objects can be explored. The development of numeracy for young children extends through many play activities: Wendy house, playshop, sand and water play. In all these situations, children are exposed to classification, in terms of weight, volume and money.

Visually handicapped children can happily share these activities with their fully sighted classmates, and will hopefully learn from them as well as from the teacher's guidance. The goal of the activity must not be lost, and both discovery and reinforcement encouraged until concepts are firmly established. A difficult, but vitally important, concept to be learned, for example, is the invariance of number, the understanding that the number remains the same, even with change of object to which the number is applied. Three dogs, three beads, three houses all have the quality of 'threeness' about them. Without useful sight this can be a difficult concept to grasp, and yet it is at the basis of mathematical thinking. Visually handicapped children sometimes learn words by rote very quickly, enjoying the sound of words and rhythm, chanting 'two and two makes four' and yet being totally unaware of the property of number.

The language of mathematics

However, there is a language of mathematics which needs to be used with real understanding by children, and this language has to be taught and used consistently by the teacher. 'Fewer', 'less', 'large', 'heavier', 'equal to' are examples of such early mathematical references. Children need to ask questions in order to gain information to verbalise their discoveries, and to postulate their ideas. From the language children use it is possible to learn much about the gaps that exist in their concept formation, so that further opportunities for discovery can be offered, and guiding questions posed. Children with defective vision or without sight will be in particular need of questioning that prompts attention to attributes. 'Are the stones rough or smooth?' 'Which is largest and smallest?' 'Which is heavier?' 'Are they all the same?' Language relating to mathematical concepts plays an important part in formulation of ideas and correct concepts, and the way in which children with visual handicaps use it requires constant evaluation in questions and discussion.

Throughout the school years, intensive pupil/teacher interaction will be needed in mathematics. As new concepts become understood, activities are needed to reinforce this understanding. Skilful teachers will perceive with their visually handicapped, as with their fully sighted, pupils when to intervene, to direct, and when to reinforce with practice. Throughout the primary school years mathematics will be closely related to real experience, to concrete material and to practical activity, but as the child progresses he or she needs to learn to record work. Initially, this is usually done by using bricks, beads and counters to record results of simple numeracy activities. This sounds a simple matter, but using such materials for calculating or recording can present problems for visually handicapped children. Moving counters around on a flat desk can lead to them being dropped on the floor, or missed visually; if the materials are contained in a tray they are easier to control. Practice in handling small objects may be needed by some visually handicapped children with poor manipulative skills before they can manage to record with concrete objects.

Recording work

As manipulative skills improve, a cubarithm board can be useful for children with severely limited sight to record early number work. This device, which can be obtained from the RNIB, is a plastic board with raised lines which form squares. Small metal cubes with braille symbols A-J (which stand for the numerals) and symbols for the four basic rules signs (addition, subtraction, multiplication and division) are put into the tray to record the sums. Although many children enjoy working with these, a few find the cubes too small to manipulate. Children with sufficient sight to do so can use dark felt-tipped pens for writing numbers on matt, white paper. As recording becomes more complex, pupils using tactile methods for learning will need to use their Perkins braillers for recording. Here again, recording calculations is a complex procedure and pupils are likely to need time and apparatus to practise it. Whittaker (1968) (in *Teaching Maths and Science to the Blind*) recommends a linear layout rather than the vertical setting out of arithmetical calculations. Class teachers must be aware of the fact that these procedures take time to master. A calculation can take a minute, yet recording it in braille can take several minutes. A useful reference book of braille notation mathematical signs and terms is *Mathematics in Braille: a reference book for teachers and students* (Danielson, 1983).

Schemes of work

As visually handicapped pupils progress through primary school, problems can arise with mathematical schemes that have nothing to do with the children's intrinsic mathematical ability. Some schemes are very visual and impossible to transcribe into braille in a meaningful way because of the amount of pictorial information. Even when adaptations are made, the result may be too confusing for the child to discriminate by tactile means, or they may need too much time to assimilate prefacing information. For those pupils who have some, but impaired, sight a whole page of material that needs to be scanned and searched and is comprised of a confusing mixture of print, diagrams and pictures presents a difficult task. Sometimes, when introducing problem-type questions, schemes present a quantity of descriptive reading material for what is, in fact, a simple computation. This form of presentation has value and can be interesting and motivating, but for visually impaired children with a slow reading speed the mathematics lesson could largely be spent in reading. Another approach should therefore be considered, possibly tape-recorded material, or a simplified and condensed presentation of the mathematical problem. There is a place for amplification and a place for economy of expression. There is a need for planning, so that adaptations can be made in good time, if necessary, to the material that is to be used. The presentation of worksheets may require checking, to ensure that they are duplicated clearly. In mathematical work fractions and decimal points can be particularly difficult to see. The equipment that children will use needs to be checked for legibility too. Rulers and protractors may bear small marks and figures that are hard to discriminate. Adapted versions of such equipment are available from the RNIB or teachers may be able to add clearer markings to standard geometry sets.

Some processes in the mathematics scheme may pose particular problems for children with poor vision. Estimation is a case in point, since it is difficult to see large quantities or long lengths when visual acuity is limited. A child with normal vision can visualise a length in terms of the football pitch or swimming pool, but these have little meaning in terms of distance for children with defective vision. Practical work can be helpful in countering such problems; walking along pathways or around the school estimating the time taken to cover prescribed distances can relate time and distance in a meaningful way. Timing with a stopwatch or audible timer, measuring with metre wheels or tapes can verify such results. Concepts of time and distance are not easy to understand, but such practical activities can be especially valuable for children who have defective vision, besides preparing them for more sophisticated later work involving calculations of speed and velocity.

Work in mathematics throughout the primary school will continue to be based on practical work and related to everyday activities, but as concepts become established the nature of work in numeracy becomes more representational. Possibly because they rely on their memories and have little or no reinforcement from visual promptings, children with visual handicaps have a somewhat legendary reputation for excelling in mental arithmetic. Research is needed to confirm this impression, but in any case calculations can become too long or too complicated for this facility to be relied upon. A cranmer abacus is a small, handy means of recording number work in a temporary form. Based on the Japanese abacus it consists of rows of beads for calculation and ephemeral recording. It is available from the RNIB and detailed descriptions of its use are given in such specialist literature as *Teaching Maths and Science to the Blind* (Whittaker, op. cit.). Adept users of this invaluable piece of equipment can operate it with considerable speed, and it can be used for basic work in the four rules or, for those able to master its use at an advanced level, for metric work, decimals and money calculations. Computer learning undoubtedly has a useful place in the practice of mathematical rules, but learning based on practical experience and understanding developed through interaction between teacher and pupil remains significant, not least for visually handicapped children. Pupils with defective sight may need to have access to an individual monitor when doing computer work in order to see displayed figures clearly. 'Talking' calculators can be an interesting and useful aid and are becoming less expensive; both blind pupils and those with defective sight can find them helpful, since the displays on standard calculators can be quite difficult to discriminate.

Pupils with some usable vision will work in the same way, and normally on the same schemes, as their fully sighted classmates, with attention given to the visibility of the materials that they use. Teachers will find it of interest to refer to a project that has given particular attention to the needs of visually handicapped pupils in this area of the curriculum. *A guide to the teaching of maths at the primary level to pupils with visual handicaps* (Heritage, 1986) is a publication from the Research Centre for the Education of the Visually Handicapped, University of Birmingham. This project details the concepts which visually handicapped children need to establish in the progressive stages of their mathematical thinking; it includes a checklist which is valuable in helping the teacher to devise an appropriate mathematics curriculum for the individual pupil. Basically intended for pupils in the primary school, the material in this publication can also be used for secondary-aged pupils who show a delay in attaining concepts. The Checklist refers to topics included in the primary school curriculum, and can be used as the basis for a recording system of individual attainment. It covers some 80 per cent of the topics that would be mastered by ordinary pupils at the ages stated in the text. Some of the ideas in the different sections are mathematically interdependent, but the teaching sequence is controlled by the user. In common with others experienced in seeking to meet the needs of visually handicapped pupils, Heritage stresses the initial need for concrete experience, emphasising that concept formation should take precedence over other activities, including recording. Early work is linked to story telling, for instance, Paddington Bear's two ears, two eyes and two coat-buttons, but it is emphasised that too much language may obscure rather than clarify numerical concepts. The checklist gives practical items relating to sets and relational topics, number, addition, subtraction, multiplication, division, fractions, concepts of shape and space, volume and capacity, time, money and pictorial representation. The second section of this publication contains a wealth of suggested activities and materials well suited to use by visually handicapped pupils, but totally acceptable in ordinary classroom mathematics work.

Mathematics at the secondary stage

Mathematical work in the secondary school has been concerned with academic attainment leading to examinations in the final school years, and possibly continuation in higher education, but it has important implications in practical everyday situations and in the management of daily life. Despite earlier delay in concept formation, outstanding success in mathematics has been shown by individual blind students, even though such achievement has been dependent on the use of tactile diagrammatic work and the braille mathematical code. The mastery of this code, introduced during the primary years, is essential for academic work by tactile users in the secondary years. Pupils will need to use the Perkins brailler, specialised graphboards and the audible calculators and the computers to which they have been introduced in their primary years. There are several ways of producing diagrammatic material in tactile form (see Chapter 6) and the student will need to practise using these, but some of the greatest difficulties will be experienced in mastering and using with facility the range of braille symbols for arithmetic and algebraic recording, and in the linear layout manageable for algebraic equations but bearing the possibility of confusion when used for setting out fractions. These are areas of management in which the teacher in an ordinary school will want to consult with an experienced specialist either in the advisory services or in one of the similar 'outreach' services for visually handicapped children run by one or two special schools (see Chapter 6). It must be remembered that when tactile material is provided in mathematics as in other areas of work, it will take longer to discriminate than visual material. It takes longer to feel along a line than to scan it visually, and it is possible but difficult for the students themselves to make graphs (Clamp, 1981). Logarithm tables are available in both braille and large print format, and mathematical texts can be brailled through the same agencies as literature. The maths teacher can read out loud the work that is being put up on the blackboard, including a description of diagrams, and this can be helpful for pupils with defective vision as well as for the blind.

It is possible with appropriate teaching and adaptations for severely visually handicapped pupils to undertake the standard examination curriculum. The requirements and the philosophy of the GCSE bring the practical and academic aspects of work in mathematics closer together, but the syllabus will need to be scrutinised carefully so that difficulties attendant upon the visual nature of work can be taken up with the appropriate examining board well in advance. Mathematics is an essential area of the curriculum for the visually handicapped pupil although a demanding one; its emphasis on logical thinking and the opportunity it offers to relate theory to practice are invaluable. Some pupils will not be able to master the higher levels of academic work in mathematics but should still have a lively programme of 'social' mathematics. Practical projects such as formulating plans for furnishing a room exemplify this. Measuring out the space available, working out the area of carpet and curtain necessary, and costing the furniture give opportunities for sharing practical activities and developing mathematical skills. Pupils who are visually handicapped should not be left out of the practical aspects of such projects when the work is shared, but they may need to use adapted and clearly marked measuring tapes and be given plenty of time to complete the recording of data. It can be valuable for them to reproduce in diagrammatic form the area that they have measured, since even in the secondary years visually handicapped pupils have difficulties in the expression of shape and in spatial concepts.

Despite the need to give particular attention to such specific areas of potential difficulty, the progression of work for the visually handicapped should be the same as for the fully sighted. The social aspect of mathematics will, however, be particularly important. A leaver's programme which includes such an element is particularly valuable for those with visual disabilities. Filling out a cheque is quite a difficult task for a visually handicapped person, as is making sense of a print-out, a bank statement, a payslip or a shopping receipt. Practice in numeracy and familiarity with the layout of such forms can be part of this programme. A leaver's programme which includes practice in the management of some of the aspects of adult life that depend on a basic level of mathematical competence are useful for all pupils but may require more specific attention for those who are visually handicapped.

ART AND CRAFT

The place of art and craft in the curriculum

> Offering any sensory stimulation fills the mind with ideas concerning the relationship between a person and that person's world. Art materials have qualities that excite senses rather than sight. Clay and paint both have a feel, a texture; and movement can be sensed when materials are manipulated. A partially sighted or even non-sighted individual can still map an internal 'image' because of the quality of these materials. (Dubowski, 1986)

Art is not necessarily synonymous with visual art, although visual aspects of creativity can be stimulating for those who have even a small amount of sight. The value of visual creativity has been documented over many years in relation to the visually handicapped. Lowenfeld's (1939) study, *Creative and Mental Growth*, is the precursor of numerous studies of the therapeutic aspects of art which are still being explored (Leavens, 1986). There are cogent reasons to justify the inclusion of art and craft in the curriculum, not least for visually handicapped pupils, but is such justification necessary?

Unfortunately, sometimes it may be, since the pressure of time can give rise to a situation in which pupils are encouraged to 'catch up' on private study, or to work on academic areas with the peripatetic teacher at the times when art or craft is timetabled. However, the need for a balanced curriculum is as great for the visually handicapped as it is for any pupil, and the areas of aesthetic appreciation and expression are not expendable.

Since it is commonly accepted that art can contribute to the full enjoyment of human experience, and that it is a sensual as well as an intellectual activity, its value is considerable for all pupils. The child cannot be compelled to express feelings and experience through art but this will be facilitated through an increasing mastery of technique. Lowenfeld (1974) emphasises the 'process' rather than the product, and all pupils need to experience the satisfaction of a task completed, an idea created and experienced. Much of the enjoyment of artistic experience will be derived from externalising in graphic or tactile form the creative dynamism of thinking and feeling. Do children with sight problems have a lesser need for this than others?

On the contrary, a build-up of stress and tension can be experienced by visually handicapped pupils because of the effort and concentration needed to operate adroitly in a world where the majority are fully sighted (Williams, 1973; Kell, 1973). Art and craft sessions should be times when pupils can feel relaxed and eased from tension and pressure. Unfortunately, this does not always apply. Sometimes children can approach these lessons with timidity, lack of interest, or even dislike if they are anxious about what is expected of them. Fukarai (1974), writing in his capacity as a teacher of art working with blind pupils, observed that the sighted find it hard to believe that visually handicapped pupils are able to create works of artistic merit. Nevertheless, he was able to inspire his students to reach into themselves and to produce artistically meaningful works of art, undaunted by the apparent difficulties in achieving this.

An absence of competition can be another advantage of the art class; preconceived notions of excellence and competitiveness with others are out of place. Varied activities can be made available. Sometimes visually handicapped children suffer from a limitation of choice in what they do; they can be somewhat too dependent on others, especially on parents and teachers to tell them what to do and how to do it. This may lead to apathy in making decisions and choosing activities. The availability of a variety of media and processes can encourage children to experiment freely with materials and ideas, and to decide after experimentation to try to follow through an idea and to express it. Balancing such freedom of choice may bring the discovery that certain laws of nature exist which have to be taken into account. Runny clay and dry sand cannot be sculpted, nor will badly designed structures balance; there are some immutable principles that are not subject to manipulation. In facing these, children learn through direct discovery something about the limitations and qualities of materials and their use. Napier (1974) observes that the intellectual aspects of art, such as form, balance, contrast and design, can have real meaning for visually handicapped people and are yet another way in which concepts can be understood and made meaningful.

Besides the release from tension that a child-centred activity can give, art and craft activities offer rich opportunities for language development. The choice of a theme to be depicted gives the chance through imaginative description and questioning to expand vocabulary and to increase expressive language. When children are intensely involved in an activity which they enjoy, and are working in a relaxed atmosphere, they are sometimes able to explore and discuss deep-seated feelings about themselves, their problems or their disabilities and their relationship with others. This is when a sensitive and perceptive teacher will know when to stop and listen and when to encourage the children to continue with their timetabled activities. It is such circumstances that reveal the fact that the needs of children in general, but those with special needs in particular, may not be fully met simply by the delivery of prescribed programmes.

A good opportunity can be provided in art and craft lessons for the encouragement of social skills. In the integrated setting, shared activities in such work can be invaluable in promoting co-operation and friendly interaction when pupils enjoy the satisfaction of producing an artefact that they have made together. Friezes and collages which incorporate colour and texture and which have been made by several pupils are an example of this.

Development of manipulative skills

Although the theoretical justification for the aesthetic and even the therapeutic value of the art and craft curriculum can be strongly argued, the 'process', which can be the source of so much satisfaction, may require particular attention for visually handicapped pupils. Some children with sight problems can have poor fine-motor co-ordination, and this can be developed and improved through the manipulation of tools and craft materials. The use of these does, however, need careful teaching, both in terms of safety and competence. This is another example of difficulties that can arise because children with poor vision do not easily see how to copy what others are doing, so that one-to-one demonstration may be needed in the way to use scissors, hold paint brushes or wield crayons. However, pupils intent on pursuing a creative idea are likely to be highly motivated to master such skills. The use of utensils for cutting, modelling and pasting, and the control of materials being used and shaped are helpful in developing both specific skills and the efficient use of hands. Children should have the chance to experiment and to explore various techniques and processes in the expression of their ideas. Many activities offering such experience immediately come to mind. Modelling in plasticine, papier mâché and clay; scrap modelling; collages of different texture using both natural and processed materials; puppet making; knitting, sewing and weaving. Crafts that might initially not seem well suited to pupils with sight problems have sometimes been shown to be both manageable and enjoyable. For instance, wood carving, wire mesh sculpture, and leather craft. Painting with textured paint can be rewarding for visually handicapped pupils, encouraging them to use what vision they possess, whilst even totally blind children can enjoy the feel of the paint on paper as they move over it with their fingers.

Drawing

There is also a place for drawing in the arts programme; some children with defective vision, especially in the case of myopia, excel in fine-line drawings and produce graphic work of a high standard. They can be highly motivated to use their vision and to work for increasing lengths of time, becoming absorbed in the enjoyable activity. Even when they do not become proficient in this skill, the worth of the process rather than the product is still relevant. Strongly coloured crayons, poster paints and felt tipped pens can be used for drawing too, and children with no sight at all can be encouraged to draw, using the techniques of plastic film on a rubber mat described in Chapter 6. In fact, Edman (1986) has ample and interesting evidence of the fact that blind children can enjoy this form of expression which reveals much about the way in which they perceive objects. It is unhelpful to impose visual ideas on blind children as they draw, and better to elicit through discussion and discovery the ideas that they want to express.

Art appreciation

An appreciation of art can be developed in the secondary school years through visits to galleries and museums; the chance to handle wood carvings, marble or clay sculptures and to learn about the history of art offers an area of interest and aesthetic enjoyment from which a pupil should not be debarred by visual disability. Enthusiasm for a particular craft may develop into a hobby that can be enjoyed long after school days are over by pupils with all levels of vision.

SCIENCE

The teaching of science to visually handicapped pupils in ordinary schools is challenging but worth while. Questions as to both its feasibility and its value may be asked. Will a pupil with little or no vision be safe using potentially dangerous apparatus and chemicals for experimental work? Will a pupil who cannot see clearly or at all be able to discover and understand scientific principles as a result of taking part in laboratory work? Will there be a need to buy expensive specialised apparatus so that the visually handicapped pupil can participate actively in practical experiments?

Safety factors

A science teacher is wise to be mindful of safety factors when bunsen burners, hot liquids, dissecting knives and strong chemicals are in the environment that visually handicapped pupils are using. Good laboratory practice is a fundamental necessity for safe work with all pupils, but most of all in the case of pupils with defective vision. Additional precautions can further reduce the risk of hazards. Cupboards, drawers and storage areas should be labelled with braille and large print, and all apparatus should be consistently stored in the same place so that pupils know where to find it and develop the habit of returning it after use. It is the muddled work bench, the glass test tubes lying about and the trailing cord from electrical apparatus that are potential dangers, especially to visually handicapped pupils, rather than experimental work that is well supervised and which rests on clearly explained procedures.

The use of laboratory glassware is recommended since it has been shown to encourage dexterity and the careful handling of delicate equipment. Pupils beginning science in the secondary school may not have had experience of work in a laboratory setting. They will be greatly helped if they have done some simple practical experimental work in the primary school. In any case, activities involving the use of water in laboratory glassware are a safe and practical introduction to experimental work. Approaching the handling of equipment carefully, learning about its construction and different parts, even gently feeling the way up the legs of tripods (for instance to locate a beacon on the tripod stand) can be a good start (Worcester College, 1978). Pupils should know how to move away quickly from an experiment that goes wrong, and unimpeded exits should always be ensured. Clear instructions, in braille or large print or put on to tape, can be prepared, so that the pupils with defective vision, like others in the class, know exactly how to proceed with the work in hand. If a good ethos has been developed in the class, the pupil with sight problems will be less reluctant to ask the teacher to demonstrate practical procedures or to ask for clarification of concepts which are unclear. Such questions, which may seem silly to other children in the class, should never be ignored or belittled, but answered with clear explanations.

Besides an orderly working environment, the manual dexterity and visual competence of pupils will be factors in the ease and safety with which they are able to undertake experimental work. The nature of the work in practical situations in the science laboratory requires pupils to use their hands in a purposeful and controlled way. Although the manipulative skills involved in weighing and measuring will be practised in other areas of the curriculum such as home economics and in hobbies and self-help skills, scientific work demands particularly precise and accurate control of the materials being used, as for instance, when very small quantities of liquids are poured into special containers such as test tubes.

It should be ensured that visually handicapped pupils work in an appropriate light, and that they have sufficient working space – factors important to all pupils but crucial for those who are visually handicapped. One potentially hazardous situation that needs to be watched can occur when pupils with near vision peer at things in the science laboratory in order to discriminate them closely. The danger of inhaling fumes or of singeing hair in the flame of a bunsen burner is a slight but possible danger. Visually handicapped children are not necessarily prone to accidents, but sensible and vigilant care needs to be exercised. There should be a confident and quiet atmosphere in the laboratory so that questions can be answered and instructions or warning clearly heard and not drowned in background noise and bustle.

Understanding scientific principles

The claim that visually handicapped pupils are unable to under-stand scientific principles as a result of practical and laboratory work is not borne out by experience. There is firm evidence that teaching science to visually handicapped pupils can be very effective, even to the extent that pupils from both special schools and integrated situations succeed in gaining places at university for degree courses in the sciences. Nevertheless, the Vernon Report (Department of Education and Science, 1972) urged that greater attention to science should be given in the education of visually handicapped children, not only at the higher academic levels, but also in more general ways. It can be particularly helpful if this is started during the primary school years, since visually handicapped pupils have at least as much need as the average pupil for the discovery and exploration of physical laws operating in the environment and for the development of the intellectual discipline involved in the logical and analytical approach of science. In fact their need may be even greater as they are less able to see cause and effect, and to learn about scientific laws as a result of incidental observation of phenomena. The principle of working from the known to the unknown and from familar concepts to new ones can be encouraged by both first-hand experience and meaningful description. Comparisons of size and shape drawn from experience, a braille dot, a handspan, can be used to bring real ideas of relationships to the study of things that are too small or fragile to handle. De Lucchi and Malone (1982) state that there are some particular goals in the teaching of science to visually handicapped pupils, and that these include the development of manipulative skills, an understanding of how to process and operate on information, and the development of scientific concepts.

Students should be encouraged to use information received through their other senses to support and reinforce the information received through their defective vision. A piece of equipment can be demonstrated tactually so that the student can understand thoroughly its components and functions. The sense of smell can be trained to distinguish various substances by their odours. Students whose listening skills are sufficiently sophisticated will be able to determine whether containers are full or empty from sound. They will also detect and identify the 'fizz' of some gases and the 'pop' of others and will recognise the noise of a burning bunsen. This use of the other senses may not develop without specific training. An alert teacher will explain the varied sounds and smells connected with a scientific procedure and help students to integrate these into an awareness of the total process.

Presentation of content

Work in science as in other areas of the curriculum should be presented in a clear way that gives the chance of maximum access to information by pupils with defective vision. An immediate consequence of this is the need for the teacher to evaluate, and if necessary to amend, the written and illustrative materials in the science scheme that work will be based on. Even at primary level, some schemes are heavily reliant on pictorial material which may have to be enlarged or simplified. Questions will need to be posed about the suitability of the schemes being considered. Are print and diagrams clear and well presented in terms of visibility? Are diagrams labelled clearly, or would children with low vision have difficulty in understanding which part of the diagram is being referred to? Is there too much information represented on one diagram for it to be clearly discriminated? Would it be better to present the pupils with two diagrams, each bearing less information? If this last adaptation is used, it must be remembered that the student will have to synthesise the two sets of information, and this will take additional time. Diagrams may need to be prepared in large, clear, black and white format, or for tactile learners, prepared by special techniques (Chapter 6). Useful and well-designed diagrams for use in human biology have been devised by Hinton (1986) and can be obtained from him at Loughborough University. Pupils using tactile diagrams or even graphic ones may need guidance as to where to begin their exploration of them, and will need some training in the interpretation of diagrams of increasing complexity.

The content of any script in a science scheme or textbook must also be considered in the light of its usefulness for pupils with defective vision. Does it describe the operations and processes coherently and in terms that are meaningful to such pupils? Will a student with sight problems need further explanation to clarify examples of what is described in the text? Can such additional material be presented in tape-recorded form or by means of verbal explanation in order to minimise further reading?

Some processes and principles evident to the fully sighted may need to be exemplified through adapted methods so that they are made clearer for those with defective vision. De Lucchi and Malone (op. cit.) illustrate this in observing that sighted pupils mixing salt and water together see the result as a clear liquid; the salt has disappeared and they are able to see the new solution. Pupils with little or no vision will need to filter the new liquid and register the absence of particles on the filter paper. The result of this experiment is to demonstrate to them the 'clearness' of the solution, and the fact that a physical change has taken place in mixing the solid and the liquid.

Adaptations to equipment

Teachers will want to follow the carefully graded explanations of scientific concepts embodied in a good standard scheme, amplifying and adapting presentation rather than disturbing the content and progression of work shared in the science class, whilst particular attention to clarity of presentation and strict supervision to ensure safe working in the laboratory will be in the interests of all. Standard approaches can and should be used as much as possible, but sometimes small but significant adaptations or additions can be helpful, such as, for instance, making the measuring marks on a thermometer or balance more clearly visible or adding brailled labels or raised marks to apparatus used by blind children ('Hi Mark' or 'Dymotape' can be useful). The RNIB catalogue of games and equipment contains information about some useful small-scale equipment that can be used in science lessons. One of these items, the light probe, a small pen-shaped article that emits a sound of varying pitch according to the intensity of light reflected from the objects on which it is beamed, is particularly effective. Because it gives an audible indication of the intensities of light, it can enable a pupil to detect changes such as litmus colour change, formations of precipitates, and 'clouds' (for example, limewater and carbon dioxide) as well as to some extent showing the differences in colour between substances. It can also be used to determine the level of liquid in a glass or beaker.

How is apparatus to be used? The short answer is with care, and in some cases visually handicapped pupils will need their own set of apparatus that has been specially adapted, marked or labelled. Passive observation will not give the full experience of discovery of a 'hands-on' situation. Small-group work can, however, be helpful when there are situations that are very difficult or impossible for visually handicapped pupils to tackle. Sometimes it can be legitimate to pair a visually handicapped pupil with a fully sighted one for practical work. Normally pupils work in pairs or small groups for practical and experimental work, but the roles of the different participants need to be clarified in advance. Microscopic work is obviously impossible for the totally blind, and very difficult for some pupils with defective vision. Problems with colour vision, relatively unimportant in some areas of the curriculum, can prove an encumbrance in the science lesson. In work with a partner the visually handicapped pupil can record and collate data, make calculations and write up findings, whilst tactile or clearly drawn diagrams can provide at least some of the information visible to the fully sighted in microscopic work. Animal dissection is another area that can be difficult for the visually handicapped pupil to manage, but real species should be used for examining whenever possible, especially when they can be pulled apart or closely observed. Although lacking the same feel and texture as the real thing, models, either commercially or school-made, can be useful aids to finding out about biological processes, as are small skeletons of real animals, or models of skeletons and human or animal organs.

The development of outreach services and resource centres is of particular help to teachers of science and mathematics, since these are areas of the curriculum in which specialised apparatus and techniques may be most needed for individual severely visually handicapped pupils. The usual arrangement is either for the science teacher concerned to visit the resource centre or service to see the specialised apparatus and have a consultation about the specific need of the individual pupil, or, better still, for a member of the outreach or resource service to visit the school and see the pupil in his own school.

The adaptation of equipment and the use of specialised techniques in the teaching of science to the visually handicapped are detailed in relevant literature which may be useful for the science specialist to consult. Articles in journals relating to visually handicapped pupils are sometimes of interest, two such examples being those by De Lucchi and Malone (1982) and Hinton (1984).

PHYSICAL EDUCATION

There will be two major considerations affecting the inclusion of visually handicapped pupils in physical education programmes alongside their fully sighted classmates. The first of these is safety and the second is the ability of the pupil to take part in activities and games which are shared and enjoyable.

Safety factors

Much can be done to reduce problems of safety by ensuring that the environment in which games and physical activities take place is well lit and without glare. The indications given in the discussions of the classroom environment (Chapter 2) are just as relevant to the gymnasium as to other places where activities take place. Clearly marked, well-contrasting boundary lines, equipment in good condition, familiarisation with the room and its contents, and predictable placing of apparatus together with normal safety precautions will be essential.

There may be a need for one-to-one demonstrations in this as in other practical subjects. The pupil may need to try a hand-grip or foothold in order to appreciate its 'feel' before confidence in an activity is established. Attention to ensuring this kind of security may be as necessary for the pupil with defective sight as for the totally blind child. In this aspect of the child's activity the same clarity of instruction as has been advocated in other curriculum areas is especially needful since the teacher can create confusion if the visually handicapped pupil is misinterpreting instructions.

There are a few eye conditions where there may be a possibility of retinal detachment (high myopia and glaucoma are instances) and in such cases contact sports and diving are examples of activities that should be avoided. The decision as to which sports should be avoided is the responsibility of the medical adviser whose opinion should be sought and adhered to. Usually visually handicapped children will only undertake what they feel able to do, but as with the sighted, there will always be one or two who need watching particularly. They may be less careful than they should be when approaching the swimming pool, or enthusiasm may overtake caution when they are in a large gymnastics hall with apparatus in it. However, the visually handicapped pupil will not benefit from being regarded as an invalid, and motivation to enjoy physical activities should be given every encouragement. There are examples of pupils who, although severely restricted by their defective vision, are so determined to play football with their sighted friends that they are able to take a very active part in the game, and, remarkably, one girl registered as blind who attended an ordinary school became regional champion gymnast, the competition involving both apparatus work and floor exercises.

Appropriate and well-graduated activities and games can help the visually handicapped pupil to gain confidence and adroitness of movement with the potential too of enjoying individual programmes (weight training, aerobics, running) and of participating in shared or competitive sports (judo, swimming).

Movement in the infant years

Active participation can begin from the beginning of school experience. In the infant classes, physical education is mainly individual and child centred. All movement activities are suitable, although when there are thirty or so young children running about, some intervention is needed. Fully sighted children must be told that they are the ones to take avoiding action, and in some activities the visually handicapped child can be allotted one side of the hall near the wall, or paired with a fully sighted partner.

Visual handicap, whether total or partial, makes imitation of movement difficult. The kinaesthetic experience of movement can be helped by side-by-side skipping and galloping with arm-linked partners; rhythmic sound, tambourine or hand-clap, can help to emphasise the beat of movement and following sound gives experience of moving about safely and quickly in space. Floor work and individual body awareness activities are vital at this age. The sensation of body awareness in relation to the floor and apparatus and in response to sound source can be experienced. By using the floor, children become aware of the feel of the separate body parts, for instance, left ear, shoulder, arm, hip, leg and foot. Directions and descriptions need to be very specific and within the child's experience, understanding and frames of reference. A 'soft play' area where there is a mass of large foam cushion is an excellent facility, since it gives the opportunity for extending body movement in a safe and enjoyable way.

Physical education in the junior school

Physical education in the junior school demands more controlled movements, and there will be greater use of apparatus with even more need for individual demonstration of movement, grips and foot position. Visual handicap can reduce a sense of distance and make co-ordination of movement difficult. Dance is an excellent activity, principally for its own enjoyment, but also for its potential benefit in these two areas. It encourages graceful movements but operates within a set limit so that confidence is increased. Dancing with a partner can be especially helpful. For some visually handicapped children, balance is difficult and its mastery may require special training. Blind children may have a poorly co-ordinated gait when walking and may not transfer balance from foot to foot appropriately. Balancing on one foot is a new concept for them, but once achieved it does much for their posture and helps self-confidence in many instances. Walking along a bench can be frightening and they need initial hand-held support, but each physical challenge overcome and new skill mastered is a 'plus' for the visually handicapped pupil.

Ball games can obviously pose difficulties and may not be possible for some children, but it is a pity for visually handicapped pupils to miss out on being members of a team and integrating fully with other pupils in the fun of games and sport. Tooze (1981) gives practical suggestions for a number of games that can be enjoyed by both visually handicapped and sighted alike.

Swimming is an activity enjoyed by many visually handicapped pupils, and can sometimes be substituted for ball games if timetabling allows, with the pupil joining a different class for this session. Swimming can help to increase strength and stamina, but safety factors must be carefully observed, particularly when pupils are approaching the swimming pool or are swimming towards the ends or sides of the pool. Basic instructions will be the same as for the fully sighted and once children are confident swimmers, guide ropes for distinguishing lanes with coloured markers showing proximity to the end of the lane should be provided. Keeping general noise levels low is important, so that directions can be heard clearly.

Physical education at the secondary stage

Physical education at the secondary school stage offers more possibilities and at the same time imposes more restrictions because of the nature of the activities in the curriculum. There may be a great emphasis on team ball games, such as rugby and cricket. Whilst, as previously noted, there may be individual pupils so highly motivated that they participate actively and with enjoyment, others may not, finding that visual handicap puts them at a considerable disadvantage, or if it is total, that it makes participation impossible.

However, there can also be a growing confidence resulting from developing control over the body and mastery of adept movement. 'Adapted' games, accepted in previous years, may be rejected, but the visually handicapped can take part in a wide variety of the activities which schools offer. Athletics, gymnastics, swimming, circuit and weight training are all possibilities, and as the pupil progresses towards leaving school, participation in sports that will become an enjoyable part of adult social life can be encouraged. Judo, yoga, archery, horse-riding, roller-skating and ice-skating, bowling, climbing, sailing, canoeing, tandem cycling are some of the well-tried possibilities. Whilst some of these activities are likely to be part of the physical education programme in many schools, there may be clubs and classes outside which can give continuing opportunities for participation. The physical education specialist within a school often has contacts within the local community which can help to open up opportunities to the school-leaver, and the advisory teacher or social worker may know of specialist groups which concentrate on specific sports or activities in which visual disability is no hindrance to taking part in challenging leisure activities.

THE VISUALLY HANDICAPPED PUPIL TAKING SCHOOL EXAMINATIONS

The introduction of the General Certificate of Secondary Education (GCSE) to replace the previous 'O' level and CSE examinations, no longer available from 1988, means that there are new challenges for teachers, and these include trying to ensure that pupils with special needs such as visual handicaps are not disadvantaged in the new procedures.

There are many positive aspects in the rearrangement of these examinations into a simple set of examinations with a single scale of grades. The aim of this is to test the application of knowledge, not merely the recall of facts. The increased flexibility of approach which is fundamental to the philosophy of this form of examination should be of as much benefit to visually handicapped pupils as to all pupils. It is particularly important that the potential of individual visually handicapped pupils should be fully recognised and that they are not penalised because their visual handicap results in a slower reading rate or their method of recording answers involves special methods or more complex arrangements than that needed by their fully sighted peers.

Since practical and course work are continually assessed during the two years of the GCSE courses, teachers can have a good understanding of the pupil's level of thinking and ability to master a range of skills, including individual study and research, essay-type answers and practical processes. It is important to judge which aspects of such course work may cause problems for the pupil with defective vision. The syllabus must be studied carefully in the light of this. Sometimes pupils will be expected to show evidence of competence in tasks that demand good hand–eye co-ordination, such as accurate measuring. Clearly, careful practice in optimum conditions, good lighting, and use of a magnifier when this is helpful will offer some assistance with this, but the possibility of offering alternative options should be investigated when the task is heavily dependent on vision.

Over the two-year period leading up to the examination, the way in which the pupil shows consistent effort is taken into consideration, and this, together with an assessment of course work, should give a more rounded basis for making judgements about the pupil's work than the previous three-hour written papers or timed practical work. The emphasis in this more global assessment is on what pupils are able to show in terms of work produced rather than on marking them down on what they don't know or can't do. The records of achievement compiled on each child during the two-year course should give visually handicapped, along with sighted pupils, the chance to be given credit for achievements including, but also in addition to, academic excellence. Personal attributes such as enthusiasm and co-operation, contributions to school activities such as debating teams, and non-academic activities such as cookery and craftwork will also be recorded and the records will be available for prospective employers to see.

These approaches to evaluating the work of pupils hold the promise of greater opportunities for individuals, including those with disabilities, to show their capabilities, but there are some inherent practical problems for visually handicapped pupils that have to be addressed. It is an interesting fact that severely visually handicapped candidates, including those who are totally blind, have sometimes done outstandingly well in the previous formal, timed examinations. With seemingly high levels of concentration, the opportunity to be taught in small classes and good auditory memory, probably with an enhanced determination to succeed, candidates have achieved good, sometimes outstanding, success in examinations in a wide rage of subjects including mathematics and the sciences, gaining university entrance in their chosen field. The examining boards have generally been co-operative with regard to agreed additional time allowance and modification in the format of the paper (braille or enlarged print). It is imperative that the close co-operation that has often existed between schools where there are visually handicapped pupils and the examining boards should continue to operate for the benefit of pupils who have sight defects, ensuring that they have as fair a chance to succeed as those who are fully sighted.

In theory this should not be difficult to achieve. Instead of the previous twenty there are now five groups of examining boards who set the examinations and award grades. This should lead to a more uniform and consistent policy with regard to the extra time allowance than has been the case with the former numerous separate boards. The appropriate board should be able to supply a leaflet enumerating accepted time allowances and modifications for disabled candidates, and this should be obtained well before the candidate embarks on the examination course. It is promising that the new boards are giving attention to the needs of handicapped pupils, but they may need persuasion to realise the full and detailed requirements of a candidate who is blind or has some sight problems. The Association for the Education and Welfare of the Visually Handicapped can represent the views of teachers to the examining boards in these matters and has a committee concerned with doing do. Tobin (1982) undertook an analysis of time allowances and modifications accepted by the previous boards, and the information in this could well be a basis for negotiating consistent procedures for visually handicapped pupils with the five examining boards now operating.

Organisational aspects are outlined in the RNIB booklet published for the National Bureau of Handicapped Students entitled *Blind and Partially Sighted Students in College* (guidance notes for students and staff) and consist of the following recommendations:

1. the provision of question papers in suitable form;
2. a flexible approach to marking;
3. attention to the needs of the visually handicapped candidate in terms of the provision of a separate room and invigilator and/or additional time allowance.

RNIB student service

It is reassuring to teachers and their candidates that the RNIB student library provides a service that can offer transcription of any public examination paper into braille, and this service can be relied upon for absolute confidentiality. The teacher responsible for examinations, or head of the school that the visually handicapped pupil attends, will need to inform the relevant examining board stating that brailled examination papers will be required. Because of the heavy demands for the RNIB service, especially in the spring and early summer, it is important to make arrangements well in advance, and the appropriate examining body will then make direct contact with the RNIB service in order to have the transcription made. Examination papers that consist of sentence-type questions or continuous prose may well be suited to a tape-recorded presentation and this has been allowed by some examining boards. The RNIB, once again, will undertake to do this recording on application. Scientific, mathematical and foreign language papers are less well suited to this medium. Candidates who work by sighted methods may be allowed to use examination papers produced in large print, and the RNIB recommend that a sample of material offered in this way should be obtained from them prior to the transcription of papers, as these large papers are cumbersome to handle and it must be ensured that the candidate will find them manageable in examination conditions.

Whatever types of adaptation are decided upon, it is important to do everything possible to ensure that teachers, invigilators and candidates are comfortable with the material chosen, and have had the opportunity for practice sessions with them. Confidence can be considerably damaged by confusion in dealing with an unfamiliar form of presentation, especially if it is in examination itself that the candidate encounters it for the first time.

Methods of recording answers

Methods of answering examination questions can be even more varied than the methods or presenting them, and familiarity and confidence in the means chosen for offering examination answers should be established considerably in advance of the examination itself.

A typewritten answer is generally considered the most straightforward presentation, since it is easily legible for examiners and offers relatively few problems for the candidate who has a fair mastery of keyboard skills. Candidates will need to use a machine with which they are familiar if they do not have their own and will also need to work in a place where the sound of typing does not disturb other candidates.

Another way of presenting answers, sometimes used by candidates who would otherwise use braille, is the amanuensis system. Each visually handicapped candidate is paired with a 'scribe' who writes the work dictated to him by the blind pupil or student and is prepared to read back answers, or parts of them, for checking. The amanuensis needs to be a person with some knowledge of the examined subject, otherwise technical terms can be a problem, and be capable of quick, clear writing. Volunteers are often found among former teachers, students and voluntary organisations.

Candidates sometimes use braille for their answers, but there may be problems in getting this transcribed. If there is access to braille/print transcription equipment such as the Vincent Work-stations (see 'Useful Addresses'), this is extemely helpful, but as in the case of direct typing of answers, the candidate must be familiar with its usage well before the examination takes place. Less frequently, the candidate is allowed to read his brailled answer on to tape immediately after the examination, and both brailled script and tape are then sent off at once to the appropriate board.

Since all of these methods are quite demanding for the candidate, and since, with the additional time allowance, the total length of the examination can be considerable, it is recommended that the candidate should have the chance of a short, timed break during the examination. Half to three quarters of an hour has generally been recognised as the accepted time extension for candidates undertaking a three-hour examination, but longer time allowances have been agreed for more complex papers or where the questions themselves form a substantial text that has to be read.

It has already been emphasised that familiarity with equipment to be used and procedures to be followed must be ensured, and this common-sense measure, important to all candidates, is particularly so for those with sight problems. In the case of those candidates who use print, but whose sight difficulties make reading the questions a slower than usual process, additional time should be sought and evidence of this need submitted to the appropriate board in good time. It will also be necessary to go through the syllabus carefully and give special attention to practical processes that may present difficulties. The storage of completed work must be planned; brailled material takes up a lot of space, and needs careful storage. In addition, the visually handicapped candidate must have enough room to work, and be able to deal with appropriate environmental conditions.

As with many other aspects of work with visually handicapped pupils, preparing for and organising examinations may appear to involve complex and time-consuming adaptations. In practice, these can quite soon become routine and have been successfully and effectively used for many candidates who, like their sighted colleagues, deserve every chance of success.

6

The special needs of blind pupils

LITERACY THROUGH BRAILLE

The braille code

The most universal tactile code remains braille, based on the configuration of six embossed dots. This system, perfected by Louis Braille (1809–1852) from a secret code used in the French army, was adopted as the most manageable form of finger reading after various systems of embossed letter outlines had been rejected as slower and more cumbersome to use. Braille texts are used as the basis of literacy for blind children, and although the system has been subject to minor revisions in terms of rules of use it is in essence the same tactile code that Louis Braille himself used. The system is based on a figure consisting of two vertical lines of three dots. Figure 7 illustrates some of the letters and also some contractions, that is, brailled signs that stand for groups of letters or short complete words or syllables such as 'tion', 'ance', 'for' (there are in fact 189 such contractions). Configurations of dots, which are subject to rules of usage, are also used for punctuation marks and for numerical figures, mathematical working signs, and musical notation. The ingenuity of the system in making available to the tactile reader such a range of symbols that are so variously represented in printed and written form simply by the use of six raised dots is remarkable. The dots or 'cells' are numbered for ease of learning and for reference. For example, dots one, two and five stand for the letter 'h'. If this configuration is replicated in a lower position and stands by itself, it represents the whole word 'his'. If the same symbol is attached to the beginning of a word it represents an opening quotation mark; whilst attached to the end of a word it represents a question mark. Thus it will be seen that the position of signs in relation to words governs meaning. There are many abbreviated words in braille, for example, 'tgr' for 'together', and completely separate codes based on the six dots for the music and mathematics codes previously referred to. A further refinement of the system is that it can be written either in Grade I braille which simply uses the 26 signs for the 26 letters of the alphabet and does not use contractions and abbreviations such as those

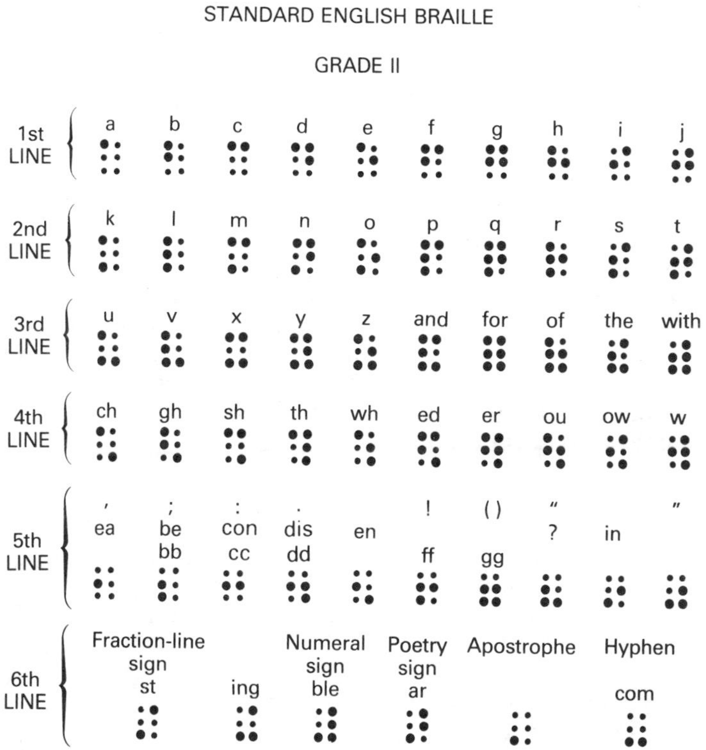

STANDARD ENGLISH BRAILLE

GRADE II

Figure 7

described above, or Grade II braille which is fully contracted. Since it is eventually quicker to read and more economical in space, Grade II braille is used by the majority of pupils in school. Acquiring literacy through braille is not just a matter of learning this somewhat complex code; tactile reading involves the use of a totally different perceptual model from that of the visual process of print reading, and therefore different approaches are needed in order to teach it, although like all forms of literacy it must be regarded as part of the pupil's total language and communication experience.

In the case of a child who has low levels of vision, consideration will have to be given to the most appropriate medium for literacy. Should it be print or braille? Although children should be encouraged to use any sight that they possess actively for learning, the use of print may be a very slow procedure, or even impossible. In such cases, braille will need to be used, with the proviso that the pupil should nevertheless continue to be motivated to use vision whenever possible to supplement and to reinforce information received through tactile learning.

Braille is read through the sensations received by the pad of one or more fingers as they travel over the page. Movement is essential since the receptors in the skin are stimulated as the finger glides lightly over the raised dots. For such movement to be possible and effective, correct posture has to be maintained. The reader should be seated with feet placed comfortably on the floor, and the table at such a height that the arm can be at an angle which enables the wrist to be relaxed. Tension can be produced through the effort of reading braille in the early stages and this must not be compounded by having an awkward seating arrangement. For the young child, teaching sessions should always be short, with the opportunity of occasionally shaking the hands and shrugging the shoulders to relieve the physical tension.

Braille reading

Both blind and sighted pupils must have achieved a certain level in intellectual, physical and emotional development before reading is possible. A sufficiently sophisticated level of listening and linguistic skills for phonic work is necessary for both groups. However, pupils who are going to use braille as their means of literacy will need to have attained a high level of tactual discrimination before reading readiness is achieved.

The child's levels of performance in these areas will need to be assessed. If sufficient motor control has not been gained so that the hands are unable to move smoothly across a piece of paper, remedial activities should be undertaken. These will include play with ring pyramids, nesting boxes, sorting cards, bead threading, and tracking with the fingers over textured lines. In order to be able to read braille the pupil must be able to discriminate between different configurations of dots. Few children entering school are likely to have this level of tactual discrimination, but it can be improved by the use of textured blocks, matching and sequencing beads by investigating 'feely' bags and exploring geometric form bricks with the hands. Lowenfeld *et al.* (1969) suggest that teacher-made materials are particularly suitable as they can be tailored to meet the needs of individual children.

The incidental exposure to literacy may well be very much less for the blind child in the pre-school years than it is for the sighted. Sighted children see words and letters in various types and in different settings by means of books, papers, labels, hoardings and television. Most blind children, however, have no access to braille in their early years. They may have encountered brailled labels which show them that toys and objects have names that can be written. Such learning, however, requires deliberate intervention from another person and cannot be the same as the ongoing environmental learning that takes place for sighted people. Blind children need enriching experiences which introduce the meaning and pleasures of the written word before formal reading skills are introduced. The mechanics of reading – finding the top of the page, page numbers, turning over pages and learning how to handle a braille book – are also necessary skills which require specific teaching.

The layout of brailled materials needs to be considered in terms of its usefulness for the reader. The principles underlying the transcription of braille are governed by different criteria from those which contribute to the visual attractiveness of a page in a printed book for children. Access to information through the tactile sense requires material that is easy to search and scan tactually. It is essential that any brailled material presented to the child is accurate; many braille signs are similar but not identical, and some have more than one meaning, dependent upon context. One dot incorrectly placed can be more confusing to the reader than a wrong letter in print that simply misspells a word. This implies the requirements for a high level of accuracy in braille transcription, and teachers who need to have material brailled should check the credentials of those offering to undertake this.

The reading readiness of children to use braille must be carefully considered, since failure in using the medium may engender long-term discouragement. Braille reading in the initial stages is not an easy undertaking for children, and their motivation to do so will need to be encouraged and maintained. In the early stages, braille is read cell by cell. This is approximately equivalent to reading letter by letter, several consecutive simulations being needed for one word, rather than the simultaneous experience of reading by sight. The braille characters differ widely in their ease of recognition by touch, the facility being affected by such factors as the number and configuration of dots, the amount of space between dots contained within the character: the frequency of its use will also be relevant. The letters a, g, l, k and y are among the simplest to recognise, but used individually have little relevance, and even groupings of these letters together would not provide many meaningful words. A large number of letters have to be recognised, remembered and then synthesised into words before braille can have real meaning for the reader. The sighted child using print has more immediate feedback in meaning from this medium which can maintain motivation to continue to find out more. In printed books, illustrations not only help to sustain interest, but also give contextual clues, and these are missing in braille. The approach to reading in braille has to have a strong phonic basis and it is impossible to transfer to another approach such as 'look and say' which can be used in reading programmes for the sighted. It needs to be appreciated, moreover, that the contractions of the braille code can cut across phonic rules. For example, the word 'paint', analysed phonetically, would emphasise the sound 'ai', whereas in braille the separate signs p-a-*in*-t would have to be identified. Braille can begin to be made meaningful within the learning experience of the child if reading is augmented and supplemented by games, activities, and oral work.

Reading schemes in braille

There are not many specially designed reading schemes for children beginning to learn braille, but the 'Family Books' obtainable from the RNIB have suggestions for supportive activities and materials which help to reinforce the story lines in the reading books. The scheme, devised by the Reading Committee of the now disbanded College of the Teachers of the Blind (College of the Teachers of the Blind, 1971), aimed to structure the cognitive and perceptual content appropriately for the young blind (Chapman, 1978). The books are small in size and easy for small hands to use: the contractions are introduced gradually and the vocabulary is based on that actually used by blind children in their early years at school. Within the limitations of vocabulary thus imposed, the stories are attractive; sentence structure, length of braille line, and the repetition of words to reinforce recognition are appropriate for the early reader. There are four sets of stories and by the end of the final book in the scheme, many of the contractions, punctuation signs and rules for sign usage have been introduced. Useful as this series has proved to be, it is time for new material to be produced, and new schemes are currently being developed for production by the RNIB. Among these, a pre-reading and beginners scheme produced by the Association for the Education and Welfare of the Visually Handicapped is already being used in some schools for five- and six-year-old pupils. Two schemes for children who need to transfer from print to braille reading (Lorimer, 1987; Fitzsimmons, 1987) are becoming available from the RNIB.

As the number of pupils using braille in ordinary schools increases, many teachers are seeking to adapt printed schemes so that children with severe visual handicap can work alongside their sighted classmates using parallel reading schemes. No printed reading scheme is likely to be able to be transcribed exactly, and such transcription should be undertaken by someone experienced in the complexities of reading in braille. Supplementary reading material which offers work of an appropriate vocabulary level and stage of competence in dealing with contractions, and yet which is still of interest and enjoyment to the pupil will take time and trouble to devise. The advice of a specialist teacher or adviser can be invaluable, but it can be an intriguing and rewarding project for a teacher to undertake and can make all the difference to a blind child in the early stages of reading.

A variety of texts in braille should be available, some of it well within the ability of the pupil, so that reading is both possible and enjoyable. If the reading level of the material offered is too difficult, the concentration needed to decode the braille results in a lack of interest in the content, with a consequent lack of comprehension.

The teaching of braille reading techniques needs to continue throughout school, even though it may appear that mastery of the code has been achieved. Attention should be given to hand movement. The relaxed movement of the hands can help to increase reading speed, as will the developing use of both hands in reading. Pupils should be encouraged to use more than one finger for discriminating the symbols, as unexpected circumstances can limit performance otherwise. A small cut on the finger can be a triviality, but for a braille reader such a small incident can interfere with reading for several weeks. Braille readers can be trained to use contextual clues, and it can be possible to eradicate bad reading habits, such as scrubbing round individual dots with the finger, before these become established and inhibit fluent reading.

Reading speeds in braille

Compared with print reading, braille reading speed is slower. Among the many studies of braille speeds that were submitted to the Vernon Committee, the study by Williams (1971) remains significant. The reduced reading speed has implications both in terms of the comprehension and the quantity of material that can be dealt with through this medium. To make a rough but relevant comparison, an average-sighted reader would normally be able to read three times as much of the content of a story in print as the average braille reader of comparable age could manage in the same amount of time. There can be problems in maintaining interest when reading speed is so slow, and academic work can become tedious, not because of the task involved, but because of the time and effort involved in the process of reading the material.

The levels and speed of the braille reader can be assessed by using one of the three easily administered tests available. Lorimer (1977) constructed a braille version of the Neale Analysis of Reading Ability Test, and this can be used diagnostically as well as to monitor progress. A second test is the Lorimer Braille Recognition Test (1962) which uses 174 braille contractions to be used for readers between the ages of 7 and 13 years. The third is the Tooze Braille Speed Test (1962). This has 120 three-letter words to be read, with the time for doing so being recorded. These tests were devised some years ago, but because of the unchanging nature of braille they are still useful. They should, however, be used in conjunction with the teacher's own knowledge of the child's progress and careful observation of the pupil's reading techniques and motivation. The results from such testing of the pupil's braille reading should in any case be considered together with information about the child's total language development; a careful analysis of errors should be made in order to find out whether tactual discrimination, or an under-developed understanding of phonics, or the reversal of signs is at the basis of poor or delayed reading competence. Such data will need to be discussed with an experienced teacher of braille, specialist teacher or adviser in order to devise remedial activities appropriate to the individual reader.

The complexities and the load on memory attendant on learning braille appear, when they are described, to be considerable. Blind children, however, do learn to read competently, both in order to gain information as well as for enjoyment. Theory and experience both bear witness to this. The teacher who wants to find out more about braille reading can turn to the well established classic *Blind Children Learn to Read* (Lowenfeld, 1969) and also be heartened by the experience of the mother of a blind eight year old hiding his braille book under the bedclothes in order to finish a story 'after hours'. Establishing literacy through braille will be likely to involve co-operation between class teacher and specialist for visually handicapped pupils. It is a fascinating and rewarding aspect of learning of key significance for the blind pupil.

Braille writing

Learning to write by using braille usually develops most happily if it is started alongside learning to read in braille. Young children sometimes find writing in braille easier than reading it, with the strange result that they sometimes race ahead with written work that they cannot read back! The machine that is used virtually universally for school work is the Perkins braillewriter which has six keys which when pressed reproduce the six dots, plus a space bar and a back spacer. This machine makes the personal production of braille simpler to learn than earlier methods, since the dots are embossed from below the paper giving instant upward embossing which can be immediately read with the fingers. Hand produced braille involved punching the dots from above by depressing an instrument into the thick manila paper; reading braille thus produced entails learning signs in reverse and removing the paper from the frame in order to read it. Some proficient braillists, however, like to use a small hand-frame for note-taking in situations in which it would be difficult to use a Perkins brailler.

At school, however, once children have been shown how to use the Perkins brailler, including the slightly tricky process of feeding in the paper, they usually learn quite quickly how to make the dots that replicate the alphabet letters. Contractions to be used in braille writing are introduced in the same order as they are learned in braille reading. The braille primer (RNIB) is useful for the sighted in order to learn the braille fully contracted code and can be used for self-instruction. It is not, however, its purpose to offer work graded on developmental lines for the school pupil learning to read and write braille, and so its use as a teaching basis for braille in school in not appropriate. It can, however, be an accurate and useful source of reference for the teacher. When texts are being brailled on a Perkins machine, pages must be fed into the machine with the binding at the top of the book, not down the side. In addition, once a piece of paper has been brailled, refeeding it into the machine can damage or erase the dots; sheets of braille work which a child has written should be kept separately from the brailled textbook.

The pupil who is working in braille will need a larger working area than the one using print. There will need to be sufficient space for the Perkins brailler, the bulky textbooks in braille, and other pieces of adapted equipment such as spur wheels and abacus.

There is a division of opinion as to whether, in encouraging pupils to write in braille, accurate and fully contracted braille should be insisted on from the beginning. To do so may have an inhibiting effect on the enjoyment children have in writing, but it is nevertheless essential that what they write should be able to be read back and not be indecipherable.

Creativity and accuracy in braille usage

Pupils are motivated to write about their own thoughts and experiences by being encouraged to write their own sentences. Once this has been attempted, the work that they have written can be read through with them, the content can be discussed and the correction of spellings and contractions explained. Correct versions can then be brailled on to the paper, preferably underneath the mistakes. This will not mean correcting every word, but selecting the items that are within the child's reading level; such work can be reinforced by the use of workcards that show phonic combinations or contractions. Accurate writing can be encouraged by the copying of a line or two from a brailled reading book, especially a favourite one. Most children find that this is a satisfying task, although it is only a small part of the writing experience. As pupils progress through school they may need a convenient way to take notes. The hand-frame previously referred to can be useful, but should only be used when braille writing has been fully mastered. These approaches to learning to write braille are teacher intensive, not only in time but in expertise, and the need for such appropriate and necessary support should be recognised when a child first comes into an ordinary school.

Braille users should be introduced to handwriting, if only to a limited extent, as they may need to sign their own name on documents. They can enjoy the movement of handwriting, and it can be made more meaningful by the use of textured paint. Pupils with low vision may need to use braille for academic work but still be able to write in large letters and should be encouraged in this dual activity.

KEYBOARD SKILLS

The increasing availability of technical equipment extends the possibility of communication for severely visually handicapped pupils, and means that the mastery of keyboard skills becomes essential. In integrated settings typed material may represent the only written communication between pupil and teacher, and it is also a valuable future means of social and vocational communication as well. Keyboard skills can be introduced at the upper junior level when the use of the Perkins brailler has become well established, and pupil's hands are of a sufficient size and strength to reach and use the keys; the pressure of time is often more intense in the secondary years and it will be very helpful if this skill has been started at least by then. It may be possible for learning to take place outside ordinary school hours, but the pupil must not be over-pressured. The technique of touch typing is essentially the same for sighted or visually handicapped pupils, although there are additional considerations for the latter because of their inability to see and check what is being typed.

Initially, personal tuition will be needed, but may be replaced by tape-recorded instruction as the pupil progresses. Students can quickly become competent enough to produce work of a good standard, and typing is usually faster and less tiring than handwriting. Well-trained blind typists have achieved excellent levels of speed and accuracy.

TACTILE APPROACHES

Developing tactile skills

Direct contact by means of touch is the only way in which severely visually handicapped children can learn about form and texture, whereas the possession of sight is a major factor in enabling pre-school children to find out about and categorise objects in terms of shape, form and pattern. The way in which hands are used has significance. Fraiberg (1977) emphasised the need for blind infants to bring their hands to the midline; in order that manual investigation of an object can take place, the use of both hands is essential, but blind children can show delay in being able to effect this. Little intrinsic motivation exists for blind children to handle objects, and they may even be deterred from doing so by the unpleasantness of some tactual experiences. Wet sand and cold food may not encourage further exploration with the hands. The importance to the child's development of tactual investigation may not always be fully understood at home, and social taboos and safety factors may further limit such activities. Underdeveloped body image and lack of physical activity can impede the development of strong hands, whilst climbing, pushing, pulling, dressing, and feeding oneself, which tend to promote it, may be insufficiently undertaken. Such activities can be encouraged in the playgroup and at home especially if expert advice on materials of the appropriate developmental level is given.

Even with such support, young blind children show a wide range of competence in their ability to recognise household objects by touch; guided tactile manipulation and exploration with supportive language can help to establish concepts of rough, smooth, hard, soft, metal, plastic, small, big and so on. Language is a key factor here, since it helps to explain and clarify what children are doing, enabling them to understand and unify the fragmented information that they receive through their tactile activities. Encouragement can be given to increase the range of such investigations by using different tactual strategies such as, for example, scanning with the flat of the hand, manipulation with finger and thumb. As tactile abilities develop and children become more competent in matching textures and shapes, they can be introduced to the handling of two-dimensional material. However, repeated exploration of three-dimensional objects of a variety of sizes and shapes is necessary before children can learn to extract information from such tasks as using braille, and the interpretation of tactile maps and diagrams that will be crucial in later school learning. There may be a tendency as children progress through school for opportunities for tactile investigation to be replaced by verbal description, but visually handicapped pupils will need to continue to have maximum opportunity for first-hand exploration of objects.

Tactile materials

Throughout the years at school, braille will be the essential and continuing source of tactile material for the blind pupil. For an individual blind child in an integrated setting, any work transcribed into this medium, apart from set reading schemes, may have to be produced specially and by arrangement with a voluntary or professional transcriber. As the pupils progress through school and their curriculum extends, their need for the transcription of more textbooks will increase. The increasing use of linked computer–braille systems facilitates the production of braille, but a variety of sources of supply of brailled material may be required, especially when some of it needs to be produced quickly. Some prison services have set up braille transcription units, and if orders for book transcription are given in good time and do not offer unusual difficulties (for instance in diagrammatic work) they can give a useful service of high standard. Braille textbooks and reading books for leisure are obtainable from the RNIB which issues a catalogue and whose textbooks committee will consider specific requests. There are also excellent braille libraries in Manchester and in London which operate a postal loan service and include school pupils among their readers. The RNIB and other voluntary bodies have transcription services (listed in Chapter 7) and sometimes local volunteers are prepared to learn braille, take the RNIB transcribers' certificate and offer their services to a school.

Braille and other tactile material can be duplicated by using a thermoform machine, which softens a sheet of plastic film and moulds it to the shape of a prepared matrix underneath; heat and vacuum processes applied for a few seconds enable the plastic sheet to take a sharp raised copy of the underlying prepared material comprising braille dots, raised lines, or textured surfaces. A map or diagram, for example, can be made by attaching string or wire to denote lines on to a firm piece of manila paper. Sand paper, rice, small grains of pasta or net can also be stuck on to similar paper to make textured areas which can be differentiated by the fingers from the smooth background of the paper. Copies of any amount can then be made on the thermoform machine using the plastic film which can be obtained from the RNIB in various weights. Addresses of manufacturers of vacuum forming machines may be found in the 'Useful Addresses' section at the end of this book.

The process of making and duplicating such material is interesting work and relatively easy provided that appropriate materials are available, but it must always be remembered that such materials need to be designed for interpretation by the finger, not the eye. It is easy to be over enthusiastic when making a tactile diagram, both in the amount of information and in the different tactual stimuli embodied in it. For example, a map for a sighted child will include visual information on population, towns, roads, hills, rivers and other geographical or topographical features. All this information presented in a tactile form would be too confusing for the student to discriminate with the fingers. Separate maps would need to be made: for example, one showing cities and road systems, another hills, rivers and topographical features, another showing population centres etc. Although this approach separates information that would be confusing if presented simultaneously, the difficulties for the blind student are obvious. Each map needs to be scanned by touch and the information gained from this procedure assimilated and interpreted in conjunction with the information gathered from the other representations. In addition the blind student has several sheets of material to keep in order rather than the one printed copy that the sighted pupil handles. It will be appreciated that the blind pupil has a time-consuming task, but one that is a useful potential source of information.

Maps and diagrams

The construction of tactile maps and diagrams can be a fascinating activity, involving the choice of a variety of materials to give definitional texture. There are some well-tried methods such as those described by Pickles (1968) in which powdered glass is used to remove tackiness from the surface of thick materials (such as used X-ray plates) on to which string, wire and textured materials have been laid. Copies are then made with a thermo-vacuum machine. A much quicker way of producing three-dimensional maps and diagrams is now available by means of the Minolta stereo copier (see 'Useful Addresses' section). The relative advantages of these two systems of producing maps and diagrams are analysed by Kirkwood (1986), who considers the two broad categories of diagram likely to be needed in school. She considers that for school purposes there are diagrams which can be reproduced and those which cannot. Diagrams to be reproduced can be made by the thermoform method described above, or by means of the newer Minolta copier. A master for use by the Minolta method can be made simply by drawing a diagram on to plain paper, adding texture effects by hatching or shading with a pen or pencil. There is no need to stick additional material on to this to create a three-dimensional effect as is the case with the matrix for the thermoform. It is possible to enlarge printed diagrams from textbooks prior to using them in the Minolta, but labelling the base diagram is time-consuming. If a Perkins machine is used for this, the dots must subsequently be coloured or the process of reproducing them on final copies will not be possible. The next stage in this process is to take photocopies on to the expanding capsule paper on which the final diagram will be shown. This stereo heat copier takes about twenty seconds to complete the process in which all the carbon marked lines and markings on the sheet are raised and show in black, clearly defined ridges on the final diagram. Diagrams can also be made by drawing with a carbon-based pencil directly on to Minolta paper and then processing the result. (Advice about compatible photocopies can be obtained from the RNIB Diagrams Co-ordinator.) Kirkwood's (op. cit.) comparison shows that skilfully produced braille on thermoformed diagrams has a high level of discriminability, making it very suitable for the 'younger, less experienced pupil', but the Minolta method is much quicker in terms of producing master copies although in terms of discriminability less versatile and with less ease of discernment of subtle differences in texture. This writer concludes her study by emphasising the need for blind pupils to be trained in interpreting tactile diagrams and recommending the use of both techniques in order to meet specific needs.

Non-reproducible diagrams (individual copies) can be made quite quickly by using a spur wheel on manila paper to follow a previously drawn outline as for freehand drawing. A thin sheet of plastic film clamped to a rubber mat can also be used for the base, with lines made by a spur wheel or biro. The embossed image can be felt by the finger.

The use of such tactile diagrammatic material is valuable in making available to the severely visually handicapped pupil a version of the diagrammatic material available to the sighted pupils in the class. However, not only are some adaptations and specific training needed, but the pupils should also have the chance to give feedback on the usefulness of the materials presented in this way.

LEARNING THROUGH LISTENING

To be able to listen critically, with concentration and with the consequent ability to retain facts presented through auditory means, must be an asset to any learner. Our environment is saturated with noise. Some people opt for more of it by wearing 'Walkman' cassette players in order to hear the sound they want while cutting out background noise; sometimes television sets and radios are left switched on indiscriminately with sound pouring out. Most pupils will be used to a high, and sometimes almost continuous, level of sound in everyday life; because of this it is relevant to consider their motivation to attend to what they may feel to be the less stimulating and exciting auditory material that they are presented with at school.

For any pupil with defective vision it is of particular importance to be able to listen critically and with concentration to information presented in this way. The reduced information that such pupils receive through visual channels increases the need for informational input in other ways. Inability to discriminate detail, a reduced visual field, the need to use specialised equipment such as closed circuit television or to use braille for reading are all likely to mean that the pupil will be receiving less information from texts and reading material in terms of rate of uptake than his classmates with unimpaired vision. Auditory learning can, to some extent, affect these deficiencies. Even the pupil with less severe visual impairment is likely to enjoy learning in this way since it offers respite from close work and visual concentration.

For the pupil who is blind and needs to use the tactile code of braille for literacy it will be important to look for additional ways of presenting information. For all its usefulness, braille is generally a slow means of reading. Texts are bulky and may be hard to obtain at the time they are needed. For practical reasons, the use of auditory material is invaluable for blind pupils, but also for those with less severe visual impairments.

There are three specific areas in which concentration on auditory work can be enhanced: firstly, by offering programmes that encourage pupils to pay attention to auditory stimuli; secondly, by attending to the quality and effective use of auditory material; and finally, by considering the advantage of providing tape-recorded material instead of, or in addition to, printed or braille texts.

Learning to listen

The question of whether attentive listening is a learned skill that can be improved by practice and teaching in a school situation must be debatable, but experienced practitioners confidently offer graded programmes of listening activities as a result of their perception of the need for this in their own work with visually handicapped pupils. Relevant literature abounds in examples of such programmes either to be used as specific training or incorporated in more general activities, and the extent to which attention to listening skills takes pride of place in literature about visually handicapped children is noteworthy. There is an implication that early attention to enhancing listening skills may pave the way for later benefits, or at least minimise problems. Barraga (1976) outlines ways in which the young visually handicapped child can be encouraged to respond to specific sounds in the environment and, basing her schemes on development factors, suggests activities which progress from awareness of sounds to discriminating between different sounds and to connecting sound with movement by using sound sequences such as a rattling ball as an encouragement for the child to follow. Her justification for such specific attention to listening skills is that in the case of the severely visually handicapped child 'the more rapidly his development in discrimination and familiarity will proceed [in terms of listening] the more stable the base for interpreting sound'.

A comparable approach is offered in *Guidelines for teachers and parents of visually handicapped children with additional handicaps* (RNIB, undated). This describes some simple and practical sound-related activities which are enjoyable for most children and need not be restricted to those referred to in the title of the booklet. Primarily intended for pre-school children, the suggested activities would be well suited to a playgroup, reception or infant class where visually handicapped children are included in the group. First activities include comparison of different sounds created by shaking containers filled with different substances (beans, sand, water, etc.) progressing to rhythmic activities such as sound patterns or clapping and tapping rhythms which replicate the sound pattern of hands and words. Orientation activities include following a drum beat or tambourine or chasing an electronic bleeping ball (obtainable from the RNIB). What is absent from these schemes is any formalisation in terms of evaluating the child's progress, and so a teacher using them will need to be especially observant of this, moving the work on and incorporating sound-related activities in general activities as discrete skills are mastered, rather than continuing to offer separate sound discriminating activities.

The value of such exercises is dependent on the eventual success of the pupil in integrating the skills he has developed through discriminating listening into day-to-day situations of learning in the classroom. In presenting listening activities there needs to be little or no difference between the way this is done for fully sighted or visually defective children. There may simply be a difference in emphasis in that visually handicapped children are likely to benefit from more intensive practice, and may find greater difficulty with the games involving mobility and orientation. Work of this kind has been perceived over the years to be valuable in integrated educational situations. Bishop (op. cit.), an influential exponent of practical aspects of work with integrated visually handicapped children for many years, gave considerable emphasis to devising programmes which aimed at helping visually handicapped pupils to give attention to listening skills. She suggests games which focus on sounds in terms of recognition, discrimination of pitch, loudness and distance, working through increasingly complex listening activities which culminate in study exercises concentrating on the analysis and criticism of verbal material which the pupils listen to and evaluate. She claims with some justification that work of this kind is a good preparation for study at higher education levels where the lecture mode of giving information is often used. There are some appropriate commercially available materials which incorporate sound recognition activities, whilst traditional stories such as 'The Three Bears' and 'Peter and the Wolf' give excellent opportunities for concentration on listening and amusing sound identification. Games that involve discrimination between words and sound similar but not identical can lead on to some preliminary work in phonics.

Salt (1986) has experienced both learning and teaching situations as a visually handicapped person and firmly advocates the inclusion of specific training in listening activities for pupils with little or no sight. He urges that auditory training should not be simply remedial, in terms of compensating for reduced information as a result of defective sight, but should build on existing strengths. Those who have worked with substantial numbers of blind pupils usually have anecdotal evidence of the skill of their pupils in recognising identity from the sound of someone's voice. There is some evidence from research too. Bull *et al.* (1983) found that in a sample of 92 young adults, voice recognition from tape-recorded samples was significantly better than for matched sighted subjects. Trowald's (1975) study showed less fatigue and greater retention of the content of taped auditory material among blind secondary school aged pupils than for their sighted peers. Such evidence underlines a potential strength for visually handicapped people in social and educational situations that should be fostered. However, Salt (op. cit.) fears that some children who seem alert may still need to strengthen and develop their capacity for discriminating listening, and advocates sound quizzes, sorting out auditory instructions against a distracting sound background, and story telling which concentrates on sound effects and dramatisation. His suggestions require more ingenuity than equipment.

Presenting auditory material

An increasing use of technical aids and equipment in the classroom can mean that there is less emphasis on the teacher's own voice and that language is less often chosen as a learning aid than when such devices were not available. Changes in teaching style, with more individual work and active learning, reduce the number of occasions when a teacher uses a lecture-oriented approach in a more formal way with the whole class. Pupils are also accustomed to highly professional and sometimes sophisticated informational programmes from the media in the form of films, videos and broadcast material. Nevertheless, the teacher is far more than an automaton controlling the use of equipment and software programmes. There is a need for the teacher to use language persuasively and effectively, and to have an audible and at times, compelling voice, especially when there are pupils in the group who cannot see well and miss visual cues. It can also be refreshing for both teacher and pupils to enjoy those aspects of learning that involve direct teacher/pupil communication. These are fresh and immediate without being processed through any interviewing device. Although helpful to all pupils, it is crucial for those with visual disabilities that when a teacher is speaking to the children the voice is clear and speech not too fast, but with enough pace and variety of tone and vocabulary to provoke and maintain interest from the listener. Definition of purpose and clarity of instruction are essential for pupils with sight problems since vagueness or inaudibility can cause real misunderstanding or confusion.

To enjoy the best conditions for attentive listening, pupils should be sitting in a reasonably comfortable way and background noise should be controlled as much as possible. When notes are written upon the blackboard or demonstrations given, these should be explained in a succinct and clear way, with care being taken to direct the voice towards the pupils. Such basic teaching techniques can be easily overlooked or forgotten, but can make a considerable difference to the learning of pupils with sight difficulties.

Tape-recorded materials

In spite of the initial time required in planning and obtaining tape-recorded material, it can be a valuable mode of presenting material to visually handicapped pupils, especially for those at secondary level who need to read a substantial number of texts. There are, however, a number of factors that must to taken into consideration when decisions to use tape-recorded materials are made.

It is essential to obtain the permission of the copyright holder, this being often best done by direct application to the publisher of the text with an explanation of why the material is needed in this form. The reproduction of any published material in large print, photo-copied or tape-recorded form must be approved before copies are made. There are a number of different ways of getting the selected material put on to tape, once the copyright is cleared. Volunteer readers who are 'friends of the school', college students, parents and teachers' aids are all potential sources of help. It must be ensured that the readers chosen speak fluently and clearly, and are able to pronounce any technical words contained in the text.

The RNIB students library has a number of texts in auditory form and is usually willing to consider others but requires advance notice. If it is envisaged that there will be a continuing need for taped material, a tape library can be built up as a resource in the school. Those special schools for the visually handicapped which operate as resource centres can also give help and advice on how to have material taped; often tape-recorded material is successfully used for academic work in such schools, particularly in preparing pupils for examination. The Audio Reading Trust (see 'Useful Addresses') can supply cassettes with a housing that bears a tactile symbol indicating the length of tape. The use of tactile symbols as an aid to efficient identifying and indexing of cassettes so that blind pupils and students can locate material easily is described in the BBC *In Touch* bulletins (Nos. 25 (5) and 24 (7)).

Although there are some negative experiences in the use of tape-recorded material, this may be because of inappropriate use, and certainly its provision is not an automatic solution to the difficulties that visually handicapped pupils may have in coping with large amounts of reading. Trowald (op. cit.) made an extensive study of listening skills for visually handicapped pupils of secondary school age, and although his study is not a recent one, the recommendations are still valid, particularly with regard to classroom practice in the effective use of tape-recorded material. He suggests that when tape-recorded material is used, lengthy periods of unbroken listening should be avoided. The listening activity should be broken at convenient times according to content, and the pupil should construct questions or make notes about the content at intervals. Varying the activities tends to keep motivation and attention high and to maintain attentive listening.

In addition to these points suggested by Trowald, teachers using tape-recorded material, especially with visually handicapped pupils, will need to consider the experiential level of the content and devise appropriate introductory and follow-up activities that are helpful in reinforcing what has been learned. There should be opportunities for the pupil to undertake activities that involve critical appraisal of the material that has been listened to and that involve self-expression in areas related to the text. Additionally, preparatory work which can help to facilitate the effective use of tape-recorded material includes the prior study of difficult or unfamiliar words, the use of study questions and the development of précis and summary techniques. If a second tape-recorder is available, it can be used by the visually handicapped student as an instant audible replacement for a notepad; small portable pocket recorders are invaluable for this (obtainable from the RNIB).

In the integrated situation the purpose of including tape-recorded material and listening skill programmes is to sharpen and speed up the pupil's capacity to use information as a result of listening, and to make available to those pupils who are visually handicapped as wide a range of study materials as possible. Mathematical and scientific material tends to be less well accepted in auditory form, partly because it may have graphical, statistical and numerical elements which are difficult or impossible to record verbally, and also because pupils prefer such materials to be 'under their fingers' in braille or produced in clear print or enlarged format that can be checked. There are limitations, too, in that auditory material does not permit scanning, but increasing skill in the use of tape-recorders gives the visually handicapped pupil the chance to study on an individual basis material that would otherwise present considerable visual tasks.

That there can be cumulative benefits from the practice of attentive listening to auditory presentations is shown by Rhyne (1982). His study indicated that in the case of 11–13 year old pupils listening to tape-recorded stories in synthetic speech taken from a Kurzweil machine (see Chapter 7), comprehension of synthetic speech significantly improved as a result of exposure to it.

In Chapter 7 descriptions are given of some of the equipment available for speeded speech in tape-recorded form. There are increasing solutions through technology to the problem of braille to print and braille to word transcriptions. Blenkhorn and Payne (1985) refer to their success in making teletext available to blind users by means of synthetic speech using a text to speech synthesiser, whilst Cassidy (1985), a visually handicapped man writing in his capacity as senior physiotherapist, refers to the value of his 'computerised workstation, using commercially available components, which by the use of superbly developed software and a synthetic speech unit can act as a braille to text to print translator, a simple talking word processor or a talking video ... this means fewer "borrowed eyes", better print accuracy and a better temper'.

Clearly, attention to listening skills has relevance for the future for visually handicapped pupils.

INDEPENDENCE TRAINING

Independence training is vital for visually handicapped children. Self-confidence, independence and self-directed decisions in terms of everyday life and work are desirable goals for all pupils, but the path to achieving them is a more difficult one, simply in terms of self-management, for those who have severe handicap. It can be a salutary experience for a teacher who has such a pupil in the class to attempt an everyday activity whilst wearing a blindfold and without the guiding sense of sight to try locating cutlery, pouring water into a glass, using the salt cellar and not the pepper pot by mistake. This is not replicating the situation of the blind pupil who has grown up with or adjusted to the condition, but it gives a useful experience of the nature of the tasks involved in self-help areas for those without sight or with very limited vision. Meeting the needs for specific training in independence skills is one of the major challenges of integration for visually handicapped pupils and one which has to be met. There are two main sets of skills which require the direct intervention of specific teaching, namely, mobility and self-help skills, and these are not normally a part of the curriculum in the ordinary school, certainly to the extent to which they will be needed by severely handicapped pupils. It is possible to encounter pupils who have a high level of academic achievement, but remain overly dependent on others for personal help in everyday situations and who cannot travel independently. Severely visually handicapped pupils, however, can and do achieve good levels of independence in these areas when they have received appropriate and consistent training. Staff expertise and time are needed in order to effect this, and special schools are well placed to offer good quality training. The integrated situation has other advantages in providing varied social conditions, a greater challenge to independence, and often a pace of daily life that encourages quick responses to ordinary events, as when pupils are changing classrooms, locating transport to go home, sharing playtime games with sighted pupils who move quickly.

Self-help skills

Basic self-care, the management of oneself and of everyday belongings involve learned skills that are influenced by watching what other people do and by imitating these behaviours from early childhood onwards, first in play and then in 'real life' situations. A child at home will watch a cup of tea being made, observing the skills and the sequence of actions involving. These may be imitated in play with dolls, and in the use of real utensils once they can be handled. The skills in this simple activity are refined by practice, becoming an achievement giving a sense of competence and satisfaction. Much learning of this kind can be missed by the child with severely defective vision with the result that structured teaching programmes may be needed, replacing cues normally gained through sight by tactile ones and guiding verbal directions. Tooze (1981) observes that a dependent child all too easily becomes a dependent adult, and emphasises the value of encouragement in independence beginning in the early years at home, and continuing throughout and beyond the years at school.

This aspect of learning and mastery of skills is so significant in the child's total development that even though school staff may not be involved in the specific teaching of self-help skills, encouragement to practise them in school should be ensured, and teachers will inevitably be involved in monitoring their visually handicapped pupils.

Teachers in the same mainstream school are in a key position to monitor the progress in their day-to-day activities, and to try to ensure that over-protection from colleagues, ancillary staff and other pupils is not so kind in intent, but over-protective in effect, that it hinders progress in self-help areas. A child with severe visual handicaps should not be left in a distressed condition through being unable to manage a small everyday task such as finding a lost shoe, but needs to be shown how to manage to fetch and return books and to move between classes and specialist rooms alongside other pupils. The additional time which can be needed by some visually handicapped children in order to do things for themselves can cause timetable problems unless care is taken. A blind or severely visually handicapped pupil may take longer, for example, to change clothing before and after physical lessons than the fully sighted children in the class. All the teachers who are involved with the child's learning will need to understand these problems and to discuss their implications frankly, so that a balance can be found between the demands of the ordinary curriculum and the particular needs of the individual blind pupil. The extent of help and the way in which it is to be given will need to be agreed, so that a consistent policy with regard to the support of the child in day-to-day situations is implemented and kept under review.

Teachers unused to blind pupils need not be unduly anxious since the children usually respond to the challenges of doing things for themselves, especially if they are shown in a practical and cheerful way how to do so. In the infant classes, independent toileting, dressing and other basic skills of self-management should have been mastered prior to admission to school, but there may, on occasion, be children who need both assistance and training in such skills. Help for parents may not have been available or well received; there may have been anxiety, protected hospital treatment or other circumstances which have impeded or prevented the basic acquisition of self-management skills by the pre-school child. The range of activities which have been mastered may be uneven. A child may be able to use a spoon but not other cutlery, or able to manage a zip but not a button. Here, the teacher is working from a positive base. Some skills have been mastered and so there is clearly potential for undertaking more. In such instances an assessment of the child's present level of functioning will need to be made and the Reynell Zinkin scales (Reynell, 1979) can be useful here. Specialist teachers and advisers of visually handicapped pupils are usually familiar with the checklist approach since it was tackled by Van der Zwan and Heslinga (1970) and will be able to help with devising a graded remedial programme along individual lines. Much of the programme implementation is carried out by ancillaries and teachers' aids, but it must be remembered that specific training in self-help areas involves perceptual activities of co-ordination, manual dexterity and directionality that need to be established and developed before success in self-help activities can be attained. Actual objects should be used whenever feasible for training, since the manipulative task of fastening buttons on real clothes, for example, is different from the experience of the same task on a doll or activity board, although these can be used for supplementary activities.

Because children with little or no sight have difficulty in reproducing processes by imitation, even comparatively simple tasks that the sighted will often take for granted may need to be analysed and broken down into sub-skills that are manageable for visually handicapped children. Backward or reverse chaining forms the basis of an instructional technique that can be effective in the teaching of self-help skills to visually handicapped children, since the task is broken down into simple discrete stages which are demonstrated with particular attention to the last stages of the process. This contrasts with forward chaining in which the task is taught step by step from the beginning. The sense of achievement in accomplishing the final stage of a self-help activity is encouraging, besides which the last stage in an activity is sometimes the easiest one to master. The first stage of eating, loading the spoon, is the most difficult for the visually handicapped child to achieve. This technique of backward chaining can also be used in the more complex skills that have to be mastered by older pupils.

Work in home economics and in health education will en-
compass learning and activities vital to self-care for all pupils. In
these areas those who are visually handicapped will need the clarity
in presentation of materials, the opportunity to handle objects and
the individual demonstration that are necessary in all their work in
practical subjects. Safety factors in home economics follow broadly
the lines recommended for science. There is no reason why totally
blind and severely visually handicapped pupils should not take part
in a full home economics programme with all its implications for
eventual independence. Careful grading and activities, beginning
with pouring liquids and spreading slices of bread, gives initial
confidence. Simple meals can be prepared, using brailled work-
sheets and recipes. Gas and electricity boards will arrange for ovens
to have brailled control markers, and convenience foods and
microwave ovens are a future boon for the visually handicapped,
though pupils need to know how to use them properly and about
the expense involved. Vigilance and clear instructions, the
predictable and orderly storage of equipment and enough time to
finish each task can be important factors in safety and success.
Brailled and large print recipe books have been produced by some of
the specialist colleges for visually handicapped students (for
example, Queen Alexandra College and the Royal National College
for the Blind) and these are generally available.

Standard equipment can be used for most processes but pupils
should be shown carefully how to hold and use knives, scissors and
sharp instruments and be given the chance to feel the position of
'on' and 'off' switches. Some specialised gadgets for cookers such as
'ping' timers are available from the RNIB, and the Disabled Living
Foundation (see 'Useful Addresses' section) has listed useful
kitchen equipment. Most cookery processes are manageable with
care but deep frying is hazardous. The ordinary school learner's
programme should have the means of ensuring that self-care and
self-management skills have been attained, and should include the
special needs of visually handicapped pupils. Choosing and caring
for clothes, managing money and shopping for food present the
same challenges for all pupils, but for those who are visually
handicapped they present extra difficulties that demand special
help. More handling of materials, more enquiries about the articles
to be purchased, more step-by-step instructions will be needed and
can be given in practical lessons. Encouragement should be given to
the discussion of meeting problems in daily life among pupils; they
will learn a great deal from each other as well as from their teachers
about coping with everyday situations.

Mobility

Training in mobility and orientation skills is a crucial area of learning for visually handicapped pupils and must receive attention whenever they are educated. Mobility can be defined as the ability to move safely from one place to another, detecting and negotiating obstacles. Orientation involves the ability to locate oneself in spatial terms and to construct a mental map of the environment. The difficulties of totally blind children in these areas will be obvious, but some low vision children also have marked problems with mobility and orientation. Recent research (Hill *et al.*, 1986) indicates that low vision children have tended to show lower scores in spatial awareness tests than totally blind children, the suggested explanation for this being that the difficulties of low vision children have been inadequately recognised and less specific teaching of the relevant skills has been afforded. Some children with defective vision whose mobility is satisfactory indoors in situations where lighting levels are controlled can have real mobility problems outdoors where there can be glare from sunlight and dim light from disturbing shadows. Such instances call for an individual appraisal of the visually handicapped pupil's needs for mobility instruction.

Early stages of independence

The beginning of independent movement starts in the earliest stages of the childs development through crawling and walking. The attitude of parents at this time is thought by Warren (op. cit.) to be crucial, since parental over-protection can be profoundly limiting in the development of mobility, whereas encouragement to move about the home environment freely, with graded exploration of the world outside, promotes the ability to move independently. The views of blind people themselves are of interest, Cutsforth (op. cit.) suggesting that a puppy can be useful in encouraging the child to move and would have the advantage of not showing either 'quarter or compassion' to its blind playmate. A dog may be an impractical mobility aid in some families but the principle of shared romping and chasing can still be a manageable one. Parents can help their children to orientate themselves by sharing the fun of discovering different auditory, tactile and olfactory clues around the house: kitchen sounds and smells, ticking clocks, the hum of the fridge, the texture of tiled and carpeted floors. These attributes and the impression they make help to build a mental plan of the home which can often be well understood. Lack of vision or limited vision can reduce the child's desire to move outside to explore new surfaces of grass, asphalt and paving stones, especially in the absence of the familiar sounds of indoors; interesting measures must be found for encouraging such exploration – going out to get an ice-cream, finding a ball.

The development of body awareness is essential if children are to acquire good mobility and orientation skills and easy posture. Concepts such as 'above your head', 'waist level', and 'knee high' need to be understood as do the meanings of 'left' and 'right'. Visually handicapped children may take a considerable time to relate their own body places to those of others, and terms such as 'in front', 'behind', 'side by side' will need to be individually demonstrated and experienced repeatedly until understood. Without sight the relative positions of left and right sides when children face each other are difficult to understand, and both laterality and directionality need to be practised in activities. The blind child will have greater difficulty than the sighted in establishing a relationship between the 'ego' and the external world, but movement and purposeful exploration can help. Sound can be a great motivator in encouraging this, moving towards sound and following sound. *Mobility Ideas* from the RNIB has some practical and enjoyable activities on these lines suitable for practice at home and also in the first years at school.

Mobility within the school campus

At school pupils need the chance to explore the new environment and if they are visually handicapped they will need to do this in detail and at a quiet time. Fixed landmarks such as doors, corridors and cupboards should be identified, and the layout of furniture explored. As security and confidence grow, other parts of the school campus and outside environment should be explored and become familiar. Such 'conducted tours' can be enjoyable, classteachers finding ways for each child to use this newly acquired knowledge. Clear directions should be given as to where lesson materials are located: 'The paper is on the table by the radiator', not 'It's over there'!

The sighted guide techniques (Chapter 2) can be learned by both visually handicapped pupils and their sighted friends. If the correct techniques are adopted it can prove to be an efficient way of getting about, and the visually handicapped pupil should be able to use different sighted guides with ease. A technique referred to as 'trailing' should be learned to help safe movement around school buildings. The back of the fingers are lightly 'trailed' over the surface of walls while the arm is held in front and slightly to the side of the body with the fingers slightly curved as they brush along the wall. This technique is particularly useful for negotiating corridors. *Independence Training for Visually Handicapped Children* (Tooze, 1981) illustrates the correct usage of this and other specific techniques for effective mobility. This invaluable text outlines the progressive stages of learning independent mobility and is based on the natural stages of children's development.

Although the class teacher can encourage and provide opportunities for independent mobility, when formal training is undertaken there will need to be a specialist input from a trained mobility officer or specialist adviser for visually handicapped pupils. This training demands trust from the pupil and is an exacting activity involving learning how to interpret information received through the unimpaired senses and use this to move about with a purposeful sense of direction. Early activities and games involving response to sound pave the way for the more sophisticated skills involved in mobility training. Echoes from buildings and obstacles such as bus shelters can be used to detect their presence by the skilful blind traveller, who can even be aware of a parked car as a result of interpretation of variations of reflected sound. Such high levels of competence are not attained by all, but competent independent mobility can and should be attained during the school years by severely visually handicapped pupils.

The class teacher's contribution to mobility skills

Much can be done by the teacher in an ordinary school to help the pupil who needs to develop orientation skills. Learning about the points of the compass is useful for orientation, whilst physical education is closely associated with both mobility and orientation skills. Games which involve walking in a straight line across an open space making exact full, half and quarter turns can be included in mathematics when concepts of time and distance are also being considered.

Specialised techniques

The use of the long white cane for mobility involves specific techniques which are different from those used with the white cane usually carried simply for identification. Long cane users are trained to detect obstacles at ground level by arcing the cane smoothly from side to side at a distance of about two paces in front of the feet. Users have to co-ordinate the movement of the cane with that of their footsteps and at the same time interpret the information that they receive through their auditory sense and retain a mental map of where they are walking; these complex skills demand a high level of concentration. Some pupils become highly proficient in long cane mobility, but learning the technique can be fatiguing and sometimes stressful. Once acquired it is an invaluable skill for life.

Proficiency in orientation involves not only an immediate sense of direction, but also the ability to read and use tactile maps and diagrams, a skill which can form part of the total mobility training.

On leaving school the blind pupil will have some choice in mobility aids and techniques. There are sonic spectacles which work on a 'radar' system of object detection by means of sound waves and there is the possibility of having a guide dog. Whatever future choice is made, basic good levels of body awareness, directionality and confident movement will enable the blind person to make the most effective use of these aids.

Even when visually handicapped pupils have attained a competent level of independence, there will be occasions when help from sighted people is needed. Being able to accept or decline help without giving offence is a valuable social skill. Opportunities for further education, for employment, for enjoying life should not be inhibited for blind school leavers because of problems with independent mobility, and supplementary teaching outside ordinary school hours should be organised if it is needed.

7

The use of technology and other resources

EDUCATIONAL TECHNOLOGY

Technical developments in recent years have offered potential solutions to many of the problems faced by visually handicapped pupils in ordinary classes. Since text material can be transcribed from print to braille and vice versa by means of specifically designed software, auditory material for study use efficiently recorded and stored, and small or detailed visual material thrown up as an enlarged image on to a television monitor, access to the curriculum for pupils with little or no sight has become increasingly easier. An area in which well-chosen equipment can be valuable is in increasing the speed of communication and informational uptake; for instance, tape-recorded material can be speeded up and diagrams in tactile form produced in minutes from printed master copies.

The judicious and effective use of technical means of making educational material available to visually handicapped pupils does not obviate the need for such pupils to have opportunities for first-hand experience in handling objects and making discoveries in their own way. Nor does the use of these techniques preclude the necessity for teachers to have an understanding of the implications of visual handicap on their pupils' learning, for example, in concept formation and language development.

As the range and sophistication of the available technology increases, so does the problem of selecting the most appropriate equipment for specific tasks and learning situations. Some equipment is still very expensive, and its purchase needs to be considered in relation to the total resources available to support the pupils requiring it. Would the money spent on equipment be better used if it were applied to more classroom help instead, or a variety of simpler, less expensive learning aids? Heads of schools, class and specialist teachers and specialist advisers for visually handicapped pupils need to consult before expensive equipment is purchased and to bear in mind practical considerations of usage. The final selection of equipment will be influenced by suitability for a particular school situation, and also cost. Arrangements for storage of the equipment and access to its use will have to be made; factors in the care and maintenance of the equipment are likely to make a difference to the extent to which it is actually used once purchased. If its size means that storage is only possible several corridors away from the classroom, obviously incidental use will be minimised, since pre-planning will be necessary. The rapid developments taking place in the design of educational and specialist equipment for visually handicapped users mean that any item purchased is likely to become superseded by a newer, more sophisticated and efficient model. Full information sought from manufacturers should include details about replacement of parts, servicing, maintenance and obsolescence in the face of newer developments.

Some equipment, such as the Optacon (see page 173), carries with it the need for specific training, both for the pupil and instructor. This has implications for the workload of both pupils and teachers. Deriving long-term benefits from the mastery of such specialised equipment requires time and expertise to be available in the early stages of use.

There is no doubt that technology will make an increasing contribution to the lives of the visually handicapped. Education, in using it efficiently and effectively, can take place in the school years, beginning with the selection of the appropriate equipment to suit the pupil's ability and need. Described below are examples of some of the equipment that is available for use by the visually handicapped. Addresses of the manufacturers are given at the end of the book.

The Vincent Workstation

This is one example of several systems now available. It consists of a Perkins brailler, BBC computer, television monitor, speech synthesiser and printer. Text is brailled on the Perkins brailler and then it either appears in printed form on the screen or is spoken through the speech synthesiser. In addition, a printed copy can be obtained from the printer. Although this system is widely used in special schools, it does have particular implications for those mainstream teachers who have a blind child amongst their pupils since it provides immediate communication between braillist and non-braillist, thus enabling the teacher to give immediate feedback on the pupil's work without the need for transcription at a later time. The system also allows for the pupil to keep a brailled copy of written work while handing a printed copy to the teacher. Using the speech synthesiser, the pupil can keep a check of the work in progress and when learning braille this audio feedback informs children of any errors in their work.

There is also a program available which enables the keys of the Perkins brailler to create musical notes, thus providing a level of enjoyment not usually experienced with a braille writer. In addition there are several games available which sighted children can enjoy alongside those who are visually handicapped. All of this software is extremely motivating for the blind child, and can be especially helpful to the pupil whose sight is deteriorating and who is having to make the difficult transfer from print to braille.

The word processor facility is particularly useful for older pupils and adults in employment in that it allows them to locate and correct errors without assistance from a sighted person, thus giving them additional independence in work involving literacy.

Closed circuit television

There are several companies manufacturing systems which consist of a television monitor, camera and reading stand. Printed material is placed on the reading stand which can be moved sideways and back and forth so that a different section can be presented to the camera resulting in a magnified image displayed on the screen. The magnification of print can be from five times to forty times, far greater than can be provided by other low vision aids. In addition, most closed circuit television systems allow a negative image to be presented on the screen, that is, white on black, instead of black on white. This has the advantage of reducing glare and many visually handicapped people find the negative image easier to see and less tiring for longer periods of viewing. There are also colour systems now available. Lewis (1986) noted that young children who previously had been unable to concentrate on a story being read to them were now able, with the added stimulus of seeing the book illustrations, to extend their periods of concentration considerably. He also suggested that the colour system might well make objects in the environment hitherto unseen by some children, such as insects, stamps and so on, accessible to their view.

Some systems also incorporate a camera but can be focused on more distant areas, such as the blackboard or demonstration table. This has particular benefits for the visually handicapped child in the integrated setting, where a very common problem for the teacher is to make information on the blackboard available to the pupil. Closed circuit television has several advantages in addition to the high level of magnification which in itself may allow the child to see print for the first time. The screen can be viewed from a normal distance, so the viewer can work in a more relaxed position than is often possible for the visually handicapped when doing desk work; this lowers the possibility of fatigue and tension. Diagrams can be seen at one viewing instead of in the small sections necessitated by many magnifiers. Handwriting and typing are examples of other activities that can be greatly helped by using these systems. In the classroom, teacher and pupil can view the screen at the same time, which facilitates the discussion on the current progress of work. Similarly, a group of children can use the equipment simultaneously, which may help to prevent the social isolation which can be caused by the working situation of visually handicapped pupils.

There are several disadvantages, however. Most of the systems are heavy and bulky, and even the portable models are not easily manoeuvrable. An integrated pupil, particularly at secondary school stage where lessons are taken in a number of different classrooms, would probably not have this aid available all the time. The systems are expensive to purchase and require not only a capital outlay, but funds for maintenance and repair. Training is needed for the pupil to manage the system independently, and a regular check must be made to see that the equipment is being used efficiently by the pupil.

Closed circuit television can make many materials and activities available to the low vision child, and a creative teacher will find a multitude of uses over and above reading and writing. Microscopic slides or photographs can all be viewed, using certain adaptations, and activities such as knitting and other crafts can be taught and practised. For many visually handicapped children these systems are of tremendous assistance and should be made available to them where this is the case.

Versabraille

The Versabraille is an example of an electronic brailler which uses cassettes to store brailled material, making the use of paper unnecessary. Text which is brailled into the machine is stored on the cassette, and the standard C60 can store four hundred pages of braille. When the user is writing, the brailler can quickly recall on to the keyboard what has been written, the information being sent back at approximately a hundred words a minute. Interfaced with a printer, typewriter or braille embosser, the Versabraille can be used to produce a printed or braille copy of the stored text. Incorporated within the machine are word-processing facilities including correction, deletion and addition to sentences and paragraphs. Easy storage and retrieval are possible because the material is organised into sections, pages and paragraphs, and to 'fast forward' the whole cassette takes under 45 seconds. The Versabraille can be linked to various computers and, with the use of appropriate software, Grade II braille can be stored on the machine. Non-braillists can prepare braille by typing it in via the computer and brailled material can also be transcribed into printed text.

The Versabraille, in common with other electronic braillers, does have limitations. Since it has a display of only twenty characters, searching for a particular item of information does take time. In addition, a knowledge of computing is necessary to transfer the stored text on to paper, and a period of training and practice will be required to master the procedures which will probably be beyond the younger pupils. The cost of the Versabraille is high and will probably remain so as the market for the electronic braillers remains small. This is likely to be the greatest limitation of these machines being available to visually handicapped pupils integrated into mainstream schools.

Microwriter

The Microwriter is a mini word processor which has a variety of functions when used in conjunction with a television monitor, speech synthesiser and printer. It is small enough to be hand held and has six keys which fit well into the span of the fingers. Various combinations of the keys form a code for letters and word-processing instructions. A small visual display is an integral part of the machine. The code for operators is simple, taking only a few hours to master, though continued practice is obviously necessary for speedy and efficient use. Operating the keys is relatively quiet and little pressure is required, so material can be typed in unobtrusively. For information to be extracted, there needs to be access to a dot matrix printer. The visual display allows the user to see what is being stored, and for the blind operator the voice synthesiser states what letters, numbers, words or processing instructions are being typed in. The memory will hold up to five pages of foolscap, and the processing facility permits very high quality papers to be produced. Visually handicapped people whose fingers are not strong or sensitive enough to produce or read braille find the Microwriter invaluable, but it is also a piece of equipment that is widely used by many braillists.

Optacon

The Optacon converts print into tactile symbols that can be felt by one finger. The machine is about the size of a small cassette recorder and comprises three components: the camera, the electronic unit and the stimulating display. The tiny camera contains two lamps and a circuit of 145 light-sensitive photo transistors. The tactile display is composed of tiny rods corresponding to the photo transistors in the camera and these rods vibrate, reproducing the image received by the camera. The reader moves the camera across the page with one hand while the index finger of the other hand feels the vibrating rods which form an image of about three by two centimetres in area. As the camera passes over each letter, the rods vibrate simultaneously and the reader perceives the enlarged letter tactually as it passes across the display. The Optacon therefore gives the blind reader immediate access to printed material. With the addition of a special lens, the electronic display of a video screen can be carried and a typewriter attachment gives the user access to what is being typed.

Unfortunately, reading with the Optacon is slow and, although highly proficient users can attain reading speeds of 70 words a minute, Best (1981) found the average speed to be under 40 words a minute. Tracking the print with the camera is extremely difficult, as is interpreting the sensations from the tactile display, and, in addition, words must be synthesised from the individually perceived letter so there are obviously limitations to its use.

An intensive training course of over 50 hours is essential for mastering the skills necessary to read effectively with the Optacon. This is usually undertaken by both user and teacher so that training can continue once the basic course is completed. The equipment is expensive, and though it has great potential, users are most likely to be those who are in the later years of education or in employment.

Kurzweil reading machine

The Kurzweil Reading Machine is the size of a standard office photocopier and has a similar layout. It speaks the text of the printed material presented to it by converting it into synthetic English speech. A page of text is placed on the scanner and almost simultaneously the listener hears it spoken. The Kurzweil can convert almost any type and style of print, including books, professional journals, letters and newsprint. However, some forms of handwriting and poorly duplicated material are not convertible. The machine is equipped with facilities for searching text, spelling out words, repeating lines and, via the variable speed mechanism, listeners are able to scan the material, obtain an overview of content, and select a passage to read in detail. Developed to produce good intelligibility of text which is necessary for clear understanding of the formation being received, the Kurzweil can read up to 250 words a minute. A separate control panel enables the listener to sit comfortably away from the machine, and in addition to the incorporated talking calculator the machine allows for other input and output devices to be connected.

However, the Kurzweil requires training as it is a complex piece of equipment and the reader must be able to feed the scanner with text by turning over pages of a book or replacing read pages with new material.

Owing to the high cost of the Kurzweil Reading Machine, it will only be available at present as a resource, and many central public libraries have now purchased these machines, which are used by a number of visually handicapped people for study or leisure. It can, currently, only be used for reading straight text and is unable to interpret graphics or maps. Nevertheless, the Kurzweil has important implications for visually handicapped users for educational, social and vacational use.

Viewscan

This is a reading system which is fully portable, weighing approximately nine pounds. It accepts print by means of a small camera which must be kept in contact with the printed page and tracked along a line of print. The image is then displayed on a screen in black print on a red background or red print on a black background. The magnification, brightness and contrast can be adjusted, and the Viewscan can be operated with rechargeable batteries, thus avoiding the problem of finding a power source.

However, the visual display is only suitable for some partially sighted and low vision children, and steering the camera across the text is a sophisticated skill. With the Viewscan, only one line of print can be seen at a time, unlike closed circuit television where whole sections of text can be viewed at once.

The Viewscan Text System is the combination of the Viewscan and a personal computer which is completely portable and which provides a number of facilities: word processor, computer terminal, calendar, clock and calculator. For visually handicapped secondary pupils who are able to read the visual display and operate the camera, the Viewscan and the Text System can be valuable tools in an integrated setting.

Variable speed cassette recorder

This recorder has great advantage over the standard forms of cassette or tape recorder as it allows the listener to hear the cassette at a faster speed than normal without loss of intelligibility. Recorded text can be heard at a rate of up to 170 words a minute. In addition the use of high-pitched tones when running the cassette in 'fast forward' allows efficient scanning of the cassette content with identification of specific sections.

Listening to recorded material can be slow and tedious and often results in a loss of concentration. The variable cassette recorder avoids this tendency and the listener is able to cover a large amount of material in a comparatively short period of time. Making effective use of the speeded-up speech requires a high level of listening skill, some specific training and strong motivation, but it can be useful for well-motivated pupils.

Photocopiers

Access to a photocopier which has an enlarging facility can be invaluable to those educating visually handicapped children in an integrated situation. Diagrams and some sections of print in textbooks used by fully sighted people may be too small for the low vision or partially sighted pupil, but enlarged either once or twice become legible for such pupils.

The quality of the paper and the print of the text selected must be good, however, as any faults and distortions will also be enlarged. Material should only be enlarged when absolutely necessary, as not only are the photocopies bulky but visually very complex for many low vision children to use. The Minolta is a recent form of photocopier which can produce embossed material (see page 153).

Microcomputers

Microcomputers are widely used in all areas of education and much of the commercially produced software, if judiciously chosen, can be used by the children with some vision. Special programs have been developed at the Research Centre for the Visually Handicap-ped (see 'Useful Addresses' section), some of these incorporating additional devices such as concept keyboards, joysticks, speech synthesisers and touch-sensitive screens. The computer monitor can be very stimulating visually and programs containing bright, moving images have been found to attract the attention of children who had not appeared to function visually before. Programs have also been devised for use in the learning and practising of specific skills, such as braille and typing. Research into braille transcription, print to braille and vice versa has led to the development of several useful programs, though the complexities of Grade II braille have led to difficulties. Blenkhorn (1986) points out that to produce individual or even adapted programs for visually handicapped pupils takes a considerable amount of time. He suggests that to make software available to these pupils, it is easier to adapt the computer, for example, to produce large print on the screen. Teletext can now be received via speech synthesisers, large print or Grade II braille. This has enabled visually handicapped people to have access to up-to-date information never possible before. Future developments will no doubt offer further exciting possibilities.

RESOURCES USEFUL FOR TEACHERS IN ORDINARY SCHOOLS

It is invaluable for teachers to know where to refer when they need to track down information about the availability of specialised equipment and educational materials or locate advisory services and resource centres. Probably the most useful and convenient source of specific information of this kind is the *Directory of Resources for those Working with Visually Handicapped Children* (Travis, 1987) published by and available from the Department of Special Education at the University of Birmingham. This publication is regularly updated and gives addresses and, where relevant, telephone numbers of providers of resources and services throughout England and Wales. It is of practical relevance to professionals working with visually handicapped pupils in these countries, and of interest to overseas readers who wish to survey the resources and support services currently available here. The six main areas covered are:

1. aids and services
2. catalogues, bibliographies and journals
3. educational services
4. societies and organisations
5. spoken word
6. sport and leisure.

Addresses of the various organisations providing these resources and services are listed in the 'Useful Addresses' section at the end of this book.

1. Aids and services

The first section of this directory, which lists sources of aids and services, can help the teacher to be aware of and to obtain items specifically useful for visually handicapped pupils, such as dark typewriter ribbons, desks with adjustable sloping tops, electronic and mobility aids. The major supplier of such materials is the Royal National Institute for the Blind which has a permanent display of aids and equipment in the showroom at 224 Great Portland Street, London W14. Details of services for enlarging print and sources of advice and information on the use and supply of magnifiers, closed circuit television and low vision aids are also listed in this section.

2. Catalogues, bibliographies and journals

Whilst it is usually an advantage to be able to visit a standing exhibition of specialised aids and equipment, this may not always be possible. The second section of the directory lists suppliers of catalogues which give precise information on the cost and availability of articles that can be sent by post or delivered to school. In this respect, the RNIB catalogue of games and equipment is invaluable.

Bibliographies on particular educational topics relating to visually handicapped people are listed under this section, as well as details of the specialised journals concerned with this field. Articles of interest and relevance to the teacher are frequently to be found in these publications; for example, recent articles in the *British Journal of Visual Impairment* have included 'Supporting visually handicapped children in ordinary schools' by Benton (1984), 'Ecological fieldwork with visually handicapped students' by Hinton (1984) and 'The role of a visual handicap department in an integrated secondary school' by Hughes (1984). This journal, which is produced three times a year, is 'addressed to all those professionally concerned with children and adults who have visual impairment'. Further information can be obtained from the Editor. *The New Beacon* is a journal published monthly in both braille and print by the RNIB. It contains articles on educational topics and gives details of recently published braille texts and large print books that can be purchased. Recent additions to the RNIB libraries are also listed. Some of the journals published in the United States which contain relevant articles on the education of visually handicapped children are listed in this second section of the directory.

3. Educational services

Although the BBC *In Touch* bulletins are not primarily concerned with educational topics, they do contain references which reflect the interest shown in these matters in some of the weekly *In Touch* programmes. These bulletins can be a useful source of information on legal matters and allowances and they also give some consumer reports on specialised aids and equipment. They are published quarterly, and can be obtained direct from the BBC.

A list of the addresses of local education authority advisers and peripatetic teachers in England and Wales is given in the third section of the directory, as well as those of the individual members of the RNIB team of advisers. The units and resource centres providing for visually handicapped pupils and the addresses of the special schools catering for such pupils are also given here.

The third section also lists a number of local educational authority schools which offer resource provision either in terms of advisory personnel or by showing examples of equipment and materials. For instance, Exhall Grange School, under the Warwickshire Education Authority, has a resource room containing examples of journals and literature, magnifiers and low vision aids. There are also instances of resource provision offered by the educational establishments sponsored by voluntary organisations for the blind. The Royal National College for the Blind has a resource centre directed towards the needs of visually handicapped students in further education and Worcester College for the Blind has inaugurated an outreach service relating to secondary pupils. Both the school and the college of further education under the auspices of the Birmingham Royal Institute for the Blind have also been sources of considerable information for teachers and lecturers in ordinary schools and colleges. This contribution is typical of the special schools for visually handicapped children, many of which are heavily involved in providing practical teaching placement for specialist teachers in training, as well as in giving information on the management of equipment and curriculum areas such as maths and science. To be able to continue to do this they must themselves be able to offer a full curriculum and have the opportunity to develop and evaluate methods and materials.

In order to minimise interruptions to the timetable, visits to special schools for visually handicapped pupils need to be carefully co-ordinated and agreed in advance, and it must be appreciated that their role is complementary to that of the advisory services and not a substitute.

4. Societies and organisations

Among the societies and organisations listed in the directory there is a considerable breadth of commitment. In general, the older societies and institutes often founded over a century ago are the ones which support educational establishments as well as providing some welfare services for visually handicapped adults. The RNIB not only sponsors educational establishments but it also has a team of advisers who will visit children at home or in school on request. Besides being the main supplier of specialised aids and equipment, the team runs a service for recording and transcription from print to braille; it also has an express reading service and publishes information leaflets, some of which are particularly useful to educators of young or multiply handicapped blind children. There is also an extensive print and braille library besides the showroom and shop at Great Portland Street.

The Disabled Living Foundation is a much more recently established organisation which has sponsored a number of projects directed towards the needs of visually handicapped people of all ages. Publications from this foundation include *Notes for Teachers* (Cameron, 1982) which is for the use of teachers in ordinary schools where there are some visually handicapped pupils. There is a special project worker who is available by appointment to discuss the comprehensive collection of aids and equipment which can be viewed. The foundation has a very active Advisory Panel on Visual Handicap which has given attention to a wide range of practical solutions to the daily living problems of handicapped people.

There are also both professional and consumer organisations which provide resources in the form of information, conferences and publications relating to the educational and social concerns of visually handicapped children and young people, notably, the Association for the Education and Welfare of the Visually Handicapped. This professional organisation has played an active role in advising government departments, negotiating with examining boards and organising regional and national conferences. Besides being co-editors of the *British Journal of Visual Impairment*, the association publishes a newsletter and holds a stock of publications obtainable from the Business Manager. This association is represented at international conferences, and its own national conferences include speakers of international reputation. It represents a unique body of experience in the education of visually handicapped pupils in both special school and integrated situations, and has contributed to research development, specialised reading schemes and attainment tests.

A consumer organisation that also offers some informational resources to the teacher is the Partially Sighted Society which now has a National Low Vision Advice Centre. The Education Committee of this organisation runs occasional national conferences for professionals and parents of visually handicapped children.

The Research Unit for the Blind at Brunel University carries out research on aids for the visually handicapped, especially with regard to increasing access to information. This unit publishes an international register on blindness and visual disability.

University departments and colleges are usually able to supply information about their training and research projects. It is helpful for them to have a stamped addressed envelope accompanying enquiries, and encouraging for them to have an acknowledgement of the information that they send.

There are a great many organisations which are either concerned with specific aspects of professional or employment matters, such as the Association of Blind Physiotherapists and the Visually Handicapped Typists and Secretaries Group, or which encourage research into specific cases of visual disabilities such as the British Retinitis Pigmentosa Society. It may be of interest to a teacher who wishes to find out details of a proposed career for a pupil or to suggest support for parents of a child with a specific visual condition to contact such organisations. Details of their addresses and telephone numbers are listed in the directory.

5. Spoken word

The value of using well-produced tape-recorded material for visually handicapped pupils is discussed in Chapter 6 and the teacher wishing to arrange for material to be taped will find Section 5 of the directory invaluable, as it lists a substantial number of volunteer and professional tape-recording services. The Audio Reading Trust, for example, has a full catalogue of the trust's audio books available in print and on cassette, whilst the Foundation for Audio Research and Services for Blind People advises on the use of sound equipment, sells good-quality cassettes at reasonable prices and also offers a range of compact cassette recorders, some with variable speed and tone. There are individual recording services such as the Hallam Tape Service, whilst the RNIB Customer Liaison Unit at Braille House will supply detailed information about tape-recording services.

6. Sport and leisure

It can be both enjoyable and beneficial for a visually handicapped pupil to develop an interest in sport whilst at school and to wish to continue to practise it after leaving. Ideally, sport and leisure provide opportunities for social interaction and enjoyment shared between visually handicapped and fully sighted enthusiasts and this attitude can be fostered during the school years. Some sports, however, may require modifications or there may be groups of visually handicapped participants who have a special skill, enthusiasm and interest in a particular sport. Sports associations are also often helpful, not only in promoting interest in the chosen sport or leisure activity, but in giving advice and information about how the blind or severely visually handicapped can take part in and enjoy it. Their enthusiasm is often contagious and can open up possibilities that may not have been envisaged. The British Association for Sporting and Recreational Activities of the Blind (BASRAB) or the

Director of Education and Leisure of the RNIB will help with all matters regarding sport and leisure activities. Details of sailing courses, nature trails for the visually handicapped and museums with facilities for the blind are also given in the directory. Blind or severely visually handicapped pupils should be encouraged to find out about and use such facilities for their own interest and enjoyment. For younger children the Toy Library at the Research Centre for the Education of the Visually Handicapped in Birmingham loans toys free to all visually handicapped children, schools and advisers, and there is a postal service available, whilst the Toy Libraries Association will supply leaflets which give advice on suitable toys for children with sensory handicap. The booklet *Toys with a Purpose* available from the RNIB is also recommended.

The resources outlined above are examples of the range of sources of information and materials that can be made available to the teacher who has visually handicapped pupils in the class, and they are there to be used.

8

Towards better practice

GUIDELINES FROM RELEVANT STUDIES

When visually handicapped pupils are taught in the ordinary school the problems that they can have in learning and the teacher's capacity to help the child to overcome them will be greatly influenced by the availability of resources and support services, and better practice is dependent upon the adequate provision of these. The route towards such better practice is by no means uncharted, since the principles of integrating pupils with special needs, including those who are visually handicapped, have received attention in relevant literature.

A study which identifies attitudes as a central issue in the integration of children with special needs is offered by Booth and Potts (1983) in *Integrating Special Education*. The section on provision for visually handicapped pupils by Lowe is largely concerned with a crucial appraisal of segregated education and advocates a complex system to include the setting-up of resource centres and advisory services on a peripatetic basis, with residential special schools for the additionally handicapped. Attitudes towards the visually handicapped are stressed as being of prime importance in this work, but the class teacher will also need to have information and advice on classroom management, special equipment and materials, since these are also germane to the pupil's successful and happy placement in the ordinary class.

The RNIB has published some valuable studies in this area of educational concern which examine current good practice and consider outstanding needs. *Towards Integration* (Jamieson *et al.*, 1977) undertakes an illuminative approach to research on the integration of special needs pupils, and has been followed by *Educating Pupils with Special Needs in the Ordinary School* (Hegarty *et al.*, op. cit.) and *Learning Together* (Hodgson *et al.*, 1984) which sets out to examine relevant classroom strategies and curriculum modifications needed for such pupils and to highlight the issues faced by mainstream teachers in this context. Some practical guidelines are given that are relevant to pupils with visual handicap, and factors that may be inimical to good practice and successful placement are exposed. In his 1981 publication, Hegarty (op. cit.) gives instances of potential concern, contending that:

> The individual needs of the child are often controlled by personality factors affecting the child's ability to adapt to varying circumstances.
>
> The difficulties of visual handicap are not always appreciated by the sighted.
>
> Vision is such an important role in the learning experience that any visual loss immediately imposes restrictions and may limit access to the full curriculum.
>
> Success in academic achievement does not necessarily result in good social adjustment and vice versa.

These caveats are cited by Benton (op. cit.) in an informative journal article which includes detailed checklists embodying 'factors requiring consideration to ensure the successful placement of visually handicapped children in mainstream schools', and which if fully and universally implemented would do much to meet the points raised by Hegarty (op. cit.). Benton claims that there can be no 'blueprint' or 'utopian system' for the support of visually handicapped pupils in ordinary classes, since the nature of these can be subsequently affected by local circumstances and financial conditions. There can also be wide differences in the extent of existing local provision, and in the interest of special education advisers in different authorities, with a corresponding range of specialist support. One clear conclusion to be drawn from this claim is that specialist advisory services for visually handicapped pupils should be increased and made available throughout the country to ensure the appropriate back-up for teachers and support for pupils in whatever locality their school is situated. Indeed, the importance of adequate personnel is a recurrent theme throughout the relevant literature.

THE ESSENTIAL ROLE OF ADVISORY SERVICES

Despite rejecting a blueprint as unrealistic in present circumstances, Benton, who draws on considerable experience of advisory work for visually handicapped children, sets out the criteria that she thinks are essential in four areas of the work of the advisory services for such pupils, namely:

> assessment and evaluation (including assessment of visual functioning and levels of independent mobility);
> supporting the children (including adaptation of materials and curriculum modification);

acting as consultant to the teacher (including giving advice on pupils' needs and arranging 'withdrawal' teaching services if needed);
involving the parents (encouraging home/school contact and home activities).

Whilst the organisation of the advisory and support services are outside the control of the teacher in the ordinary school, the first line of support is through these services, and providers of them should be made aware of what teachers feel they need in the way of support and help if they are to be happy about the integration of pupils with visual handicap in their classes. The specialist teacher adviser needs to be appropriately experienced and qualified in order to be able to assess the circumstances of visually handicapped pupils in the classroom and to offer strategies to meet the children's needs that are practical, immediate and well founded.

The administrative base from which the specialist service operates may be the psychological services in the local education authority offices or in a special school for visually handicapped children. In any case advisory and support work will be likely to involve a considerable amount of travelling between the different schools attended by visually handicapped pupils.

It has been customary for some local educational authorities to appoint a single adviser when they initially set up integrated services for visually handicapped pupils, but as increasing numbers of pupils with special needs related to visual handicap are identified in mainstream schools, and others are moved there from special schools, small teams of advisers are sometimes appointed. Such a development has many advantages, since it enables an adviser to give specific attention to a particular age group, such as pre-school or adolescent pupils. However, because of the relatively low incidence of severe visual handicap among the school-aged population, some local education authorities have not been able to adopt this practice, and a few are without specialist advisory services for visually handicapped children. The RNIB has an increasing role in providing advisory services for teachers of integrated pupils and may be the only support in such cases.

It is important for teachers who have visually handicapped pupils in their classes to feel that they have access to information and advice when it is required, and they should be given a contact telephone number as well as the address of the relevant advisory services. Because advisers have many and diverse demands on their time, it is mutually helpful to make regular and advance appointments for school visits from the service whenever possible. Some pupils will be regarded as 'contact' cases whose progress needs to be monitored but who only need to be seen once or twice a term, whilst other pupils with more severe or complex difficulties may require visits, especially in the early stages of their placement.

The organisation of the advisory services is clearly going to affect the availability of help for the classroom teacher. Whilst literature which examines different models of providing this is interesting and has some relevance to practice, the classroom teacher will want to know what lines of approach can readily be adopted in order to support the visually handicapped pupils already in the class or about to join it. A 'recipe book' approach at first looks like an attractive and quick way of offering information, but the variations and individual differences in the requirements of visually handicapped pupils can make this fallible and inadequate. It is more valuable to acquire some understanding of the implications of visual handicap in general terms and then apply these to the individual pupil.

ASSESSMENT OF INDIVIDUAL NEEDS

It is stressed by Hodgson *et al.* (1984) that thorough assessment is needed before the individual needs of children can be understood and met in practical terms of curriculum access. The educational assessment of the pupil provides the basic information that the teacher will need in order to plan appropriate programmes and learning materials. The educational psychologist and specialist adviser will usually undertake the assessment which may contain results from standardised procedures such as the 'Williams Test' (Williams, 1956) and also a profile drawn from information derived from the *Look and Think* Checklist (Tobin, Chapman *et al.*, 1978). Specific assessment procedures for visually handicapped pupils are described by Tobin (1982). Class teachers can also add greatly to the information derived from formal assessment procedures by compiling their own observation of the child's levels of independent mobility and self-help; even the way in which the child handles and tries to find out about objects can provide useful information about the pupil is using vision for learning. Such observations when discussed with the adviser can be very helpful in deciding on the format of materials to be used for learning and the need for individual teaching in some curriculum areas.

Good practice demands that it is not only the pupil's special needs that should be recorded; it must also be ensured that in any given educational situation they can be realistically met. There are already likely to be pupils within the school who have some degree of visual handicap even though this may not be severe, and it will be pertinent to observe how their needs are being met, or whether they are being ignored.

STRATEGIES FOR THE CLASSROOM TEACHER

For the classroom teacher the path to better practice in supporting visually handicapped pupils will involve the following strategies:

1. establishing co-operative and regular contact with the specialist adviser, and planning the future pattern of visits;
2. reviewing the environment in the classroom and effecting as many changes as possible to facilitate the work of the visually handicapped pupil;
3. enumerating and obtaining any specialist equipment that the pupil needs (closed circuit television etc.);
4. checking sources/supply of specialist materials and transcription services;
5. discussing curriculum implications with school head and relevant colleagues
6. requesting relevant literature for the school library, including details of resources;
7. making application for in-service training opportunities (day and short courses);
8. seeking opportunities for discussion with parents on the pupil's general progress and social adjustment.

There is a continuing need for the progress of visually handicapped pupils to be monitored, and for research to compile information on effective strategies as well as for the philosophical debate that at present attends the integration issue. In practical terms, the contribution of training is a crucial one in providing teachers with strategies to meet the individual needs of the visually handicapped pupils in their classes.

SPECIALIST TRAINING REQUIREMENTS AND OPPORTUNITIES FOR TEACHERS

The roles that teachers fulfil in educating visually handicapped pupils in ordinary schools are diverse and they need to be forearmed by appropriate training. A key figure in the successful interpretation of such pupils' needs is often the adviser for visually handicapped children who as a professional offering information and support needs to be well trained and experienced in the education of pupils with the full range of visual disabilities. The professional demands incumbent upon teachers in this advisory role are considerable, since their knowledge about visual handicap and their attitude to its implications are likely to influence the way in which these pupils are regarded, taught and supported by other teachers. It is consequently essential that the training of those undertaking advisory work or undertaking the work of visiting teacher must be thorough and objectively evaluated, preparing them to give specific and well-defined solutions to help classroom teachers deal with the needs of their visually handicapped pupils. Theoretical generalisations will not do, and whilst training must incorporate essential theoretical background, it must also offer the opportunity to develop practical professional competence and skill in teaching children who have this particular form of special need. Administrators are increasingly considering the training needs of such personnel, as opportunities for educational placement of visually handicapped pupils become increasingly diversified, so that the most effective use can be made of teaching expertise in different settings. The adviser will need to be skilful in interacting with other professionals, in predicting the need for providing aids and adapted material, in suggesting curriculum adaptations and modifications to lighting, furniture or classroom layout.

Advisers will also need to be able to discuss with the class teacher the keeping of appropriate records of the specific needs and educational progress of pupils with different kinds and degrees of vision, and they will need to know the strengths and limitations of the social and physical environment of each school that they support. Since specialist teachers and advisers will be in a position both formally and informally to generate expectations about visually handicapped pupils, they will require knowledge of the needs of these pupils that is current, accurate and extensive. Pupils with severe visual handicap are in a minority even among other handicapped children and can run the risk of having their real needs underestimated or brushed aside in the face of expediency in providing for the majority. Training must therefore equip the adviser to present facts, not simply subjective opinions, and to present these clearly and fearlessly, sometimes in the face of ignorance or prejudice. In addition to interacting with teaching colleges and administrators, advisers may be in contact with parents and have a contribution to make to public education relating to the visually handicapped.

All these demands presuppose a professional training that has an appropriate balance of practical and theoretical elements. If an adviser has had training with a low theoretical base there is the risk that he or she may proffer generalisations based on the assumption that instances of the behaviour or learning of individual visually handicapped children show universal relevance. A superficial level of information in an adviser could be detrimental to both the teacher and pupils reliant upon sound guidance, and the adviser must be knowledgeable about what has been discovered through research and good practice about the implications of visual handicap on the way children develop and learn. Teachers will need to be reassured that the needs of their visually handicapped pupils can be realistically met, since some teachers do have anxieties about accepting pupils with vision problems. Tobin (1972a) showed this in his study on 'The attitudes of non-specialist teachers towards visually handicapped pupils'. In a large sample of teachers and trainee teachers studying on postgraduate and educational degree courses at Birmingham University, the majority were somewhat daunted by the prospect of including visually handicapped pupils in their classes and rated them low in terms of pupils whom they would feel confident to accept in their classes. These negative views must be faced and teachers given the information, training and support to overcome them. It would be interesting to see the results of such a study undertaken more recently, as since that date special education modules have been incorporated into initial teacher training.

There have been some heartening examples of good practice recorded in which visually handicapped pupils have been well supported in ordinary classes by their teachers (Hegarty *et al.*, op. cit.). An appropriately trained and experienced adviser can do much to reduce the apprehensions that may be experienced by other teachers and can give soundly based and practical guidance in overcoming, rather than dwelling on, difficulties when they do arise. The class teacher can gain in confidence and in knowledge of how to help visually handicapped pupils through in-service training which complements this advice from specialists.

There is a clearly expressed need for intensive specialist training for those teachers principally concerned with the education of visually handicapped pupils and with advising other professionals, and for 'orientation' courses alongside advisory help from expert and trained personnel for those who have visually handicapped pupils in their classes in ordinary schools, or for those teaching children with other handicaps.

Currently the courses available for teachers who choose to specialise in the education of visually handicapped pupils are based in the Department of Special Education of Birmingham University and in Scotland at Moray House College of Education.

Courses offered by the University of Birmingham

Bachelor of Philosophy of Education

To fulfil the requirements of specialist teachers of the visually handicapped and advisory teachers the preference is for full-time training. At present the degree course is offered on the basis of one academic year at the university, followed by six months' part-time study in order to complete a dissertation. This is extensive training, but it would be false economy to attempt to reduce or dilute it. The theoretical, practical and experimental elements all need to be there in effective specialist training. The present course includes group visits to special schools, units and integrated provision for pupils within the full range of visual handicap from nursery schools to further education establishments. Visits in groups tend to promote discussion and questioning more readily than individual visits.

Clearly training must provide experience of the adaptations and techniques relating to the special needs of pupils with visual handicap, but the fact that some of these pupils will need to write, read, compute and move about in ways that are different from those of other pupils must be balanced against a need to understand the total developmental needs of children. The training at Birmingham is intended to help the teacher to find out about, and translate into operational terms, the means by which problems arising from the presence of visual handicap can be minimised in the learning situation. There can be a real danger that without appropriate training or experience a teacher may attribute a pupil's lack of competence to not understanding, rather than not seeing, a process or task clearly. The advisory teacher can, through training and experience, help the class teacher to seek out the underlying course of classroom failure in pupils who have sight problems, offer appropriate solutions, and also give background information and promote an understanding and interest in the needs of these children through generating short in-service courses and general discussions with teachers throughout the school. In order to equip the specialist teacher or adviser to meet these demands the training includes in-depth study of the following areas of concern:

1. the implication of visual handicap in the learning and development of children: the principal causes of sight defect in children; the anatomy and physiology of the eye; clinical assessment of vision; medical records. Sections of this element of training are given by a paediatric ophthalmologist;

2. the assessment of functional vision and the design and use of visual enhancement programmes; the use and care of optical and low vision aids; the compilation of profiles of pupils with residual vision; use of standardised tests (STYCAR and BUST);

3. the use of specialised equipment and materials for visually handicapped pupils; the presentation of learning materials to pupils with residual and low vision;

4. the effects of visual handicap on the development of pupils; cognitive, physical and language development; the special needs of pre-school and adolescent pupils; social and emotional aspects of development;

5. curricular implications: curriculum development for visually handicapped pupils with special needs; the ordinary school and special school curriculum; modifications and adaptations required for curriculum access; additional areas of curriculum for visually handicapped pupils (orientation and mobility, self-help skills, specialised communication skills, including a full knowledge of braille and the teaching of literacy through braille); perceptual training in auditory skills;

6. educational provision for visually handicapped pupils in the United Kingdom; relevant legislation; interpreting and contributing to statements of educational need;

7. the special needs of children with handicaps that are additional to those of vision;

8. interaction with other professionals and with parents;

9. leavers' programmes: further education and vocational training opportunities; exam adaptations; independence training.

These theoretical elements are essential basic knowledge necessary in order to do an advisory job properly, but teachers, like their pupils, learn through doing. Therefore, on the training course practical teaching placements are carefully assessed so that the real challenge of translating growing knowledge into effective practice can be tackled. It would be inept to advise others on areas of competence that have not been fully mastered in practical terms by those giving such advice. The final dissertation gives an opportunity for in-depth study or small-scale research on a particular educational topic relating to visually handicapped pupils.

An effective training course can never be static, although it must embody certain enduring elements such as proficiency in braille and a knowledge of the physical bases of disabilities. Rather it will reflect changes in educational thinking and practice, whilst at the same time contributing to them and helping to shape ways in which new concepts and developments can become operational.

Diploma and distance-taught courses

There is an urgent need to devise ways of offering specialist training which are flexible but nevertheless retain essential content and standards. One successful innovation in training offered by the University of Birmingham is the Diploma in Special Education (Visually Handicapped) on a distance-taught basis. This was first offered in 1981 with an intake of 38 students, and it has had a rapidly increasing intake since then. By 1986 this number had more than doubled, even though every teacher on the course has been required to undertake assessed practical work in an established school or unit in integrated provision where there are already trained staff with specialist qualifications in visual handicap. This requirement has a limiting effect on the number of trainees accepted but is essential for the control of quality of practical experience.

This distance teaching mode of offering training means that attendance at the university is reduced to a five-day summer school during each of the two years of the course. The remaining work is based on individual units which have been written by experienced specialists in social, medical, developmental and educational aspects relating to visually handicapped pupils, with major contributions to the writing having been made by permanent members of the teaching staff in the Department of Education. The academic content of this course reflects the area of study covered by the full-time course, but these are presented and evaluated in a different way: successful completion of this course, including the writing of a dissertation and assessed practical teaching placements, leads to the qualification of Diploma in Special Education (VH). This award is recognised by the Department of Education and Science as a qualification essential to teachers working in special schools for blind pupils in England and Wales.

Moray House College of Education offers a one year full-time course (SPX4) leading to the award of a diploma, which has comparable acceptance in Scotland.

The diploma courses have been found to be useful and popular with teachers from a wide range of different kinds of schools and units for visually handicapped pupils. It is strongly recommended, however, that teachers undertaking an advisory role should undertake full-time training with all its advantages of tutorial and individual work with tutors. Advisers will need to give guidance that is specific and directed towards solving problems that may be quite complex and demanding of a high level of expertise and confidence which is best mastered through full-time training opportunities.

But a training course is only the beginning, and students from both the B.Phil. and Diploma courses are invited to an annual short course which focuses on a particular area of new development or concern for those working with visually handicapped pupils. Many of these teachers will, in time, be organising short courses and contributing to in-service training of classroom teachers, and so it is essential that they should consider the content, presentation and evaluation of relevant material for this purpose for themselves.

Training needs of teachers in mainstream schools

Following the changes in the 1981 Education Act which give parents a much greater choice with regard to what kind of educational placement their child should have – special school or integrated setting – attention has been given to the inclusion in basic teacher training of modules concerned with children with special educational needs.

For example, at Birmingham University, those undertaking the Post Graduate Certificate in Education, who will be teaching in ordinary schools, are increasingly able to choose to undertake some basic work on visual handicap, to visit establishments where such children are placed and to study in greater depth a particular aspect of work with them, for instance, the teaching of science or maths to visually handicapped pupils. These young teachers have the guidance of tutors of the visual handicap course, but there may be some justifiable anxiety that this level of experience in visual handicap is not always available in training establishments, and the expertise and knowledge of teacher trainees in this area of special education needs to be extended. Nevertheless, excellent modules have been devised in colleges and university departments which draw contributions from both academic staff and practising teachers within a particular region.

Short courses and conferences

Voluntary bodies such as the RNIB and the Spastics Society run short 'awareness' courses on particular aspects of work with visually handicapped children. For example, the RNIB Conference Centre has held courses on pre-school activities for visually handicapped children, on adolescent problems, and has given attention to various curriculum areas, including mobility and self-help skills.

A number of local education authorities also run short courses for teachers in ordinary schools who have visually handicapped children in their classes. Those courses are extremely useful as 'awareness' courses but must not be confused with more substantial, carefully evaluated professional training. Their purpose and direction are such that they can provide practical suggestions to be implemented in the classroom rather than extensive and in-depth training. An example of the content of such a short course includes:

causes and implications of visual handicap in children;
screening and early intervention;
presentation of learning materials;
the enhancement of residual vision;
early activities;
development of visually handicapped children;
the integration of visually handicapped children into normal schools;
the visually handicapped adolescent;
self-help skills;
communication;
leavers' programmes;
working with parents.

Clearly a short course can only give a limited amount of information and must be very carefully planned in order to make the best use of time.

The Department of Education and Science holds a one-week conference for teachers of visually handicapped pupils every three years or so. This includes international speakers, visits to places of current interest, and discussion. Although not officially called 'teacher training', it is invaluable in considering sound educational practice, particularly of integrated situations, and is especially valuable for teachers who so far do not have much experience in dealing with the visually handicapped.

Some of the professional organisations also contribute to in-service training. The Association for the Education and Welfare of the Visually Handicapped holds a conference either annually or every few years. Frequently there are exhibitions and demonstrations of new technology, speakers of both national and international level considering topics of educational relevance, and opportunities for discussion with teachers sharing similar concerns.

The Partially Sighted Society holds occasional one-day conferences at a national level. These are geared to the interest of both parents and teachers.

Clearly a major step towards better practice in the teaching and support of visually handicapped pupils would be in the increased availability of well-planned short courses and in-service training for teachers with visually handicapped children in their classes. Greater co-operation between local education authorities and voluntary bodies offering short courses is needed in order to reduce duplication and increase the effectiveness of the courses that they offer. The expertise of those offering such courses needs to be constantly updated and feedback on the relevance of the content of courses constantly supplied from the teachers who attend them.

For their part, teachers can request that they should be given the opportunity to attend courses and insist that they must have these opportunities if they are to be able to help their visually handicapped pupils. They can have direct contact with the organisation concerned with offering training at various levels and put to them requests for the consideration of topics which they would find useful in their day-to-day work with pupils who have specialised needs.

THE CONCEPT OF A CONTINUUM OF EDUCATIONAL PROVISION

A major step towards better practice in the education of visually handicapped pupils rests in the strengthening of a continuum of educational provision for such pupils, which offers a real, not simply a theoretical, choice of educational placement suited to individual needs. A range of educational programmes is needed in order to offer the least restrictive placement for the pupil with sight problems. It must be confusing for parents if they encounter a divided or even antagonistic point of view from providers of such programmes rather than a complementary and flexible educational service. The strong historical traditions, voluntary-body funding and examination successes encountered in many special schools for visually handicapped pupils put a strong case for the status quo which is widely respected. Local education authorities, on the other hand, have considerably increased their peripatetic advisory services for visually handicapped children from one such service in 1972 to 60 services in 1985, each comprising one or more specialist advisers. In addition, the RNIB team of peripatetic advisers, initiated in 1972 by a single professional, records a team of twelve highly experienced advisers in 1985.

Clearly, there has been a marked increase in the support of integrated visually handicapped pupils in ordinary schools, and more specific help for multi-handicapped pupils in a whole range of educational establishments when they are deemed to have sight problems. The implementation of the 1981 Education Act is significant in making local educational authorities look first at the viability of a placement for a visually handicapped pupil in an ordinary school, only considering special school placement as a second option if special circumstances warrant it. However, there is still some strong evidence of burgeoning activity and growth in the special educational provision sector, with the advent of colleges of further education for visually handicapped pupils and the selective secondary school. Worcester College was full in 1986 and accepting increasing numbers of students. Not all integrated placements have proved to be educationally successful, and not all parents make integrated school placements their first choice. The number of pupils in different kinds of placement fluctuate from year to year, and it will take time for newly set up support services to become strongly established, but it is clear that a range of educational placements is needed in order to meet the diverse needs of visually handicapped pupils.

The dilemma of how to provide such a range of placements for a low-incidence group of pupils such as those with a visual handicap is not a problem unique to the United Kingdom, but is also encountered in those western countries with a relatively high standard of living and control of the infectious diseases that cause widespread blindness in children. In parts of the United States, where the relative autonomy of the individual states with regard to educational provision allows for a variety of approaches to meeting the needs of visually handicapped pupils, the special schools for such children are under review and in many cases radical changes have been made in the whole ethos and role of these schools.

Hatlen (1986) enumerates the characteristics of viable, stable healthy schools for visually handicapped pupils in the United States: they are providers of creative lifestyle programmes for those pupils who are also multiply handicapped; they support multi-disciplinary teaching teams; they have developed evaluated non-academic curricula; they support community involvement; and they provide for academically capable students from rural areas. Finally their aim is to co-operate rather than to compete with main-stream school programmes. These developments contrast with the unstable, endangered schools which are characterised by poor co-operation with other programmes, lack of clear direction, and resistance to change.

This view of the future of such special schools in the United States has much in common with the Danish model, described by Stockhelm (1986). Here the special school is a hub for the advisory educational services supporting visually handicapped pupils in integrated provision throughout Denmark. The records of these pupils are held in the special school which is a base for regular meetings of the advisers, for courses for teachers in ordinary schools and for parents and ancillary workers. But the school is a real part of the educational continuum, not simply a resource base, since it is a viable and lively school for some 120 pupils, as well as being a centre for the full assessment of visually handicapped children. Braille materials for use in all schools and tactile and enlarged materials are produced here too. Finally, the school offers summer residential courses for visually handicapped pupils in ordinary schools, providing them with mobility, braille and recreational seminars, as well as giving an opportunity to meet and form friendships with other young people who are visually handicapped and who have faced similar problems. Stockhelm (op. cit.) contends that they both need and enjoy such interaction with others who can understand and share difficulties from the perspective of their own personal experience.

This concern for the total needs of the pupil with visual handicap epitomises good practice, but lest it should seem a Utopian picture and one which the teacher in the ordinary classroom would question in terms of relevance, it is interesting to note the gradual way in which this philosophy of an educational continuum is becoming more universally accepted. Hopefully in the future it will be an accepted and viable aspect of provision for visually handicapped pupils, part of a unifying trend that seeks to provide for the pupils' real needs in real terms.

There is already an increasing interaction between special schools and integrated services for visually handicapped pupils in the United Kingdom. Some special schools are offering or planning to provide consultancy advice for teachers in ordinary schools who have visually handicapped pupils in their classes. For example, Worcester College for the Blind, which has a tradition of academic excellence, has an outreach service geared to the needs of secondary school pupils which should be particularly helpful in curriculum areas such as mathematics and science which require adaptations for totally blind pupils (Chapman, 1985).

The services for visually handicapped pupils based on Shawgrove School, Manchester, the 'open' education scheme for such pupils at Tapton Comprehensive School, Sheffield, and the support for pupils in the neighbourhood comprehensive school in Ysgol Penybont, Bridgend, all exemplify the successful development of aspects of an educational continuum for pupils with severe visual handicap, despite restrictive economic conditions. Better practice would see such developments taken further. Pupils with severe visual handicaps do require some special educational methods, the use of expensive equipment and the guidance of teachers, who are able to deal with their needs confidently because they are themselves receiving the expert information and provision of materials required to help the pupils to learn.

References

Adams, O. F., (1985a), 'How the Blind See, 2. What low vision looks like', *The New Beacon*, LXIX (814), pp. 41–44.

Adams, O. F., (1985b), 'Special building and design considerations for the blind and partially sighted', *Official Architecture and Planning*, 32, pp. 1077–1081.

Anderson, D. W., (1984), 'Mental Imagery in Congenitally Blind Children', *Journal of Visual Impairment and Blindness*, 78 (5), pp. 206–210.

Anderson, E. S., Dunlea, A. and Kakelis, L. S. (1985) 'Blind Children's Language: resolving some difficulties', *Journal of Child Language*, 11 (3), pp. 645–664.

Ashcroft, S. (1982), 'Bridges from Classroom to Community', in *Proceedings of the VIIth Quinquennial Conference of the International Congress of the Education of the Visually Handicapped*. Nairobi: ICEVH.

Barraga, N. (1964), *Increased Visual Behaviour in Low-Vision Children*. New York: American Foundation for the Blind.

Barraga, N. (1974) 'Utilisation of Sensory-Perceptual Abilities', in Lowenfeld, B. (ed.), *The Visually Handicapped Child in School*. London: Constable.

Barraga, N. (1976) *Visual Handicaps and Learning: a Development Approach*. Belmont, California: Wadsworth.

Bauman, M. K. (1964) 'Group Differences Disclosed by Inventory Items', *International Journal for Education of the Blind*, 13, pp. 101–106.

Benton, S. (1984) 'Supporting Visually Handicapped Children in Ordinary Schools', *British Journal of Visual Impairment*, 11 (1), pp. 3–6.

Best, A. B. (1981), *Microelectronic Technology and the Visually Handicapped* (monograph), University of Birmingham.

Birch *et al.*, (1966) *School achievement and the effect of type size on reading in visually handicapped children*. Co-operative Research Project, 1766, University of Pittsburgh.

Bishop, V. (1971), *Teaching the Visually Limited Child*. Springfield, IL: Charles C. Thomas.

Blenkhorn, P. (1986) 'The RCEUH Project on micro computer systems and computer assisted learning', *British Journal of Visual Impairment*, IV (3), pp. 101–104.

Blenkhorn, P. and Payne, B. (1985) 'Teletext for the Visually Impaired', *The New Beacon*, LXIX (824), p. 384.

Booth, T and Potts, P. (eds) (1983), *Integrating Special Education*. Oxford: Blackwell.

Braf, P. G. (1984) *The Physical Environment and the Visually Impaired*. Bromma, Sweden: ICTA Information Centre.

Brennan, W. (1985) *Curriculum for Special Needs*. Milton Keynes: Open University Press.

British Broadcasting Corporation, *In Touch* bulletins. London: BBC.

Budge, A., Thomas, G., Buultjens, M. and Lee, M. (1986) 'Parental Preferences in Educational Provision for the Visually Handicapped', *The New Beacon*, LXX (833), pp. 261–265.

Buell, C. E. (1966) *Physical Education for Blind Children*. Springfield, IL: Charles C. Thomas.

Bull, R., Rathborn, H. and Clifford, B. R. (1983) 'The voice recognition accuracy of blind listeners', *Perception*, 12 (2), pp. 223–226.

Cameron, A. (1982) *Notes for Teachers of Visually Handicapped Children*. London: Disabled Living Foundation.

Cassidy, M. (1985) 'Keeping an ear on things', *The New Beacon*, LXIX (824), p. 364.

Chapman, E. K. (1978) *Visually Handicapped Children and Young People*. London: Routledge and Kegan Paul.

Chapman, E. K. (1982), *Suzy*. London: Bodley Head.

Chapman, E. K. (1986) *Report on merger of Chorleywood and Worcester Colleges*. London: RNIB.

Clamp, S. A. (1981) 'Primary Mathematics for Visually Handicapped Children', *Insight*, **3** (2).

Colbourne-Brown, M. S. and Tobin, M. J. (1982) 'Integration of the Educationally Blind: numbers and placement', *The New Beacon*, LXVI (781), pp. 113–117.

College of the Teachers of the Blind (1971) *Handbook for the Family Books*.

Cratty, B. J. (1971) *Movement and Spatial Awareness in Blind Children and Youth*. Springfield, IL: Charles C. Thomas.

Cratty, B. J. and Sams, T. A. (1968) *The Body Image of Blind Children*. New York: American Foundation for the Blind.

Cutsforth, I. D. (1951) *The Blind in School and Society*. New York: American Foundation for the Blind.

Danielson, E. (1983) *Mathematics in Braille: a reference book for teachers and students*. Burwood, Melbourne: Royal Victoria Institute for the Blind.

Danielson, E. and Lamb, G. (1983) *Beginning Reading/Writing for Braille/Print Users*. Burwood, Melbourne: Royal Institute for the Blind.

De Lucchi, L. and Malone, L. (1982) 'Science activities for the visually impaired', in Mangold, S. (ed.), *Teachers' Guide to the Special Needs of Blind and Visually Handicapped Children*. New York: American Foundation for the Blind.

Department of Education and Science (1972) *Education of the Visually Handicapped* (the Vernon Report). London: HMSO.

Department of Education and Science (1978) *Special Educational Needs* (the Warnock Report). London: HMSO.

Dodd, B. (1983), 'The Visual and Auditory Modalities in Phonological Acquisition', in Mills, A. F. (ed.), *Language Acquisition in the Blind Child*. San Diego, CA: College Hill Press.

Dubowski, J. K. (1986) 'Art Therapy with the Visually Impaired', *British Journal of Visual Impairment*, IV (3), pp. 109–110.

Edman, P. K. (1986) *Integrated Education of Visually Handicapped Children*, Conference Paper of the International Congress of the Education of the Visually Handicapped, Barcelona, ICEVH.

Fagan, T., Mabert, A. and Cowen, O. (1985) 'Visually impaired children; the need for a team approach', *British Journal of Visual Impairment*, III (3), pp. 78–79.

Faye, E. E. (1984) *Clinical Low Vision*. Edinburgh: Churchill Livingstone.

Fine, S. R. (1975) 'Registration and Notification', *Child Care, Health and Development*, **5** (1), pp. 309–313.

Fitt, R. A. and Mason, H. (1986) *Sensory Handicaps in Children*. Stratford-upon-Avon: National Council for Special Education.

Fitzsimmons, S. (1987) *Spot the Dot*. London: RNIB.

Fraiberg, S. (1977) *Insights from the Blind*. London: Souvenir Press.

Fraiberg, S., Smith, M. and Adelson, E. (1969) 'An educational programme for blind infants', *Journal of Special Education*, **3**, pp. 121–139.

Fukarai, S. (1974) *'How can I make what I cannot see?'*. New York: Van Nostrand Reinhold.

Fullwood, D. (1984) *A Start to Independence for your Visually Handicapped Child*. Burwood, Melbourne: Royal Victoria Institute for the Blind.

Gardiner, R. A. (1982) *The Development of Vision*. Lancaster: M T P Press.

Gazeley, D. (1968) *Light and Low Vision*, Report No. 1, Loughborough University of

Technology, Dept of Technology.

Gibson, E. J. (1953) 'Improvement in perceptual judgements as a function of controlled practice or training', *Psychological Bulletin*, **50**, pp. 401–443.

Gomulicki, B. R. (1961) *The Development of Perception and Learning in Blind Children*. Psychological Laboratory, University of Cambridge.

Halliday, C. (1971) *The Visually Impaired Child: growth, learning, development, infancy to school age*. Frankfurt, KY: American Printing House for the Blind.

Halliday, D. and Kurzhals, I. W. (1976) *Stimulating Environments for Children who are Visually Impaired*. Springfield, IL: Charles C. Thomas.

Hanninken, K. *Teaching the Visually Handicapped*. Blindness Publications, USA.

Hathaway, W. (1959) *Education and Health of the Partially Seeing Child*. London: Columbia University Press.

Hatlen, P. (1986) *Education of the Visually Handicapped in the USA*, Proceedings of ACWVH Conference Birmingham, Association for the Education and Welfare of the Visually Handicapped.

Hebb, D. A. (1937) 'The innate organisation of visual activity: perception of figures by rats in total darkness', *Journal of Genetic Psychology*, **52**, pp. 101–126.

Hegarty, S., Pocklington, K. and Lucas, D. (1981) *Educating Children with Special Needs in the Ordinary School*. Windsor: NFER.

Heritage, R. S. (1986) *A guide to the teaching of maths at the primary level to pupils with visual handicaps*. Research Centre for the Education of the Visually Handicapped, University of Birmingham.

Hill, E. and Ponder, P. (1976) *Orientation and Mobility Techniques*. New York: American Foundation for the Blind.

Hill, E. W., Gruth, D. A. and Hill, M. (1986) 'Spatial concept instruction for children with low vision', *Education of the Visually Handicapped*, XVI (4).

Hinton, R. (1984) 'Ecological fieldwork with visually handicapped students', *British Journal of Visual Impairment*, II (2), pp. 41–44.

Hinton, R. and Ayres, D. (1986) 'A collection of tactile diagrams for first examinations in biology', *British Journal of Visual Impairment*, IV (1), pp. 13–16.

Hocken, S. (1978) *Emma and I*. London: Sphere.

Hodgson, A., (1985) 'How to integrate the visually impaired', *British Journal of Special Education*, **12** (1), pp. 35–37.

Hodgson, A. Clunies-Ross, L. and Hegarty, S. (1984) *Learning Together: Teaching pupils with special needs in the ordinary school*. Windsor: NFER/Nelson.

Hughes, D. (1984) 'The role of a visual handicap department in an integrated secondary school', *British Journal of Visual Impairment*, II (1), pp. 8–11.

Illuminating Engineering Society (1977) *Code for Interior Lighting*. London: IES.

Imamura, S., (1965) *Mother and Blind Child*. New York: American Foundation for the Blind.

Jamieson, M., Partlett, M. and Pocklington, K. (1977) *Towards Integration*. Windsor: NFER.

Jan, J., Freeman, R. and Scott, E. (1977) *Visual Impairment in Children and Adolescents*. London: Grune and Stratton.

Jay, P. A. (1978) 'Lighting for the Partially Sighted', in *Proceedings of the conference on light for low vision*. Chartered Institute of Building Services and The Partially Sighted Society, London. pp. 7–15.

Jones, H. (1970) 'A peripatetic counselling service for visually handicapped children', *Teacher of the Blind*, **58** (3), pp. 56–57.

Jose, R. (1983) *Understanding Low Vision*. New York: American Foundation for the Blind.

Kakelis, L. S. and Andersen, E. S. (1984) 'Family communication styles and language development', *Journal of Visual Impairment and Blindness*, **78** (2), pp. 54–65.

Kell, J. (1973) 'Partially sighted children', in Varma, V. (ed.) *Stresses in Children*. London: University of London Press.

Kirkwood, R. (1986) 'Tactile diagrams: their production by current day methods and their relative suitabilities in use', *British Journal of Visual Impairment*, IV (3), pp. 95–99.

Kitzinger, M. (1984) 'Role of repeated and echoed utterances in communication with a blind child', *British Journal of Disorders of Communication*, **19** (2), pp. 135–146.

Kurzhals, J. W. (1968) 'Fashioning learning opportunities for the child with impaired vision', *New Outlook for the Blind*, 62, pp. 160–166.

Landau, B. (1983) 'Blind children's language is not meaning less' in Mills, A. (ed.), *Language Acquisition in the Blind Child*. London: Croom Helm.

Langdon, J. N. (1968) 'A Matter of Concern', *The New Beacon*, **52** (612), pp. 282–286.

Langdon, J. N. (1970) 'Parents Talking', *The New Beacon*, **54** (643). pp. 282–288.

Lansdown, R. (1975) 'Partial sight – partial achievement', *Southern and Western Regional Association for the Blind Regional Review*, 60.

Leavens, M. (1986) 'Art Therapy with the Visually Impaired', *British Journal of Visual Impairment*, IV (1).

Lewis, C. (1986) 'Consumer report: colour closed circuit television', *British Journal of Visual Impairment*, IV (3), p. 105.

Lindstedt, E. (1986) 'Early vision assessment in visually handicapped children at the T R C, Sweden', *British Journal of Visual Impairment*, IV (2), pp. 49–51.

Lindstedt, E. and Hyrvarinnen, L., *The BUST LH Playing Cards*, available from Elisyn, Eva Lindstedt, Hogbergtg, 30 S-11620, Stockholm.

Lorimer, J. (1962) *The Lorimer Braille Recognition Test*. College of the Teachers of the Blind.

Lorimer, J. (1977) 'The Neale Analysis of Reading Ability: standardised for use with blind children'. Windsor: NFER.

Lorimer, J. (1987) *Braille in Easy Stages*. London: RNIB.

Lowe, C. (1983) 'Visually Handicapped Children' in Booth, T. and Potts, P. (eds), *Integrating Special Education*. Oxford: Blackwell.

Lowenfeld, B. (1971) *Our Blind Children: growing and learning with them*. Springfield, IL: Charles C. Thomas.

Lowenfeld, B. (ed.) (1974) 'Psychological Considerations', in *The Visually Handicapped Child in School*. London: Constable.

Lowenfeld, B., Abel, G. L. and Hatlen, P. H. (1969) *Blind Children Learn to Read*. Springfield, IL: Charles C. Thomas.

Lowenfeld, V. (1939) (3rd edition 1957) *Creative and Mental Growth*. New York: Macmillan.

Lukoff, I. F. and Whiteman, M. (1960) *The Social Sources of Adjustment to Blindness*. New York: American Foundation for the Blind.

Madden, N. and Slavin, R., 'Mainstreaming students with mild handicaps: academic and social outcomes', *Review of Educational Research*, 53, pp. 519–569.

Madge, N. and Fassam, M. (1982) *Ask the Children: Experiences of physical disability in the school years*. London: Batsford.

Mann, I. and Pirie, A. (1946) *The Science of Seeing*. Harmondsworth: Penguin.

Marshall, G. (1969) 'Detecting Visual Dysfunction', *Special Education*, III, pp. 21–23.

Mason, H. and Tobin, M. (1986) 'Speed of information processing and the visually handicapped child', *British Journal of Special Education*, **13** (2), pp. 69–70.

Matsuda, M. (1985) 'Facilitating the language acquisition skill of blind infants', *Journal of Visual Impairment and Blindness*, **79** (3), pp. 111–112.

McClure, G. M. *Reading Types Test*, London: Clement Clarke International.

McGurk, H. (1983) 'Effective motivation and the development of communicative competence in blind and sighted children', in Mills, A. F. (ed.), *Language Acquisition in the Blind Child*. San Diego, CA: College Hill Press.

Mills, A. F. (ed.) (1983a) *Language Acquisition in the Blind Child*. San Diego, CA: College Hill Press.

Mills, A. F. (1983b) 'Acquisition of speech sounds in the visually handicapped child', in *Language Acquisition in the Blind Child*. San Diego, CA: College Hill Press.

Napier, G. (1974) 'Special subject adjustments and skills', in Lowenfeld, B. (ed.), *The Visually Handicapped Child in School*. London: Constable.

Nemeth, A. (1959) 'Teaching meaningful mathematics to blind and partially sighted children', *New Outlook for the Blind*, 53, pp. 381–421.

Norris, M., Spaulding, P. J. and Brodie, F. H. (1957) *Blindness in Children*. Chicago: University of Chicago Press.

Parmalee, A. M. (1966) 'Development Studies of Blind Children', *New Outlook for the Blind*, pp. 177–179.

Parsons, S. (1986) 'Function of play in low vision children's development: emerging patterns of behaviour', *Journal of Visual Impairment and Blindness*, June, pp. 777–784.

Pickles, W. J. (1968) 'Raised Diagrams' in Fletcher, R. C. (ed.), *Teaching of Maths and Science to the Blind*. London: RNIB.

Reynell, J. (1978) 'Developmental Patterns of Visually Handicapped Children', *Childcare, Health and Development*, 14 (5)

Reynell, J. (1979) *Manual for Reynell-Zinkin Scales*. Windsor: NFER.

Rhyne, J. M. (1982) 'Comprehension of synthetic speech by blind children', *Journal of Visual Impairment and Blindness*, 76 (8), pp. 313–316.

Royal Institute of British Architects (1981) *Lighting and Acoustic Criteria for the Visually Handicapped and Hearing Impaired in Schools*. London: HMSO.

Royal National Institute for the Blind, *Blind and partially sighted students in college*. London: RNIB.

Royal National Institute for the Blind, *Guidelines for teachers and parents of visually handicapped children with additional handicaps*. London: RNIB.

Royal National Institute for the Blind, *Mobility Ideas*. London: RNIB.

Ryan, P. (1985) 'European Mobility Centres', *The New Beacon*, LXIX (814), pp. 37–40.

Salt, J. P. (1986) 'The development of listening skills in visually handicapped children', *The New Beacon*, LXX (825), pp. 1–3.

Scott, E. (1982) *The Visually Impaired Student*. Baltimore: University Park Press.

Shaw, A. (1969) *Print for Partial Sight*, Research Report, Library Association.

Sheridan, M. D. 1975, *Children's Developmental Progress*. Windsor: NFER.

Sommers, V. S. (1944) *The Influence of Parental Attitudes and Social Environment on the Personality Development of the Adolescent Blind*. New York: American Foundation for the Blind.

Sonsker, P. M., Levitt, S. and Kitzinger, M. (1984) 'Identification of constraints on motor development in young visually disabled children and principles of remediation', *Child Care, Health and Development*, 10, pp. 273–286.

Stockhelm, K. (1986) *Danish Model of Integrated Education*, ICEVH Conference Paper, Barcelona.

Svenson, H. (1978) *The School Situation of the Partially Sighted*. Bromma: Swedish Institute for the Handicapped.

Svenson, H. (1986) *School attendance at home: Experiences of the School Attendance of 68 Blind Students*. Proceedings of European Conference ICEVH, Barcelona.

Tillman, M. H. (1967) 'The performance of the blind and sighted students on the Wechsler Intelligence Scale for children, Study 2', *International Journal for the Education of the Blind*, 16, pp. 106–112.

Tobin, M. J. (1972a) 'The attitude of non-specialist teachers towards visually handicapped pupils', *Teacher of the Blind*, LX (2), pp. 60–64.

Tobin, M. J. (1972b) *The Vocabulary of the Young Blind Schoolchild*. College of the Teachers of the Blind.

Tobin, M. J. (1972c) 'Conservation of substance in the blind and partially sighted', *British Journal of Educational Psychology*, 42 (2), pp. 192–197.

Tobin, M. J. (1977) *Testing the Blind and Partially Sighted*. Research Centre for the Education of the Visually Handicapped, University of Birmingham.

Tobin, M. J. (1979) *A Longitudinal Study of Blind and Partially Sighted Children in Special Schools in England and Wales*. Research Centre for the Visually Handicapped, University of Birmingham.

Tobin, M. J. (1982) *A Survey of Arrangements for Assessing Blind and Partially Sighted Students in Public Examinations*. Research Centre for the Education of the Visually Handicapped, University of Birmingham.

Tobin, M. J., Chapman, E. K., Tooze, F. H. and Moss, S. C. (1978) *Look and Think: Handbook for Teachers; Teachers' File* (School Council Project), available from the RNIB.

Tooze, D. (1981) *Independence Training for Visually Handicapped Children*. London: Croom Helm.

Tooze, F. H. G. (1962) *Braille Speed Test*. College of the Teachers of the Blind.

Travis, P. (1987) *Directory of Resources for those Working with Visually Handicapped Children*. Department of Special Education, University of Birmingham.

Trowald, N. (1975) *Learning Strategies for Blind Listeners*, Southern Regional Association for the Blind, Report No. 66, pp. 115–127.

Urwin, C. (1983) 'Dialogue and cognitive functioning in the early language development of three blind children', in Mills, A. F. (ed.), *Language Acquisition in the Blind Child*. San Diego, CA: College Hill Press.

Van der Zwan, J. L. and Heslinga, K. (1970) 'What should we teach?', *Teacher of the Blind*, 59, pp. 18–29.

Vernon, M. D. (1966) 'Perception in relation to cognition', in Kidd, A. J. *Perceptual Development in Children*. London: University of London Press.

Vernon, M. D. (1971) *Reading and its Difficulties*. Cambridge: Cambridge University Press.

Von Tetzchner, S. and Martinson, N. (1980) 'A psycholinguistic study of the language of the blind; 1. Verbalism', *International Journal of Psycholinguistics*, 7 (3), pp. 49–61.

Warren, D. H., (1984) *Blindness and Early Childhood Development*. New York: American Foundation for the Blind.

Welsh Office (1984) *Staff Development Package on Visual Handicap*. London: HMSO.

Whittaker, J. (1968), 'Graphical Representation', in Fletcher, R. (ed.) *Teaching Maths and Science to the Blind*. London: RNIB.

Williams, M. (1956) *Intelligence Test for Children with Defective Vision*. Windsor: NFER.

Williams, M. (1971) 'Braille reading', *Teacher of the Blind*, 59 (3).

Williams, M. (1973) 'The Blind Child', in Varma, V. P. (ed.) *Stresses in Children*. London: University of London Press.

Wills, D. (1965) 'Some observations on blind nursery school children's understanding of their world', *Psycho-analytic Study of the Child*, 20, pp. 344–364.

Wills, D. (1979) 'The ordinary devoted mother and her blind baby', *Psycho-analytic Study of the Child*, 34.

Wilson, M. D. (1981) *Curriculum in Special Schools*. Schools Council.

Worcester College for the Blind (1978) *Proceedings of Conference on the Curriculum*. Worcester College.

Useful Addresses

ORGANISATIONS

ASSOCIATION FOR THE EDUCATION AND WELFARE OF THE VISUALLY HANDICAPPED (AEWVH), Hon. Sec. Mrs S. A. Clamp, St John's School House, Hazdor, Nr. Droitwich, Worcs. WR9 7DR.

AUDIO READING TRUST, c/o RNIB, 224 Great Portland Street, London W1N 6AA.

BRITISH ASSOCIATION FOR SPORTING AND RECREATIONAL ACTIVITIES OF THE BLIND, 2 Westwood Road, Hillmorton, Rugby CV22 5QL.

BRITISH JOURNAL OF VISUAL IMPAIRMENT, Editor, c/o South Regional Association for the Blind, 55 Eton Avenue, London NW3 3ET.

DISABLED LIVING FOUNDATION, 380 Harrow Road, London W9 2HG, Tel. 01–289–6111

FOUNDATION FOR AUDIO RESEARCH AND SERVICES FOR BLIND PEOPLE, 12 Netley Dell, Letchworth, Herts. SG6 2TF.

KENT ASSOCIATION FOR THE BLIND, 15 Ashford Road, Maidstone, Kent ME14 5DB.

NATIONAL LIBRARY FOR THE BLIND, Cromwell Road, Bredbury, Stockport SK6 2SG.

NATIONAL LOW VISION ADVICE CENTRE, 3 Colleton Crescent, Exeter, Devon EX2 4DG.

PARTIALLY SIGHTED SOCIETY, Queens Road, Doncaster DN1 2NX. Tel. 0302–68998

RESEARCH CENTRE FOR THE EDUCATION OF THE VISUALLY HANDICAPPED, University of Birmingham, PO Box 363, Birmingham B15 2TT.

RESEARCH UNIT FOR THE BLIND, Institute of Bioengineering, Brunel University, Uxbridge, Middlesex UX8 3PM.

ROYAL NATIONAL COLLEGE FOR THE BLIND, College Road, Hereford HR1 1EB.

ROYAL NATIONAL INSTITUTE FOR THE BLIND, 224 Great Portland Street, London W1N 6AA. Tel. 01–388–1266. Also at Braille House, 338 Goswell Road, London EC1V 73E. Tel. 01–837–9921.

SENSE (NATIONAL ASSOCIATION FOR DEAF/BLIND AND RUBELLA HANDICAPPED), 311 Grays Inn Road, London WC1. Tel. 01–278–1005.

SOUTHERN REGIONAL ASSOCIATION FOR THE BLIND, 55 Eton Avenue, London NW3 3ET.

TACTILE DIAGRAMS RESEARCH PROJECT, c/o Mr Ron Hinton, Dept of Education, Loughborough University of Technology, Loughborough, Leics. LE11 3TU.

TOY LIBRARIES ASSOCIATION, 68 Church Way, London NW1 1LT.

WORCESTER COLLEGE FOR THE BLIND, Whittington Road, Worcester WR5 2JU.

MANUFACTURERS OF EQUIPMENT

Closed circuit television

ALPHAMED LTD (Alphavision), 61 Beechtree Avenue, Marlow Bottom, Bucks. Tel. 06284–71370
STEAM STORAGE CO (Focus), Castle Works, Castle Street, Tiverton, Devon EX16 6RG. Tel. 0884–254172
C. DAVIS KEELER LTD, Low Vision Dept (Magnavision and Magnilink), 29 Marylebone Lane, London W1M 6DS. Tel. 01–935–8512
VISIONAID SYSTEMS (Visualtek) 25 Easthorpe Street, Ruddington, Notts. NG11 6CB. Tel. 0602–847849

Large print typewriters

ADLER OEM LTD, 140/154 Borough High Street, London SE1 1LH. Tel. 01–407–3191
IBM UNITED KINGDOM LTD, Perivale Buildings, Rockware Avenue, Greenford, Middlesex. Tel. 01–578–4399
OLYMPIA BUSINESS MACHINES CO LTD, 203/205 Old Marylebone Road, London NW1 5QS. Tel. 01–262–6788

Lighting

L80 ASYMMETRIC LIGHT, 1001 Lamps, 4 Barneston Road, Catford, London SE6.
WALDMAN LIGHTS, c/o Athrodax Ltd, Athrodax House, Priory Road, Bicester, Oxfordshire.

Thermoform (vacuum forming machines)

AMERICAN THERMOFORM CORPORATION, 8640 East Slauson Avenue, Pico Rivera, California 90660.
C. R. CLARKE AND CO, Carregammon Lane, Ammanford, Dyfed SA18 3EL.
MINOLTA (UK) LTD, 1/3 Tanners Drive, Blakelands North, Milton Keynes, Bucks.

Other Aids

HALLAM TAPE SERVICE, 2 Parkview Court, Cobner Road, Sheffield 18.
KURZWEIL READING MACHINE, John Bradburn (Computer Systems) Ltd, Quantel House, St James Mill Road, Northampton NM5 5JW. Tel. 0604–55142.
MICROWRITER, c/o The Foundation for Communication for the Disabled, 25 High Street, Woking, Surrey GU21 1BW. Tel. 01–405–1019
OPTACON, c/o Sensory Information Systems, Unit 10, Cameron House, 12 Castlehaven Road, London NW1 8QU.
VERSABRAILLE, c/o Sensory Information Systems, *see* OPTACON.
VIEWSCAN TEXT SYSTEM, LVA Marketing, 7 Musters Road, West Bridgford, Nottingham N62 7PP.
VINCENT WORKSTATION, c/o Sensory Information Systems, *see* OPTACON.

Index